NICHOLSON

GUIDE TO THE WATERWAYS ❻

Nottingham, York & the North East

Nicholson

An imprint of HarperCollins*Publishers*

Also available:

Nicholson Guide to the Waterways

1. **London, Grand Union, Oxford & Lee**
2. **Severn, Avon & Birmingham**
3. **Birmingham & the Heart of England**
4. **Four Counties & the Welsh Canals**
5. **North West & the Pennines**
7. **Thames, Wey, Kennet & Avon**

Nicholson Inland Waterways Map of Great Britain

Published by Nicholson
An imprint of HarperCollins*Publishers*
77-85 Fulham Palace Road
Hammersmith, London W6 8JB

www.**fire**and**water**.com
www.bartholomewmaps.com

First published by Nicholson and Ordnance Survey 1997
Reprinted 1998
New edition published by Nicholson 2000

Researched and written by David Perrott and Jonathan Mosse.
Design by Bob Vickers.

The publishers gratefully acknowledge the assistance given by British Waterways
and its staff in the preparation of this guide.

Grateful thanks is also due to members of the Inland Waterways Association and
CAMRA representatives and branch members.

Photographs reproduced by kind permission of the following picture libraries:
British Waterways Photo Library pages 71, 102; Bill Meadows Picture Library pages 50, 57, 59;
Derek Pratt Photography pages 12, 97.

Printed in Italy.

ISBN 0 7028 4166 8
ME10292
97/2/33

The publishers welcome comments from readers. Please address your letters to:
Nicholson/OS Guides to the Waterways, HarperCollins Cartographic,
HarperCollins Publishers, Westerhill Road, Bishopbriggs, Glasgow, G64 2QT.

The canals and river navigations of Britain were built as a system of new trade routes, at a time when roads were virtually non-existent. After their desperately short boom period in the late 18th and early 19th centuries, they gracefully declined in the face of competition from the railways. A few canals disappeared completely, but thankfully most just decayed gently, carrying the odd working boat, and becoming havens for wildlife and the retreat of the waterways devotee.

It was two such enthusiasts, L.T.C. Rolt and Robert Aickman who, in 1946, formed the Inland Waterways Association, bringing together like-minded people from all walks of life to campaign for the preservation and restoration of the inland waterways. Their far-sightedness has at last seen its reward for, all over the country, an amazing transformation is taking place. British Waterways, the IWA, local councils, canal societies and volunteers have brought back to life great lengths of canal, and much of the dereliction which was once commonplace has been replaced with a network of 'linear parks'.

The canals provide something for everyone to enjoy: engineering feats such as aqueducts, tunnels and flights of locks; the brightly decorated narrowboats; a wealth of birds, animals and plants; the mellow unpretentious architecture of canalside buildings; friendly waterside pubs and the sheer beauty and quiet isolation that is a feature of so much of our inland waterways.

It is easy to enjoy this remarkable facet of our history, either on foot, often by bicycle, or on a boat. This book, with its splendid Ordnance Survey® mapping, is one of a series covering the waterways network, and gives you all the information you need.

▌CONTENTS

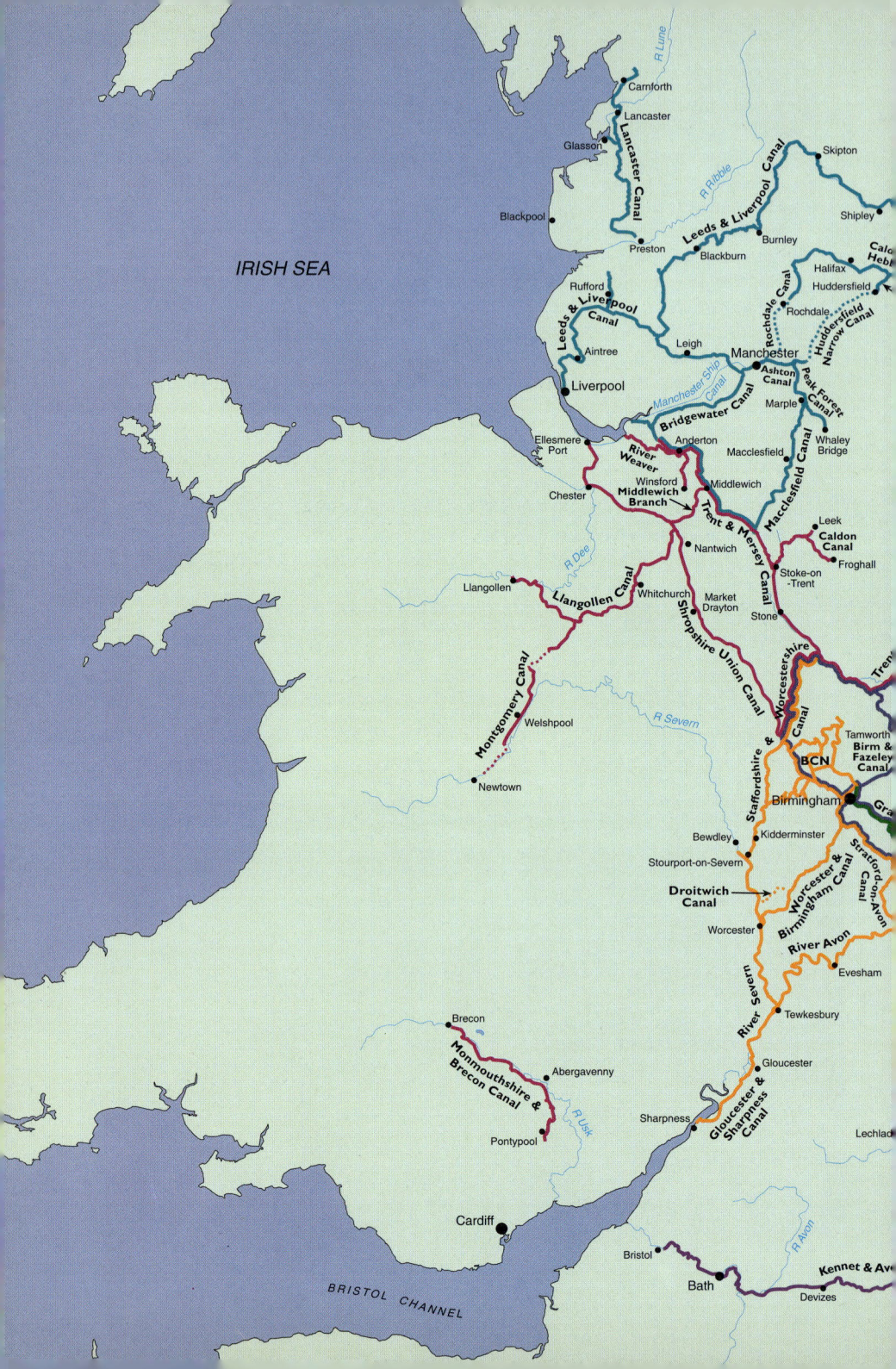

The Waterways of England and Wales

KEY

Waterways featured in this guide

Unnavigable section

Waterways featured in:
Guide 1
Guide 2
Guide 3
Guide 4
Guide 5
Guide 7

NORTH SEA

THE WASH

Ripon Canal
River Ure
Stamford Bridge
York
Pocklington
River Ouse
River Derwent
Pocklington Canal
Selby
Selby Canal
Aire & Calder Navigation
Leeds
Castleford
R Aire
Kingston upon Hull
R Hull
R Humber
Goole
Wakefield
Navigation
Huddersfield Broad Canal
Keadby
Stainforth
South Yorkshire Navigations
Doncaster
West Stockwith
River Trent
Sheffield
Rotherham
Chesterfield Canal
Worksop
Retford
Gainsborough
Torksey
Chesterfield
Lincoln
Fossdyke & Witham Navigations
R Ancholme
River Trent
Newark-on-Trent
Kyme Eau
South Kyme
Boston
Erewash Canal
Langley Mill
Gunthorpe
Nottingham
King's Lynn
Wisbech
R Bure
R Yare
Mersey Canal
Grand Union Canal
R Trent
Burton upon Trent
Peterborough
R Nene
Ashby Canal
Barestone
Leicester
Coventry Canal
Leicester Section
Foxton
Market Harborough
R Waveney
Oxford Canal
Coventry
Welford
Rugby
Crick
Union Canal
Northampton
Cambridge
R Great Ouse
Stratford-on-Avon
Stoke Bruerne
Cosgrove
Banbury
Oxford Canal
Grand Union Canal
Leighton Buzzard
Bishop's Stortford
Aylesbury
Hertford
River Stort
Thrupp
Hemel Hempstead
River Lee
Oxford
Watford
River Thames
Slough
London
Hungerford
Reading
R Thames
Newbury
R Medway
Chatham
Basingstoke Canal
River Wey
Basingstoke
Greywell
Guildford
Maidstone

The slogan Waterways For All was coined to take account of the wide diversity of people using the inland waterways for recreation.

Today boaters, walkers, fishermen, cyclists and gongoozlers (on-lookers) throng our canals and rivers, to share in the enjoyment of our quite amazing waterway heritage. British Waterways (BW), along with other navigation authorities, is empowered to develop, maintain and control this resource in order to maximise its potential: namely our enjoyment. It is to this end that a series of guides, codes, and regulations have come into existence over the years, evolving to match a burgeoning – and occasionally conflicting – demand. Set out below are the key points as they relate to everyone wishing to enjoy the waterways.

LICENSING – BOATS

The majority of the navigations covered in this book are controlled by BW and are managed on a day-to-day basis by local waterway offices. Waterway Managers are detailed in the introduction to each waterway. All craft using BW waterways must be licenced and charges are based on the length of the craft. This licence covers all navigable waterways under BW's control and in a few cases includes reciprocal agreements with other waterway authorities (as indicated in the text). As this edition goes to print, BW and the Environment Agency are preparing to go to consultation on an optional joint licence to cover both authorities' waterways. Permits for permanent mooring on the canals are also issued by BW. For further information contact BW Customer Services (see inside front cover). You can download licence fees and charges and an application form from the BW website (see inside front cover).

Since 1 January 1997, BW and the Environment Agency have introduced the Boat Safety Scheme, setting technical requirements for good and safe boat-building practice. A Boat Safety Certificate or, for new boats, a Declaration of Conformity, is necessary to obtain a craft licence. For powered boats proof of insurance for Third Party Liability for a minimum of £1,000,000 is also required. Further details from BW Customer Services. Other navigational authorities relevant to this book are mentioned where appropriate.

LICENSING – CYCLISTS

Not all towpaths are open to cyclists. This is because many stretches are too rough or narrow, or because cyclists cause too great a risk to other users. The maps on the BW website show which stretches of towpaths are open to cyclists. This information is also available from your local waterway office, which you should contact in any case to obtain the necessary permit to cycle on the towpath and a copy of the Waterways Code. When using the towpaths for cycling, you will encounter other

towpath users, such as fishermen, walkers and boaters. The Waterways Code gives advice on taking care and staying safe, considering others and helping to look after the waterways. A complete list of towpaths available for cycling is available in a National Cycle Pack, price £5.00 from BW Customer Services.

TOWPATHS

Few, if any, artificial cuts or canals in this country are without an intact towpath accessible to the walker at least. However, on river navigations towpaths have on occasion fallen into disuse or, sometimes, been lost to erosion. In today's leisure climate considerable efforts are being made to provide access to all towpaths with some available to the disabled. Notes on individual waterways in this book detail the supposed status of the path, but the indication of a towpath does not necessarily imply a public right of way or mean that a right to cycle along it exists. Maps on the BW website show all towpaths on the BW network, and whether they are open to cyclists. Motorcycling and horse riding are forbidden on all towpaths.

INDIVIDUAL WATERWAY GUIDES

No national guide can cover the minutiae of individual waterways and some Waterway Managers produce guides to specific navigations under their charge. Copies of individual guides (where they are available) can be obtained from the Waterway Office detailed in the introduction. Please note that times – such as operating times of bridges and locks – do change year by year and from winter to summer.

STOPPAGES

BW works hard to programme its major engineering works into the winter period when demand for cruising is low. It publishes a National Stoppage Programme and Winter Opening Hours leaflet which is sent out to all licence holders, boatyards and hire companies. Inevitably, emergencies occur necessitating the unexpected closure of a waterway, perhaps during the peak season. You can check for stoppages on individual waterways between specific dates on the BW website. Details are also announced on lockside noticeboards and on Canalphone (see inside front cover).

STARTING OUT

Extensive information and advice on booking a boating holiday is available on the BW website. Please book a waterway holiday from a licenced operator – only in this way can you be sure that you have proper insurance cover, service and support during your holiday. It is illegal for private boat owners to hire out their craft. If in doubt, please contact BW Customer Services. If you are hiring a canal boat for the first time, the boatyard will brief you thoroughly. Take notes, follow their instructions and *don't be afraid to ask* if there is anything you do not understand. BW have produced a short video giving basic information on using a boat safely. Copies of the video, and the Waterways Code for Boaters, are available free of charge from BW Customer Services.

GENERAL CRUISING NOTES

Most canals are saucer-shaped in section so are deepest at the middle. Few have more than 3–4ft of water and many have much less. Keep to the centre of the channel except on bends, where the deepest water is on the outside of the bend. When you meet another boat, keep to the right, slow down and aim to miss the approaching craft by a couple of yards: do not steer right over to the bank or you are likely to run aground. If you meet a loaded commercial boat keep right out of the way and be prepared to follow his instructions. Do not assume that you should pass on the right. If you meet a boat being towed from the bank, pass it on the outside. When overtaking, keep the other boat on your right side.

A large number of BW facilities in their north-east region – pump-outs, showers, electrical hook-ups and so on – are currently operated by smart cards, obtainable from BW Regional Office, Neptune Street, Leeds (0113 281 6800); local waterways offices (see introductions to individual navigations); lock keepers and some boatyards within the region. At the time of printing, a £6 card will purchase one pump-out, about 12 showers and electricity pro rata. Please note that if you are a week-end visitor, you should purchase cards *in advance*.

Speed

There is a general speed limit of 4 mph on most BW canals. This is not just an arbitrary limit: there is no need to go any faster and in many cases it is impossible to cruise even at this speed: if the wash is breaking against the bank or causing large waves, slow down.

Slow down also when passing moored craft, engineering works and anglers; when there is a lot of floating rubbish on the water (and try to drift over obvious obstructions in neutral); when approaching blind corners, narrow bridges and junctions.

Mooring

Generally speaking you may moor where you wish on BW property, as long as there is sufficient depth of water, and you are *not causing an obstruction*. Your boat should carry metal mooring stakes, and these should be driven firmly into the ground with a mallet if there are no mooring rings. Do not stretch mooring lines across the towpath. Always consider the security of your boat when there is no one aboard. On tideways and commercial waterways it is advisable to moor only at recognised sites, and allow for any rise or fall of the tide.

Bridges

On narrow canals slow down and aim to miss one side (usually the towpath side) by about 9 inches. *Keep everyone inboard when passing under bridges*, and take special care with moveable structures – the crew member operating the bridge should hold it steady as the boat passes through.

Tunnels

Make sure the tunnel is clear before you enter, and use your headlight. Follow any instructions given on notice boards by the entrance.

Fuel

Hire craft usually carry fuel sufficient for the rental period.

Water

It is advisable to top up every day.

Lavatories

Hire craft usually have pump-out toilets. Have these emptied *before* things become critical. Keep the receipt and your boatyard will usually reimburse you for this expense.

Boatyards

Hire fleets are usually turned around on a Saturday, making this a bad time to call in for services. Remember that moorings at popular destinations fill quickly during the summer months, so do not assume there will be room for your boat. Always ask.

LOCKS AND THEIR USE

A lock is a simple and ingenious device for trans-porting your craft from one water level to another.

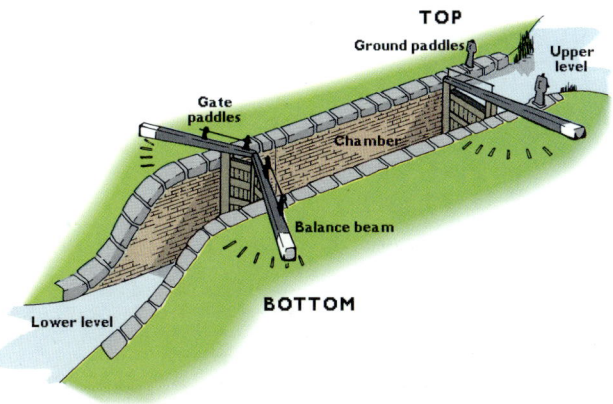

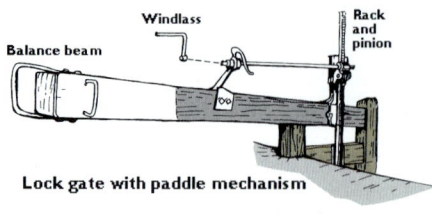

Lock gate with paddle mechanism

When both sets of gates are closed it may be filled or emptied using gate or ground paddles at the top or bottom of the lock. These are operated with a windlass.

General tips

- Make safety your prime concern. *Keep a close eye on young children.*
- Always take your time, and do not leap about.
- Never open the paddles at one end without ensuring those at the other are closed.
- Never drop the paddles – always wind them down.
- Keep to the landward side of the balance beam when opening and closing gates.
- Never leave your windlass slotted onto the paddle spindle – it will be dangerous should anything slip.
- Keep your boat away from the top and bottom gates to prevent it getting caught on the gate or the lock cill.
- Be wary of fierce *top gate* paddles, especially in wide locks. Operate them slowly, and close them if there is *any* adverse effect.
- Always follow the navigation authority's instructions, where these are given on notices or by their staff.

PLANNING A CRUISE

Many a canal holiday has been spoiled by trying to go too far too fast. Go slowly, don't be too ambitious, and enjoy the experience. Note that mileages indicated on the maps are for guidance only.

A *rough* calculation of time taken to cover the ground is the lock-miles system:

Add the number of *miles* to the number of *locks* on your proposed journey, and divide the resulting figure by three. This will give you a guide to the number of *hours* it will take. But don't forget your service stops (water, shopping, pump-out), and allow plenty of time to visit that special pub!

TIDAL WATERWAYS

The typical steel narrow boat found on the inland waterways system has the sea-going characteristics of a bathtub, which renders it totally unsuitable for all-weather cruising on tidal estuaries. However, the more adventurous will inevitably wish to add additional ring cruises to the more predictable circuits within the calm havens of inland Britain. Passage is possible in most estuaries if careful consideration is given to the key factors of weather

conditions, crew experience, the condition of the boat and its equipment and, perhaps of overriding importance, the need to take expert advice. In many cases it will be prudent to employ the skilled services of a local pilot. Within the text, where inland navigations connect with a tidal waterway, details are given of sources of both advice and pilotage. This guide is to the inland waterways of Britain and therefore recognizes that tideways – and especially estuaries – require a different skill and approach. We therefore do not hesitate to draw the boater's attention to the appropriate source material.

GENERAL

Most inland navigations are managed by BW or the Environment Agency, but there are several other navigation authorities responsible for smaller stretches of canals and rivers. For details of these, contact the Association of Inland Navigation Authorities at www.cam.net.uk/home/aina or BW Customer Services. The boater, conditioned perhaps by the uniformity of our national road network, should be sensitive to the need to observe different codes and operating practices. Similarly it is important to be aware that some waterways are only available for navigation today solely because of the care and dedication of a particular restoration body, often using volunteer labour and usually taking several decades to complete the project. This is the reason that, in cruising the national waterways network, additional licence charges are sometimes incurred. The introduction to each waterway gives its background history, details of recent restoration (where relevant) and also lists the operating authority.

BW is a public corporation, responsible to the Department of the Environment, Transport and the Regions and, as subscribers to the Citizen's Charter, they are linked with an ombudsman. BW has a comprehensive complaints procedure and a free explanatory leaflet is available from Customer Services. Problems and complaints should be addressed to the local Waterway Manager in the first instance – the telephone number is listed in the introduction to individual waterways.

The Inland Waterways Association campaigns for the 'conservation, use, maintenance, restoration and development of the inland waterways', through branches all over the country. For more information contact them at PO Box 114, Rickmansworth, WD3 1ZY, telephone 01923 711114, fax 01923 897000, email iwa@waterways.org.uk or visit their website at www.waterways.org.uk/index.htm.

FREEPHONE CANALS

Emergency help is available from BW outside normal office hours on weekdays and throughout weekends via Freephone Canals (see inside front cover). You should give details of the problem and your location.

AIRE & CALDER NAVIGATION

MAXIMUM DIMENSIONS

Castleford to Goole
Length: 200'
Beam: 20'
Headroom: 11' 10" *(see note 5 on page 21)*

MANAGER

01977 554351

MILEAGE

CASTLEFORD to:
Bank Dole: 7 miles, 3 locks including Castleford
New Junction Canal: 16½ miles, 5 locks
Goole: 24 miles, 5 locks

SAFETY NOTES

BW produce excellent Cruising Notes for the pleasure boater using this waterway, obtainable from the manager's office. This is both a commercial waterway and one developed from a river navigation: both pose their own disciplines highlighted in the notes.
Each lock on the waterway has a set of traffic lights both upstream and downstream of the lock chamber. The purpose of these lights is to convey instructions and advice to approaching craft.

Red light

Stop and moor up on the lock approach. The lock is currently in use.

Amber light *(between the red and green lights)*

The lock keeper is not on duty. You will need to self-operate.

Green light

Proceed into lock.

Red & green lights together

The lock is available for use. The lock keeper will prepare and operate the lock for you.

Flashing red light

Flood conditions – unsafe for navigation.

Most lock approach moorings are immediately upstream and downstream of the lock chamber however, **please note:**

Ferrybridge Lock upstream approach mooring is located on the river side of the lock island.

Locks at Castleford, Bulholme, Ferrybridge and Bank Dole allow access to river sections of the navigation. River level gauge boards indicate conditions as follows:

GREEN BAND – Normal river levels safe for navigation.

AMBER BAND – River levels are above normal. If you wish to navigate the river section you are advised to proceed on to and through the next lock.

RED BAND – Flood conditions unsafe for navigation. Lock closed.

All locks between Castleford and Goole (except Bank Dole) are equipped with VHF Marine Band Radio. They monitor and operate on channel 74.

See page 15 for details of self-operation of these locks.

In an emergency non-VHF users contact the manager's office or out of office hours dial 100 and ask for Freephone Canals. Mobile phone users dial 01384 215785.

The River Aire was first made navigable to Leeds in 1700 and rapidly became a great commercial success, taking coal out of the Yorkshire coalfield and bringing back raw wool, corn and agricultural produce. Improvements were then made to the difficult lower reaches, with first Selby and later Goole becoming Yorkshire's principal inland port. The opening of the New Junction Canal in 1905 further secured its suitability for commercial traffic, which today still amounts to some 2 million tonnes, mainly coal, sand and petroleum.

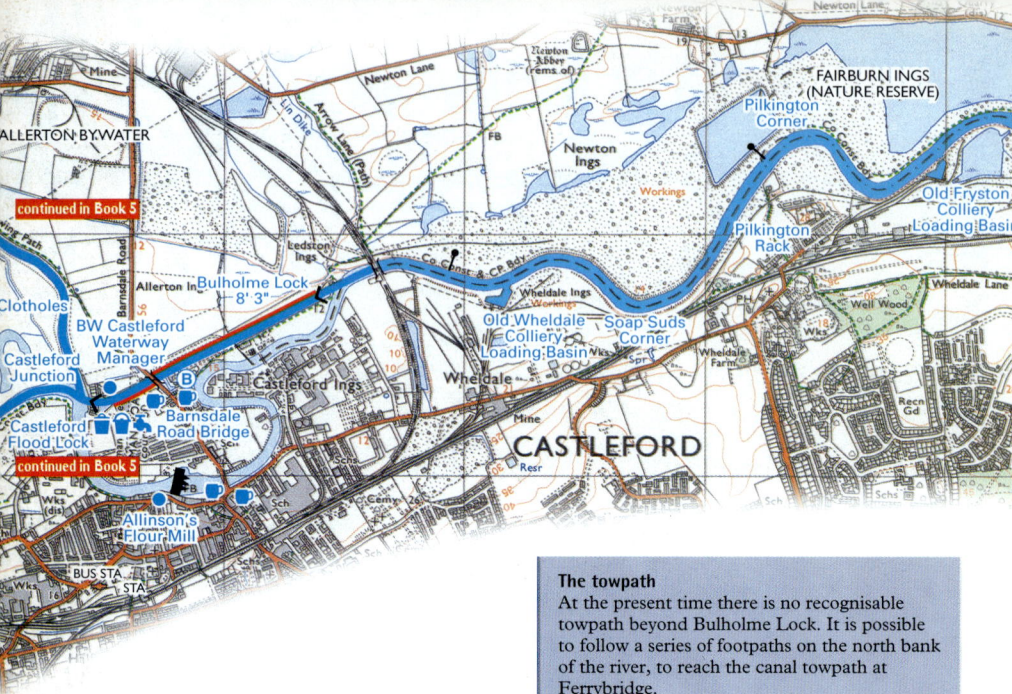

continued in Book 5

continued in Book 5

> **The towpath**
> At the present time there is no recognisable towpath beyond Bulholme Lock. It is possible to follow a series of footpaths on the north bank of the river, to reach the canal towpath at Ferrybridge.

Ferrybridge

Leaving Castleford Junction the canal is dominated by the extensive works of Hickson and Welch. The company, founded in 1905 by a Mr Hickson, is now a multinational chemical giant best known in this country for developing the pressure treatment process used to preserve timber. Also in the vicinity of the basin is the maintenance depot of Cawood Hargreaves, one of the largest haulage companies on the Aire & Calder. At Bulholme Lock is a sign directing walkers to Newton. This walk should not be attempted in wet weather as the footpath becomes waterlogged. The lock keeper's bungalow, built on stilts, replaces a traditional canalside cottage. At this point the canal enters the river which is surrounded by large areas of derelict land. Landscaping of the now abandoned Fryston and Wheldale collieries is still being undertaken but will, no doubt, lead to the establishment of plants and trees in the area. The lower land to the north of the navigation forms the Ings, a word dating back to Viking times which denotes areas of riverside water meadows which are subject to seasonal flooding. Mining subsidence in the area, particularly over the last 50 years, has meant that much of this land has now become permanently waterlogged, resulting in the loss of a considerable area of agricultural land. These wetlands have, however, provided a habitat to all forms of wildlife, the area between the river and the village of Fairburn being recognised as a nature reserve since 1957. Owned by the Coal Authority, formerly the National Coal Board, and leased to the RSPB, the 618-acre site was designated a statutory bird sanctuary in 1968 – 251 species of birds have been recorded, of which about 170 are regular visitors. Originally the land was acquired in order to provide space for tipping spoil from the collieries. The Coal Authority still retains tipping rights in the area but, in the interest of wildlife, has restricted its activities. Continued work on the spoil heaps prevents the natural establishment of

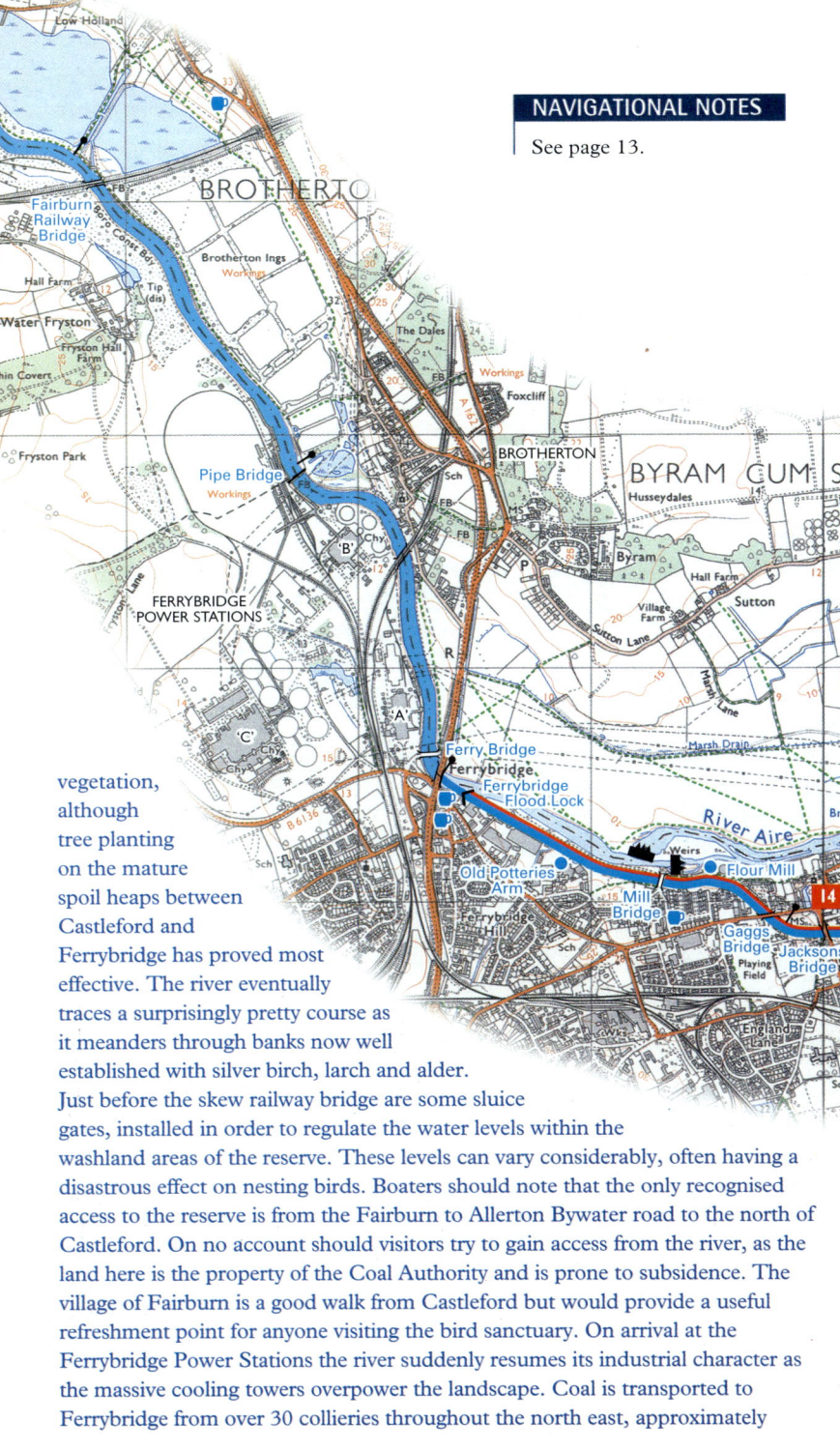

NAVIGATIONAL NOTES

See page 13.

vegetation, although tree planting on the mature spoil heaps between Castleford and Ferrybridge has proved most effective. The river eventually traces a surprisingly pretty course as it meanders through banks now well established with silver birch, larch and alder.

Just before the skew railway bridge are some sluice gates, installed in order to regulate the water levels within the washland areas of the reserve. These levels can vary considerably, often having a disastrous effect on nesting birds. Boaters should note that the only recognised access to the reserve is from the Fairburn to Allerton Bywater road to the north of Castleford. On no account should visitors try to gain access from the river, as the land here is the property of the Coal Authority and is prone to subsidence. The village of Fairburn is a good walk from Castleford but would provide a useful refreshment point for anyone visiting the bird sanctuary. On arrival at the Ferrybridge Power Stations the river suddenly resumes its industrial character as the massive cooling towers overpower the landscape. Coal is transported to Ferrybridge from over 30 collieries throughout the north east, approximately

25 per cent of this being carried by water. Hargreaves alone carry well over 1,000,000 tonnes of coal to Ferrybridge C each year. Navigators should therefore be prepared for the movement of heavily-laden commercial craft in the area – ¼ mile upstream of the railway bridge there is a build-up of traffic as coal barges and trains of compartment boats manoeuvre in the stream waiting to unload. Once alongside the wharf a large overhead gantry takes over, propelling individual pans, each holding approximately 170 tonnes, into position under a giant hoist capable of handling 1000 tonnes of coal an hour. This in turn lifts the pan 40 feet into the air, tipping it into a concrete hopper. Leaving behind the frantic activity of the power stations, the graceful 18thC bridge which once carried the Great North Road comes into sight. This has now been superseded by the concrete viaduct which carries the A1 dual carriageway. Here the River Aire leaves the navigation, flowing off to the left, as the canal traces a more southerly course through Knottingley. All craft should bear right and await the traffic lights controlling the entrance to the Ferrybridge Flood Lock. Moorings immediately beneath the viaduct are for the use of boats waiting to enter the lock only. Long-stay moorings are to be found on the river to the left of the lock. Care should be exercised on this section as the river terminates in a weir. Pubs and shops in Ferrybridge can be reached from the lock. The navigation now enters an artificial cut which continues all the way to Goole. The canal skirts an industrial complex on the right and passes the tall gaunt buildings of King's Flour Mills on the left, before entering a pleasantly green, wooded cutting. Here is evidence of limestone quarrying over and above the need to make passage for the waterway and indeed the approaches to both Gaggs and Jacksons Bridges remain as solid rock.

Ferrybridge power stations

● **Fairburn**

W. Yorks. PO, tel, stores. Limestone and alabaster were once quarried here. There is also a record of a tunnel, 350yds long, which extended under the village connecting it to the river. Perched on the hillside above the Ings, the village has several pubs and shops.

● **Ferrybridge**

W. Yorks. PO, tel, stores, garage. The town takes its name from the bridge over the River Aire which was built at the point where, for many centuries, travellers were ferried across the water. Possession of the site has been contested in the past by the Romans and much later by the armies of York and Lancaster. The area is now dominated by the three power stations, Ferrybridge A, B and C. Ferrybridge A is now given over to workshops devoted to the repair and testing of machinery, Ferrybridge B has recently closed whilst C station still produces electricity for the national grid. The power stations are open to visitors by telephoning (01977) 674188.

NAVIGATIONAL NOTES

1 All the locks on the Aire & Calder operate mechanically and, although largely under the control of mobile lock keepers, can be boater-operated out of hours. Obey the traffic light signals.

2 Remember that this is a river navigation. Many of the locks are accompanied by large weirs, so keep a sharp lookout for the signs which direct you safely into the locks.

3 When the river level rises after prolonged heavy rain, the flood locks will be closed. Pleasure craft should stay put until they are advised by a lock keeper that it is safe to proceed.

4 This is a commercial waterway, used by 600-tonne tanker barges and push-tow coal pans. Keep a lookout for them, and give them a clear passage, especially on the many bends that the river describes on this stretch. Moor carefully on the canal sections of the navigation, using bollards or fixed rings rather than mooring stakes, since the wash from these craft can be substantial.

5 Ferrybridge power station is not far away and navigators should be prepared for the sudden activity in that area. There is nowhere suitable to moor on this part of the river.

Pubs and Restaurants

● ✕ **Golden Lion** The Square, Knottingley (01977 673527). Riverside at Ferrybridge Lock. A friendly pub overlooking the River Aire serving Tetley's real ale. Meals available *lunchtimes and evenings (except Sun evenings)*. Vegetarians and children catered for. Outside seating. Quiz *Sun.* B & B.

● **Magnet Inn** 100yds south of Ferrybridge Lock. A basic John Smith's real ale pub, popular with the locals. Bar food. Pub games. *Open all day.*

Boatyards

Ⓑ **CPL Hargreaves** Navigation Road Dockyard, Lock Lane, Castleford (01977 553685). Boat repairs, dry dock, wet dock, DIY facilities, crane.

Heck Bridge

Immediately through Shepherds Bridge the navigation forks: straight ahead to Bank Dole Lock into the River Aire and thence to the Selby Canal, while the main line bends right. Care should be exercised here on account of both moored commercial craft and laden coal pans approaching under Skew Bridge. They require first call on the available water to line up for Shepherds Bridge. For much of this journey the canal is

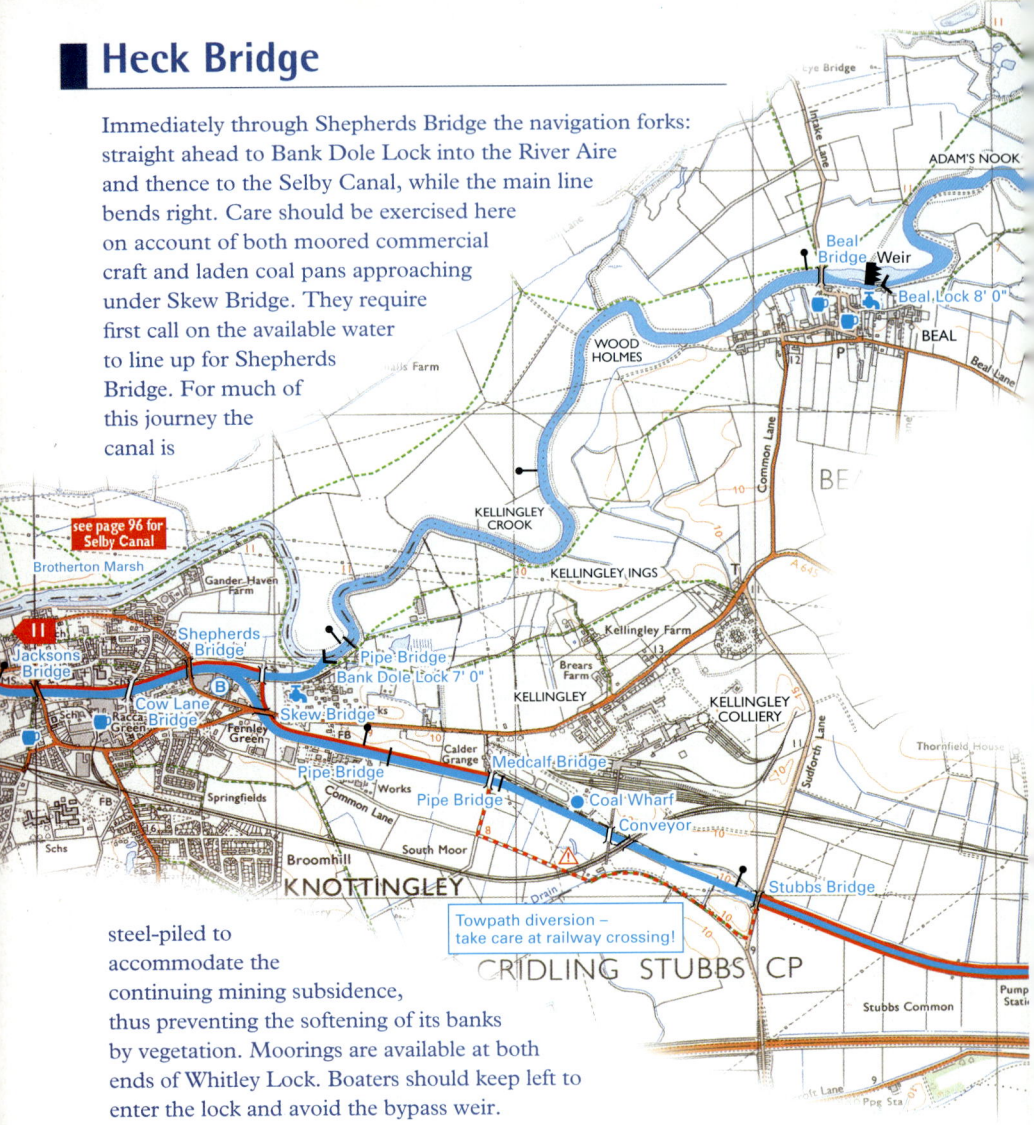

steel-piled to accommodate the continuing mining subsidence, thus preventing the softening of its banks by vegetation. Moorings are available at both ends of Whitley Lock. Boaters should keep left to enter the lock and avoid the bypass weir.

● **Knottingley**

W. Yorks. All services. Once famous for the making of clay tobacco pipes and for its pottery, Knottingley now depends on the manufacture of synthetic chemicals, hydro-carbons, cosmetics and glassware. The famous Rockware Glass Works produces the majority of the glass containers in our homes and supermarkets. The pretty church of St Botolph can be seen at the north end of Jacksons Bridge. The church has some impressive carvings around the doorway and an interesting campanile tower. The area next to the church was once the site of

Knottingley Old Hall, an Elizabethan residence demolished in 1830 'for the sake of the lime-stone beneath it'.

● **Whitley Bridge**

N. Yorks. PO, tel, stores, station (limited service). The original settlement of Whitley Bridge has now been lost amidst a sprawling development of new housing in Low Eggborough. There are two feed mills in the area. Eggborough Power Station, one of the largest in Yorkshire, is situated halfway between the canal and the old course of the River Aire.

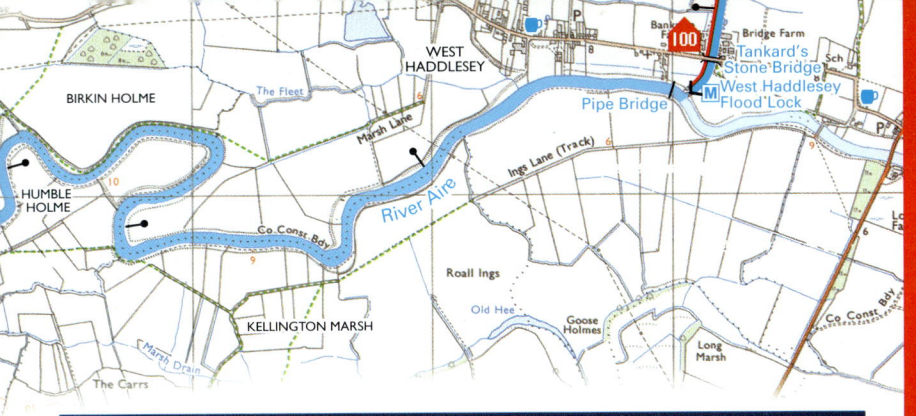

NAVIGATIONAL NOTES

1 **Lock operation** Lock gate and sluice operating pedestals are located adjacent to the upstream and downstream gates. You will need to insert a BW sanitary station key into the pedestal to activate the system and allow use. Follow the step by step instructions on the operating panel in order to open the gates/sluices safely. Each pedestal can only be used to operate the adjacent gate/sluice.

2 **Emergency breakdown telephone** In the event of a breakdown in the operating system a red fault light will illuminate. Should this occur an emergency telephone is located in the front of the lockside control building. The cabinet door will automatically unlock or use your BW key. Dial 100 and advise Freephone Canals of your location and fault details. Remain by the telephone in case the duty engineer calls back for further information.

Boatyards

ⓑ **Hirst Boatbuilders** The Slipway, Fernley Green Ind Estate, Knottingley (01977 670834). 🅳 Gas, overnight and long-term moorings, slipway, engine installation, DIY facilities, electrical and plumbing, boat fitting-out, solid fuel.

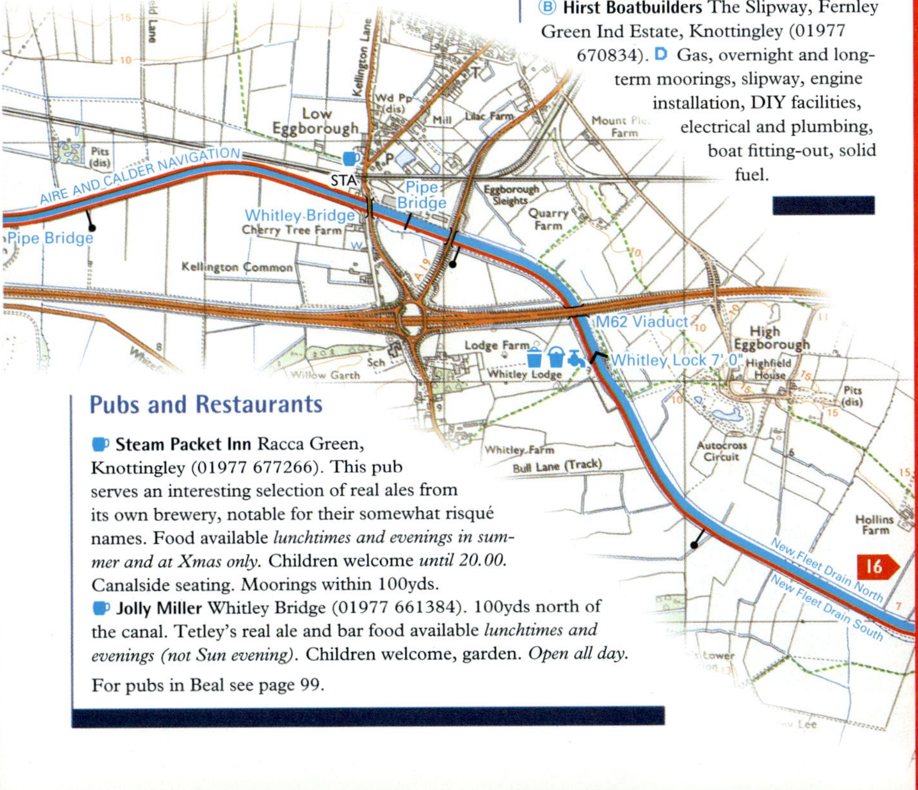

Pubs and Restaurants

🍺 **Steam Packet Inn** Racca Green, Knottingley (01977 677266). This pub serves an interesting selection of real ales from its own brewery, notable for their somewhat risqué names. Food available *lunchtimes and evenings in summer and at Xmas only*. Children welcome *until 20.00*. Canalside seating. Moorings within 100yds.

🍺 **Jolly Miller** Whitley Bridge (01977 661384). 100yds north of the canal. Tetley's real ale and bar food available *lunchtimes and evenings (not Sun evening)*. Children welcome, garden. *Open all day*.

For pubs in Beal see page 99.

Pollington

Soon Heck Bridge appears giving access to local pubs. Until recently there was a quaint village shop, where only the sign outside gave the visitor any indication of its function. Once inside it soon became apparent that the shop was no more than a room set aside in someone's house. Sadly this is yet another whimsical feature of English village life that has passed away. Just beyond Heck Bridge is the home of the South Yorkshire Boat Club. The site makes use of the basin once excavated to provide transhipment of stone to Goole from the local quarry. Immediately beyond the village the east coast main railway from London to Edinburgh crosses the navigation. Now electrified, this line carries the new Class 91 Electra locomotives capable of hauling passenger trains at speeds of up to 140 mph, since an automatic in-cab signalling system has been approved and installed. To the north stand the twin chimneys of the disused quarry, now the site of a concrete pipe works. The navigation now adopts a fairly bleak and monotonous course through a flat but fertile landscape. Trees are scarce, and hedges and livestock are nowhere to be seen. There are numerous drainage ditches. The straggling village of Pollington lies to the north of Pollington Bridge; there is a post office and two pubs. The school and a brick-built chapel with a bell tower are on the south side of the bridge. To the west of the village, facing the canal, stands Pollington Hall, an attractive 18th-C house with pleasingly proportioned narrow windows and a door canopy. Beyond the lock is Manor Farm where there is evidence of a moat. These buildings, along with Pollington Grange to the south of the navigation, indicate a former prosperity. At Pollington Lock the lock

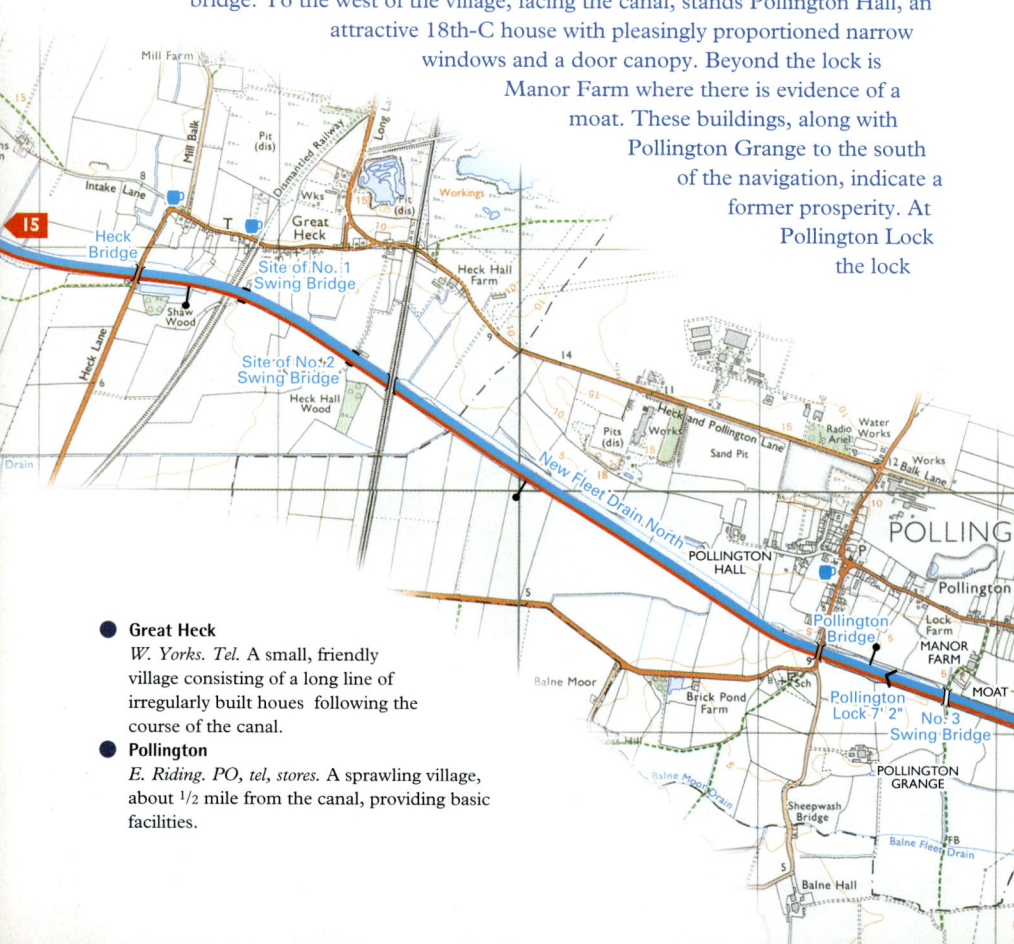

● **Great Heck**
  W. Yorks. Tel. A small, friendly village consisting of a long line of irregularly built houes following the course of the canal.
● **Pollington**
  E. Riding. PO, tel, stores. A sprawling village, about 1/2 mile from the canal, providing basic facilities.

keeper's pretty cottage is one of the best examples of its type, with attractively rounded brick arches above the windows and a particularly deep overhang to the roof at the gable ends. Beyond Crow Croft Bridge the demolished abutments of an old railway bridge can be seen, unusual in that it once pivoted upwards at one end. At this point the River Went draws close and follows the line of the navigation towards Goole. The dinghies of the Beaver Sailing Club at Southfield Reservoir add an unexpected and welcome splash of colour to the landscape. The 110-acre reservoir, built at the turn of the century, marks the beginning of the New Junction Canal leading south to Sheffield. Its construction provided a water supply to meet the needs of the much larger locks installed on the navigation, and it effectively maintains the water levels of the docks at Goole.

NAVIGATIONAL NOTES

See page 15 for details of self-operation of locks.

Pubs and Restaurants

Bay Horse Great Heck (01977 661125). 300yds north of Heck Bridge. A cosy pub, popular with boaters, serving Tetley's and Boddingtons real ales. Bar meals available *lunchtimes and evenings, 7 days a week.* Children welcome, outside seating. Music *Wed.* Quiz night *Thur.*

New Inn Great Heck (01977 661414). On the Pollington Road out of the village. John Smith's real ale and food served *evenings and Sunday lunchtimes.* Vegetarians and children catered for. Outside seating. Quiz *Sun.*

George & Dragon Pollington (01405 862668). In the square directly north of Pollington Bridge. A basic John Smith's real ale pub, popular with the local youngsters. Food available *evenings and lunchtimes Fri–Sun.* Patio seating, children welcome. Live music *Fri & Sat.* B & B.

King's Head Pollington (01405 861507). At the east end of the village. Tetley's and guest real ales together with bar meals served *lunchtimes and evenings, 7 days a week.* Vegetarians catered for. Garden and children's play area. Quiz *alternate Tue.*

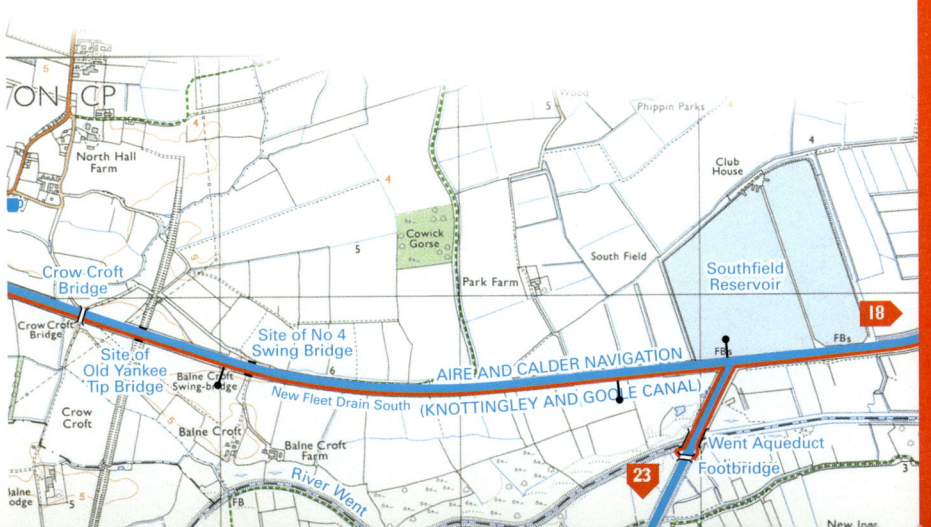

Rawcliffe Bridge

Beyond the turning to Keadby and Sheffield, up the unerringly straight New Junction Canal, the Aire & Calder performs an exaggerated dogleg and then sets off on an equally straight course for its terminus in Goole Docks. This manoeuvre is brought about by the appearance of the River Don from the south, joined near Beever Bridge by the diminutive River Went. In times of high rainfall the Went becomes more aggressive, flooding the surrounding farmland and leaving large deposits of silt in its wake. The turf growing enterprise in this area bears witness to the inherent fertility of this regular fluvial performance and to man's ability to capitalise on one of nature's excesses. Having swung hard left, the boater is now in alignment with the Dutch River, the artificial channel cut by Cornelius Vermuyden to contain the River Don's previous exuberance. Before his intervention the Don had two mouths: one across the Isle of Axholme into the Trent near Trent Falls and a second into the River Aire, little more than a mile north of here. Were the boater not to swing right, under New Bridge, but to carry on straight ahead (with the addition of the odd wiggle or two) he would, in fact, be following the Don's old course. As the tidal Dutch River, Vermuyden's Don now

● **Rawcliffe Bridge**
E. Riding. Tel, stores, station (limited service). A small, straggling settlement, running down to the canal and Dutch River to the south and up to the main village of Rawcliffe 1½ miles to the north.

accompanies the canal all the way to Goole. Both navigations – the Dutch River is used by experienced skippers – duck under the M18 (a sheltered 'berth' much fancied by local barge owners for painting their boats) and passes the site of both an old tar works and of a disused brickworks. Both works used to rely heavily on the canal for raw materials and the export of their finished products. To the east of Rawcliffe Bridge BW have established a safe haven mooring available for craft on either a short- or long-term basis. Contact the Castleford office for further details.

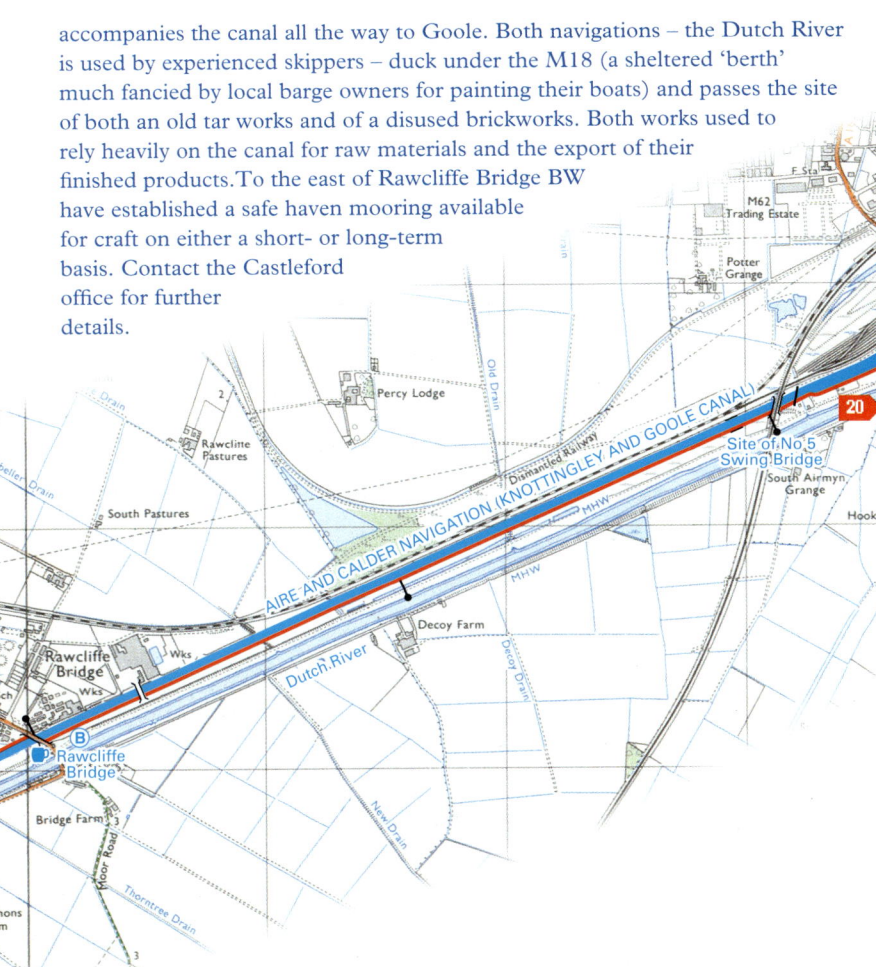

Pubs and Restaurants

🛥 **Black Horse** Rawcliffe Bridge (01405 839019). Canalside. A comfortable, nicely furnished and welcoming pub dispensing Tetley's and a guest real ale. Traditional bar meals available *lunchtimes and evenings, 7 days a week.* Children and vegetarians catered for. *Sunday* lunches are a speciality. Canalside seating and moorings available. Quiz *Sun.* Pool. The landlord keeps his own boat outside and appreciates boaters *slowing down* to pass.
🛥 **Rawcliffe Bridge Hotel** Rawcliffe Bridge (01405 839251). ¹⁄₄ mile north of the canal. John Smith's and Tetley's real ales. Food to

order. Children and vegetarians catered for. Pub games. Occasional B & B.
🛥 **Royal Hotel** Rawcliffe (01405 839232). ³⁄₄ mile north of canal, beside the station. John Smith's and Tetley's real ales available in this friendly pub. Children welcome. Live music *Sat.* Pool, darts and dominoes.
🛥 **Downe Arms** Market Place, Snaith (01405 860544). Not straightforward to access from the canal but the attached brewery and range of Mansfield real ales might act as a strong draw. Meals served *lunchtimes and evenings* in this historic, listed, village-centre building. *Open all day.* B & B. Station (limited service). Disabled access.

Goole

Immediately before the railway bridge, marking the effective start of Goole docks, is the site of the old No 5 swing bridge, replaced by a device replicating the stop planks found on narrow canals. A 'curtain' resting in the bottom of the waterway is winched across from one bank to the other. It was originally installed at the outbreak of World War II in anticipation of the docks being bombed. Once through the bridge, it can be plainly seen that there is far more boat capacity than there is waterborne traffic to fill it. To the north is a small basin, the remains of what was a proposed connection to the West Dock. It was here that Humber keels removed their lee-boards, masts and cog boats before heading inland. Fuel barges berth beside a boatyard in the first basin on the left (known as the 'dog and duck'), followed by John Branford's sand barges (cargoes from the Trent to Leeds) at the aggregate wharf, and the occasional Waddington's boat. On the right is a concrete plant which recieves materials by water, the Waterways Museum, commercial wharves and finally William Bartholomew's No 5 Boat Hoist, now restored and soon to be opened to the public. Bartholomew devised the system of trains of floating tubs – known as Tom Puddings – towed in a long snaking line (as many as 19 at a time) behind a tug, to be up-ended into a coaster, via the Boat Hoist, on their arrival in the docks.

Boatyards

Ⓑ **Goole Boathouse** The Timber Pond, Dutch Riverside, Goole (01405 763985). ⚓ D E Gas, overnight mooring and long-term mooring (6' *max draught)*, winter storage, slipway, crane, dry dock, boat repairs, chandlery, books, maps and gifts, toilets, showers, groceries.

NAVIGATIONAL NOTES

1 There are British Waterways visitor moorings by the sanitary station, by Goole Boathouse.
2 At the west end of South Dock the navigation ceases to be the responsibility of BW and comes under the jurisdiction of Associated British Ports (ABP). They may be contacted on VHF radio channels 14 and 19 – call *Goole Docks* – or by telephoning (01405) 760924.
3 Beyond this point ocean-going shipping is manoeuvring and contact must be made with Ocean Lock Control before continuing.
4 Overnight mooring in this area will incur a substantial charge and temporary mooring, whilst awaiting a lock or bridge swing, is only permitted if the crew are in attendance. Mooring on any pier whilst on the tideway (unless awaiting a lock) will also incur a charge.
5 Headroom under the swing bridge is approximately 11' 6" (the level of the dock can vary) and contact should be made with the lock keeper to arrange for it to be opened.
6 Lock operating times are *2^1/$_2$ hours before high tide and 1 hour after* for which no charge is made. Outside these times special pens are always available on payment of a fee, which is in turn dependent on the time of day or night.
7 The lock keeper will willingly offer advice and information on navigating the tideway. For his part the boater must inform ABP that he is on the river and make his position known. ABP maintain a continuous watch on channel 14. **At high tide the River Ouse is a busy navigation, carrying ocean-going shipping.**

● **Goole**
E. Riding. MD Wed & Fri. All services. When the Aire & Calder Navigation applied for an Act to build a canal from Knottingley to Goole in 1819, Goole was no more than a few cottages scattered around the marshes on the banks of the Ouse. Work commenced on cutting the canal in 1822 and by the following year a new town was developing rapidly as dwellings were built for the employees of the company. By 1828 foreign trade had begun with Hamburg and the local people entertained themselves by going down to the docks in the evening to await the arrival of foreign vessels on the spring tides. It is said of Goole that it was 'born under Victoria and died with her'. The docks are still very much the focal point of Goole, handling cargoes from Europe and Scandinavia. Lock Hill, near the Leisure Centre, is a good vantage point for watching vessels manoeuvring.

Boothferry Leisure Centre North Street, Goole (01405 769005). Excellent facilities for the whole family.
Goole Library and Museum Carlisle Street, Goole (01405 762187). The museum houses an interesting exhibition depicting the development of Goole and the surrounding area. Free.
Waterways Museum & Adventure Centre Dutch Riverside, Goole (01405 768730). Museum displays, boat tours of Goole docks. Café. *Open Mon-Fri 10.30–15.30 and Sat & Sun Easter-Sep 12.00-17.00.* Charge.

BOAT TRIPS
Waterways Museum & Adventure Centre Dutch Riverside, Goole (01405 768730). Hourly tours around the docks *weekends, Easter–Sep. Other times by appointment.*

Pubs and Restaurants

⬤ **Old George** Market Place, Goole (01405 763147). Formerly the George IV, and decorated with local antiques, this friendly pub houses many photographs of Goole in its former days. John Smith's, Stones and Worthingtons real ales. Bar food *lunchtimes only, not Sun.* Children welcome, and a quiz *every Sun.*
⬤ **Macintosh Arms** 13 Aire Street, Goole (01405 763850). Close to the main docks, this former courthouse offers a friendly welcome together with John Smith's, Tetley's and guest real ales. Outside seating and pub games. Open all day.
⬤ **Victoria Hotel** Hook Road, Goole (01405 763839). The landlord prides himself on his well kept Tetley's, John Smith's and guest real ales. A typical homely northern pub with dark wooden panelling and cream paintwork, built in 1794. Beer garden, pool, darts and dominoes. Other pubs in Goole, close to the docks and frequented by boaters, include the Vermuyden, the Bridge Inn and the Middle House.

New Junction Canal

The New Junction Canal provides a link between the Aire & Calder and the South Yorkshire Navigations and is one of the last canals to be constructed in this country. The waterway is 5¹/₂ miles long and completely straight all the way, the monotony being broken only by a series of swing and lift bridges, all of which can be manned during working hours (see navigational notes). There are aqueducts at each end of the long corridor formed by the navigation, the first carrying the canal over the River Went. Two smaller aqueducts are to be found at Chequer Lane and Westfields. Although the countryside here is flat, it is not without character. Moorings are available to the north of Sykehouse Bridge and from here the village of Sykehouse and its two pubs may be reached, approximately ³/₄ mile to the west of the canal. Further moorings are available to the north of Kirkhouse Green Bridge. Beyond Top Lane Lift Bridge is Low Lane Swing Bridge, carrying the road leading into Kirk Bramwith, with its interesting Norman church. Then the Don aqueduct appears. It presents a rather foreboding feature as it is contained by large guillotine gates at either end. Passing boats, although protected by a barrier on one side, have no more than a girder fixed at water level on the other side, to prevent their descent into the river below. Once over the aqueduct, the canal is joined by the Stainforth & Keadby section of the navigation meeting at a very fine angle from the left. Its junction is masked by trees growing on the narrow spit of land formed between the two canals.

NAVIGATIONAL NOTES

All locks and moveable bridges can be boater-operated using the BW sanitary station key. There are three lengthsmen who will assist passage if working in the area. This canal comes under the BW Waterway Manager based in Doncaster who can be contacted on 01302 340610.

● **Sykehouse**
S. Yorks. Tel, stores, garage. A linear settlement which sprawls extensively to either side of the canal. A pub and a shop will be found to the west where there is some attractive new housing, much of which has been thoughtfully constructed of old brick. The Holy Trinity Church has an attractive brick tower which was added to the original stone structure in 1724. The stone was subsequently replaced by a Victorian brick edifice. The village seems to virtually close down during the winter months.

Pubs and Restaurants

Old George Inn Sykehouse (01405 785635). It is a brave man who would interfere with a Yorkshireman's cricket! Once the home of the local cricket team, the adjoining field now contains an extensive adventure playground which has made this a popular pub with families from the surrounding towns and villages. The summer months attract visitors from far and wide who come to enjoy the swimming pool, boules and short mat bowls. There is also a regular karaoke night on *Thur*. The building dates back some 500 years, the pub having been formed from what was once a terrace of cottages consisting over the years of a shop, a dame school, a farrier, a butcher and a slaughter house. The original wheel for hoisting the animals aloft for slaughter still hangs in the dining area. One room in the pub has its ceiling covered with old coins, all stuck there with the froth off the beer. Tetley's real ale is served here and food is available *lunchtimes (weekends and during school holidays only)* and *evenings, 7 days a week. Closed Oct-Easter.*

16

17

Site of Old Yankee
Tip Bridge
Crow Croft
Bridge
Site of No 4
Swing Bridge

Crow
Croft

AIRE AND CALDER NAVIGATION

Balne Croft
Swing-bridge

New Fleet Drain South (KNOTTINGLEY AND GOOLE CANAL)

FBs

The Fleet Drain

FB

Balne Croft

Balne Croft
Farm

Went Aque
Footbridge

River Went

Balne
Lodge

Old
Ings

FB

Eskholme

Place Hills
Farm

FB

Moor House

Ferry Bridge

Topham

Station
House

Thorseby
Hall

PH

Sch

Poplar's
Farm

Marsh Hill
Farm

Sykehouse
Lift Bridge

Warren
Hall

Starkbridge
Farm

Turpin
Farm

Sykehouse

Mawson
Green

Mawson Green
Farm

Pinetrees
Farm

London
Hill

Tithedale
Farm

SYKEHOUSE

Holmpton

Kirk Lane
Bridge

Kirk Lane Bridge

Peartree
Corner

Claybridge

Manor
Farm

Sykehouse Lock
Bridge
(swing)

Sykehouse Lock
and Lift Bridge

Clay Dike

Clay
Bridge

Little Fen
Field

Hannes Ing
Covert

Smallhedge Rein

NEW JUNCTION CANAL

Smallhedge
Farm

Smallhedge Swing Bridge
(disused)

Gle

Fishlake Covert

FIS

Westfield House

Kirkhouse
Green Gorse

Westfield
Bridge House

Site of
Westfield Bridge

Neville
Hall

Flood
Arches

West Field

Kirkhouse
Green

Hobbledehoy
Wood

White
Gates
Farm

Hotel

Kirkhouse Green
Road Bridge
(swing)

Wood
End

Pear Tree
Farm

Kirkhouse Green
Lift Bridge

KIRK BRAMWITH CP

114

Woodhouse Field

Braithwaite Hall
Sch

Top Lane Lift Bridge

River Don

CHESTERFIELD CANAL

MAXIMUM DIMENSIONS

Length: 72'
Beam: 6' 10"
Headroom: 7' 6"
(Craft of 8' 6" beam *may* be able to proceed as far as Clayworth, depending on the height of the superstructure.)

MANAGER
01636 704481

MILEAGE

WEST STOCKWITH to
Drakeholes Tunnel: 6$\frac{1}{2}$ miles
Haydon: 12 miles
Retford Lock: 15$\frac{1}{4}$ miles
Osberton Lock: 22$\frac{1}{4}$ miles
Worksop Town Lock: 25$\frac{1}{2}$ miles
Shireoaks Aqueduct: 28$\frac{1}{4}$ miles
NORWOOD TUNNEL East End: 31$\frac{3}{4}$ miles
Locks: 47

The Chesterfield Canal was initially surveyed in 1768 by John Varley to follow a line between Chesterfield and Bawtry on the River Idle, as an improvement on the trade route already in use. However, both Worksop and Retford were anxious to benefit from the proposed waterway, so Varley undertook a second survey a year later along a route to West Stockwith that bypassed the Idle altogether.

In 1769 James Brindley who had, due to pressure of other work, delegated the initial survey to Varley, called a public meeting at the Red Lion in Worksop. Here he proposed a draft line, terminating near Gainsborough and costing £105,000. This was later re-amended, on the grounds of cost and speed of construction, to meet the Trent at West Stockwith.

Work started in October 1771 with John Varley as resident engineer, Brindley being still too busy with other schemes to be permanently on site. Most of the work, including digging the 2893yd long Norwood Tunnel, constructing the summit level reservoir and building the lock flights, was let as separate contracts and carried out by individual contractors. Brindley's method was to make each section of the canal navigable as soon as it was completed to enable the company to benefit from the carriage of the heavy construction materials.

Brindley's death in September 1772 was a sad blow to the project and led to Varley being placed in overall charge of this, his first large project. Ultimately Hugh Henshall, Brindley's brother-in-law, was made inspector of works, later to become chief engineer with a salary of £250 per annum. In the following year he discovered work, carried out by John Varley's father and two brothers, in the construction of Norwood Tunnel, to be unsatisfactory. Soon other examples of dubious contractual arrangements and slack management came to light, all reflecting badly on the Varley family. The extent of John Varley's complicity in these matters remains to this day a matter for debate.

On 4th June 1777 the canal was officially opened from West Stockwith to Chesterfield. Norwood Tunnel caused problems from the outset, as did the shortage of water to the summit pound. Boats travelling less than 12 miles empty, or lightly laden, were penalised when using a lock. Over the next 25 years a more satisfactory solution was provided by the building of three large reservoirs at Killamarsh, Woodhall and Harthill.

As had always been envisaged by the canal's promoters, coal was the principal cargo carried, followed by stone, corn, lime, lead, timber and iron. Pottery and ale were also regular cargoes. Traffic peaked at over 200,000 tons in 1848, when records show the average load as 22 tons. Early in 1840 a cargo of Anston Stone, bound for the construction of the new Houses of Parliament, was carried for transhipment at West Stockwith: the first of approximately 250,000 tons despatched in total. As always, amalgamation with a railway company, in this case the Manchester & Lincoln Union Railway, led to a steady decline in the canal's fortunes and a reduction in maintenance. By 1904 it was reported that the minimum headroom in Norwood Tunnel was reduced to 4' 10", owing to subsidence, while a roof collapse in 1907 led to its final closure.

Between the wars, now under London & North Eastern Railway (LNER) ownership, the canal was reasonably maintained, while the tidal lock into the Trent was enlarged and repaired in 1923–5. Attempts were also made to reduce the weed which had appeared in 1852 and remains, to some extent, a problem today. The navigation was temporarily resuscitated by the transport of munitions during World War II, but traffic virtually came to an end in 1955 when the small trade from Walkeringham brickworks (near Gringley) to the Trent finished. One cargo that did linger on into the early 1960s was that of warp: a fine natural silt dredged from the Trent at Idle Mouth and used as a metal polishing material in the Sheffield cutlery trade. To the end all boats remained horse-drawn.

On 24 May 1960 a public enquiry into the canal's future was held in Chesterfield at which BW proposed the retention of the waterway from the Trent to Worksop for pleasure boating. The remainder was to be either utilised for water supply or infilled. The 1968 Transport act finally confirmed its status as a cruiseway.

By 1976 it was generally considered desirable that the waterway be restored beyond Worksop and the Chesterfield Canal Society was formed with the ultimate aim of full restoration to Chesterfield. Work on both the western and eastern ends is moving on rapidly, aided by a great deal of volunteer work, together with industrial and European Union money. The major difficulties remaining are the restoration of Norwood Tunnel and bypassing the houses built on the infilled line at Killamarsh. An exciting scheme has been proposed whereby the canal is linked into the River Rother; the river itself is made navigable, so providing a link to the South Yorkshire Navigations at Rotherham.

SELF-DISCOVERY OR WATERWAYS RECOVERY?

Messing about in the mud has long been the pursuit of little boys (and girls) and is an occupation that some of us have great difficulty in shrugging off, even in later life. Imagine, then, having the opportunity to legitimise this sensory indulgence in the respectable form (in the eyes of some, at least) of canal restoration. There are still many muddy, overgrown ditches festering in their own private world of decay that were once illustrious watery highways. As the more straightforward canal restorations are successfully accomplished, so the more difficult ones become the targets for the doyens of dirty digging, namely the Waterways Recovery Group. Formed with the express purpose of resurrecting fallen waterways and familiar to many a boater as the driving force behind the annual National Waterway Festivals, this organisation is able to dig the dirt with the best of them. The Chesterfield Canal is one of many navigations to have benefited from their unstinting ability to mix endeavour with cheerfulness, pleasure with muck and sand with cement.

West Stockwith

The church spire of East Stockwith stands opposite the entrance to the Chesterfield Canal. The lock here is power-operated. Just above the lock is a basin housing a boatyard, a boat club, a hire boat company, a slipway (apply to the lock keeper), and plenty of moored pleasure boats. Pump-out facilities, diesel and gas are also available from the lock keeper *when on duty*. A pub is nearby. At Misterton there are two locks close together, with a canalside pub at the bottom. The course of the canal is entirely rural and pleasant, passing well-established, but often decaying, farm buildings.

● **West Stockwith**

Notts. PO, tel, stores. At the junction not only of the Chesterfield Canal with the Trent but also of the River Idle with the Trent. East Stockwith is just across the river, tantalisingly out of reach. The two communities used to be connected by a ferry. In a way, the total lack of communication with the other village, only 50yds away, serves to enhance the magical sense of remoteness that Stockwith possesses – especially when one sees big barges appearing round the bend, churning past the two villages and then as quickly disappearing again.

Cuckoo Walk It is possible to follow the towpath (and the boat-horse route over Norwood Tunnel) along the entire length of the waterway to Chesterfield. Whilst still incomplete as a through navigation, this is by far the best way to appreciate fully the marvel of this, one of the early Brindley-conceived canals. Further details from: The Secretary, Chesterfield Canal Society, 18 Rosedale Avenue, Chesterfield, S40 2UY (01246 559054).

● **Misterton**

Notts. PO, tel, stores, garage. The village has a thriving Methodist church, as do most of the places in this area. John Wesley came from nearby Epworth.

● **Gringley on the Hill**

Notts. PO, tel, stores. The village is about a mile's walk up from the canal. A small rise on a level with the church tower gives a good view. On a clear day the pinnacles of Lincoln Cathedral can sometimes be seen, nearly 20 miles to the south east.

Boatyards

ⓑ **Chesterfield Canal Boat Company** West Stockwith Basin (01522 514774). Narrow boat hire, maps. The following facilities are available in the basin and are obtainable by contacting the lock keeper on 01427 890204.

🚿 🚽 ⚓ D Pump-out, gas, short- and long-term mooring, winter storage, slipway, toilets, showers.

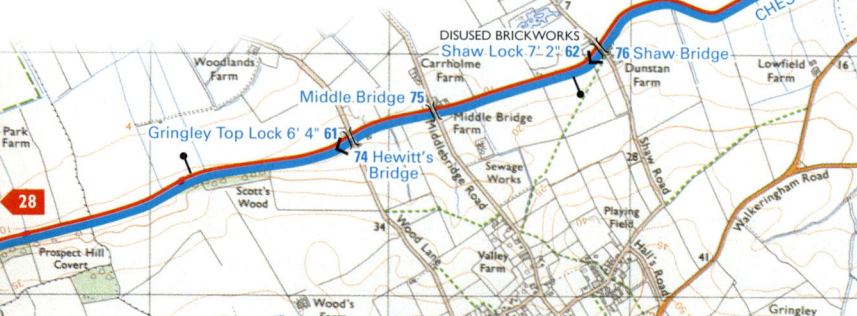

28

Pubs and Restaurants

🔵 **Waterfront Inn** West Stockwith (01427 891223). Canalside at West Stockwith Basin. John Smith's, Marston's and guest real ales together with excellent food *(lunchtimes and evenings)*. *Sun lunchtimes* carvery. Vegetarians and children catered for. Garden seating. Take-away menu. B&B. Live music *Fri. Open all day*.

🔵 **White Hart** West Stockwith (01427 890176). By the junction of the rivers Idle and Trent. John Smith's and Worthington real ales. Bar food available *lunchtimes and evenings, 7 days a week*. Children and vegetarians catered for. Garden. Karaoke *Sat*. B & B.

🔵 **Packet Inn** Misterton (01427 890559). Canalside at Misterton Low Lock. John Smith's and guest real ales. Good choice of reasonably priced meals, including vegetarian, *lunchtimes and evenings (not Mon lunchtimes)*. Beer garden. Music *Thur evenings*.

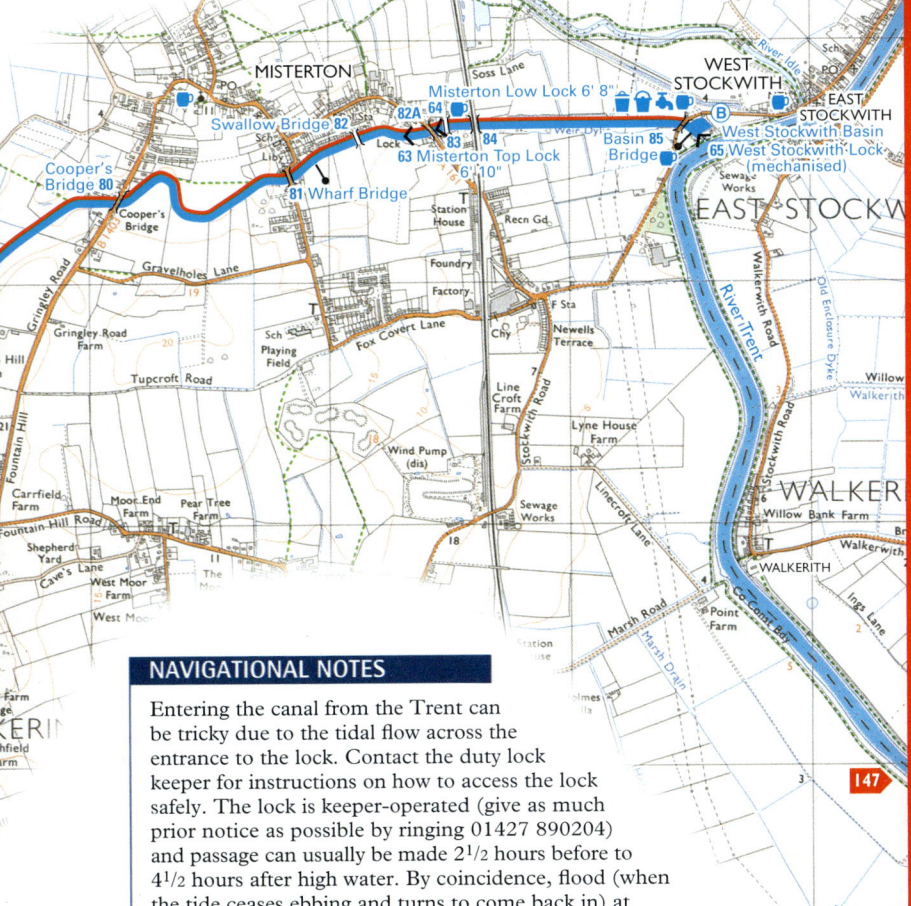

NAVIGATIONAL NOTES

Entering the canal from the Trent can be tricky due to the tidal flow across the entrance to the lock. Contact the duty lock keeper for instructions on how to access the lock safely. The lock is keeper-operated (give as much prior notice as possible by ringing 01427 890204) and passage can usually be made 2½ hours before to 4½ hours after high water. By coincidence, flood (when the tide ceases ebbing and turns to come back in) at Stockwith is the same time as high water at Hull. The flood runs for approximately 2½ hours and the direction of flow changes very rapidly. VHF radio frequencies: calling channel 16, working channel 74. The radio is not constantly manned. Commercial river traffic operate on channel 6 upstream of Keadby Bridge and it is useful for VHF users to monitor this channel to establish the whereabouts of large craft.

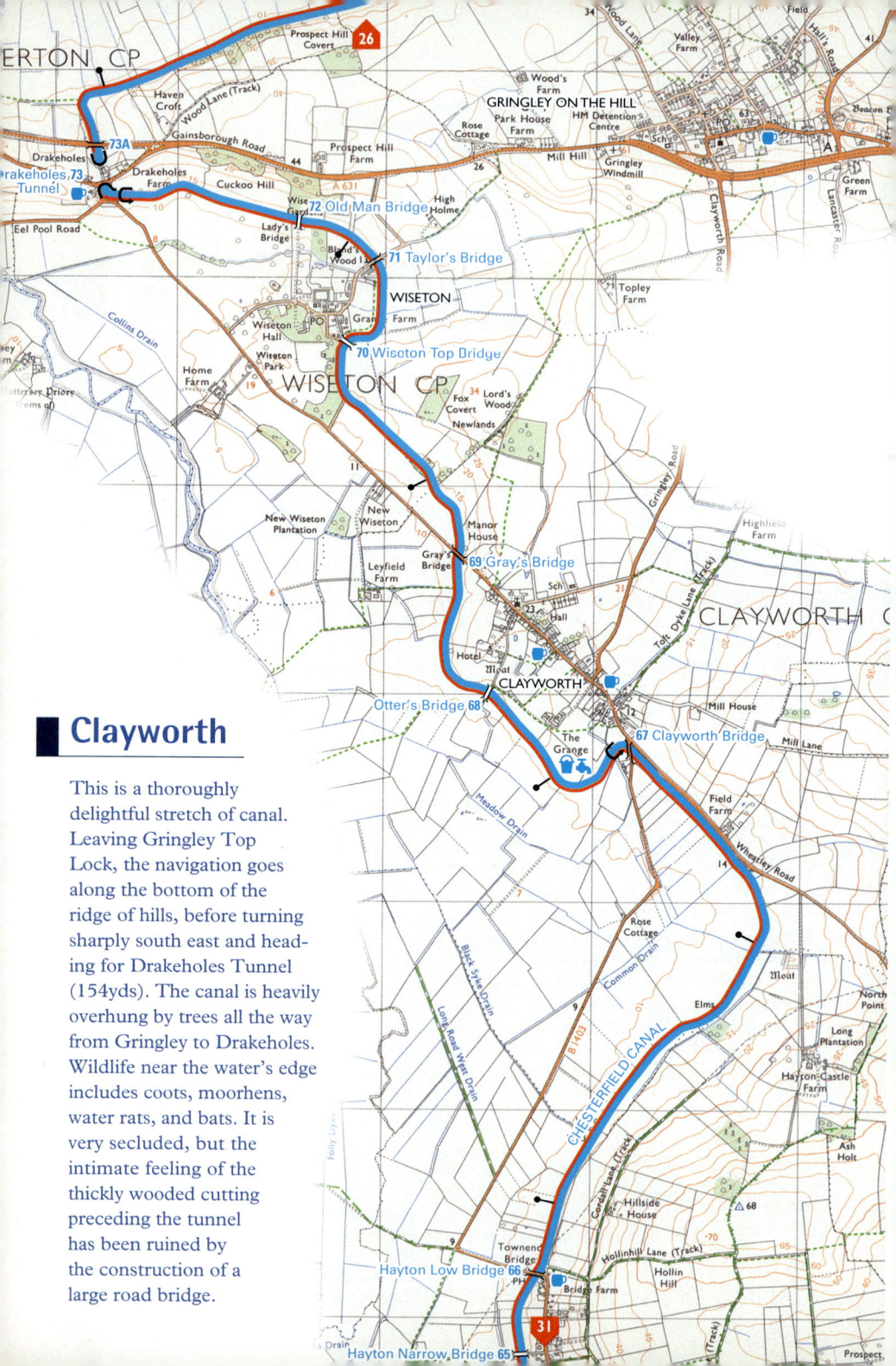

Clayworth

This is a thoroughly
delightful stretch of canal.
Leaving Gringley Top
Lock, the navigation goes
along the bottom of the
ridge of hills, before turning
sharply south east and heading for Drakeholes Tunnel
(154yds). The canal is heavily
overhung by trees all the way
from Gringley to Drakeholes.
Wildlife near the water's edge
includes coots, moorhens,
water rats, and bats. It is
very secluded, but the
intimate feeling of the
thickly wooded cutting
preceding the tunnel
has been ruined by
the construction of a
large road bridge.

The tunnel is cut through rock and is mostly unlined. At the south end one emerges to find a sharp corner at a mooring site, where there is also a turning place for full-length narrow boats and a slipway owned by the Retford & Worksop Boat Club. A handsome pub stands nearby. Leaving Drakeholes, the canal is still accompanied by woods as it reaches Wiseton Park, passing the stern features of a bearded man on the parapet of Old Man Bridge. The canal now skirts an attractive courtyard housing development built on the site of the park's old walled kitchen garden. The brick from the enclosing walls has been put to good use in the construction of many of the houses. The straight road that crosses the canal at Gray's Bridge is of Roman origin. The navigation circles the village, ending up with a sharp turn to the right at Clayworth Bridge. The white building by the bridge used to be a pub (the White Hart). It is now a boat club base, so a good lookout for other boats should be maintained when negotiating the bridge. There are visitor moorings immediately north of Hayton Low Bridge.

● **Wiseton**
Notts. Tel. A superbly elegant estate village set in a landscaped park, still clearly fulfilling its original manorial function. Trees and grass separate the various buildings, of which the large stable with its handsome clock tower is the most significant. The hall, a modern red brick building, which replaced the original in 1962, is well hidden behind high walls.

● **Clayworth**
Notts. PO, tel, stores. A quiet and pleasant village extending along a single main street. The houses are of all periods, the new blending well with the old. The Retford & Worksop Boat Club is based at the old pub at Clayworth and welcomes visitors to the clubhouse. There are good moorings and all facilities here. In the old days a passenger boat used to run every Saturday from this pub to Retford, so that the villagers of Clayworth, Hayton and Clarborough could take their produce to Retford Market. The goods were loaded into the 'packet' boat on the Friday night, then the people would return early on Saturday morning, leaving at 06.30 to reach Retford by 08.30. The boat used to return in the evening when the market closed. A handsome sundial sits over the porch of the pretty village church inscribed with the words "Our days on earth are as a shadow". Inside there is a series of beautiful wall paintings.

Pubs and Restaurants

🍺 ✕ **White Swan** Drakeholes, Wiseton (01777 817206). Canalside at Drakeholes Tunnel. A smart and fairly pricey establishment serving Castle Eden, Boddingtons and Flowers real ale. There is an extensive bar menu, offering a good choice for vegetarians, as well as a carvery and restaurant. *Food available lunchtimes and evenings (pub closed Sun evenings and Mon all day during winter until Easter).* Outside seating. Children welcome. B & B.

🍺 ✕ **Blacksmith's Arms and Wiseton Restaurant** Town Street, Clayworth (01777 818171). A smartly refurbished pub and restaurant with a good choice of real ale including Stones, Bass, Worthington and a guest. Excellent meals are available *lunchtimes and evenings* in both the bar and restaurant (à la carte and table d'hôte), both of which offer a wide choice, including vegetarian and children's menus. *(Restaurant closed Sun evenings).* Patio seating.

🍺 **Brewers Arms** Town Street, Clayworth (01777 816522). Unadulterated village local that once brewed its own beers now serving Castle Eden, Boddingtons, Whitbread and guest real ales. (The brewing vats are still buried under the car park!) Traditional bar meals available *lunchtimes and evenings except Mon.* Beer garden and swings. *Thur* quiz in winter. Traditional pub games. The pub is combined with a quality country clothing shop supplying outdoor wear.

🍺 ✕ **Boat Inn** Main Street, Hayton (01777 700158). Canalside near Hayton Low Bridge. A popular and nicely kept pub offering Bass, Stones and Tetley's real ales. A wide range of reasonably priced food (including vegetarian) is available in the bar *lunchtimes and evenings, 7 days a week.* The carvery restaurant is *open all day Sun and evenings Mon–Sat.* Garden and play area. B & B.

Retford

The canal now leaves the woods and low hills to the north and heads southwards through more open farmland towards East Retford. In the town centre is the first of the narrow locks, with a large canal warehouse beside it. West of here the canal crosses three minute aqueducts, then a double bend and an old iron footbridge lead to West Retford Lock. In the open countryside along here are the four Forest Locks, complete with boater facilities that include a shower. At the third one is a British Waterways permanent mooring site and the water point is right beside the top gate. The straight road crossing at the nearby Barnby Wharf Bridge was a Roman highway. It was, in fact, the original course of the Great North Road but 200 years ago the citizens of Retford got the road diverted to pass through their town, thereby increasing its importance and prosperity. They must now be equally relieved to have rid themselves of it again. There is a useful supermarket on the towpath side above Retford Lock and a café and take-away south of bridge 56.

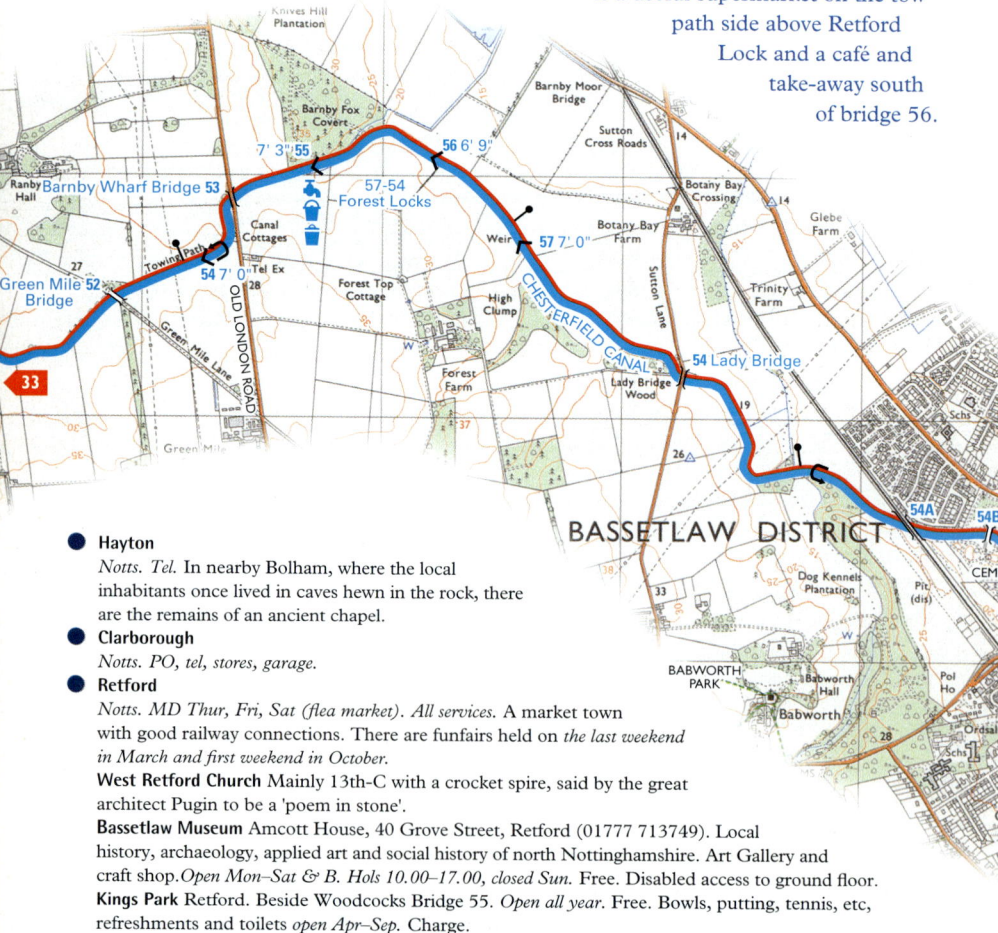

● **Hayton**
Notts. Tel. In nearby Bolham, where the local inhabitants once lived in caves hewn in the rock, there are the remains of an ancient chapel.

● **Clarborough**
Notts. PO, tel, stores, garage.

● **Retford**
Notts. MD Thur, Fri, Sat (flea market). All services. A market town with good railway connections. There are funfairs held on *the last weekend in March and first weekend in October.*
West Retford Church Mainly 13th-C with a crocket spire, said by the great architect Pugin to be a 'poem in stone'.
Bassetlaw Museum Amcott House, 40 Grove Street, Retford (01777 713749). Local history, archaeology, applied art and social history of north Nottinghamshire. Art Gallery and craft shop. *Open Mon–Sat & B. Hols 10.00–17.00, closed Sun.* Free. Disabled access to ground floor.
Kings Park Retford. Beside Woodcocks Bridge 55. *Open all year.* Free. Bowls, putting, tennis, etc, refreshments and toilets *open Apr–Sep.* Charge.
Tourist Information Centre Amcott House, 40 Grove Street, Retford (01777 860780). There is a local heritage trail guide and mini-guide available here.

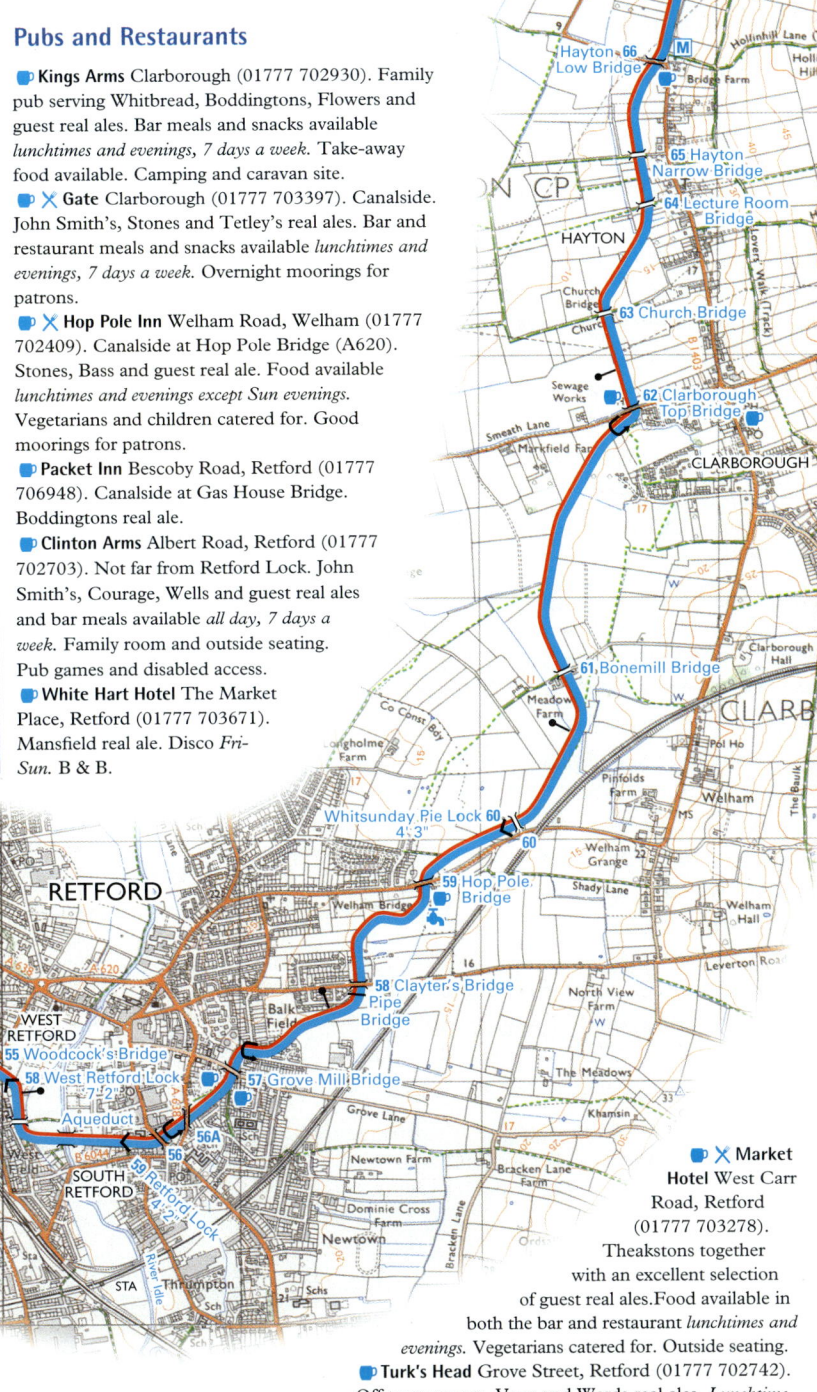

Pubs and Restaurants

Kings Arms Clarborough (01777 702930). Family pub serving Whitbread, Boddingtons, Flowers and guest real ales. Bar meals and snacks available *lunchtimes and evenings, 7 days a week.* Take-away food available. Camping and caravan site.

Gate Clarborough (01777 703397). Canalside. John Smith's, Stones and Tetley's real ales. Bar and restaurant meals and snacks available *lunchtimes and evenings, 7 days a week.* Overnight moorings for patrons.

Hop Pole Inn Welham Road, Welham (01777 702409). Canalside at Hop Pole Bridge (A620). Stones, Bass and guest real ale. Food available *lunchtimes and evenings except Sun evenings.* Vegetarians and children catered for. Good moorings for patrons.

Packet Inn Bescoby Road, Retford (01777 706948). Canalside at Gas House Bridge. Boddingtons real ale.

Clinton Arms Albert Road, Retford (01777 702703). Not far from Retford Lock. John Smith's, Courage, Wells and guest real ales and bar meals available *all day, 7 days a week.* Family room and outside seating. Pub games and disabled access.

White Hart Hotel The Market Place, Retford (01777 703671). Mansfield real ale. Disco *Fri-Sun.* B & B.

Market Hotel West Carr Road, Retford (01777 703278). Theakstons together with an excellent selection of guest real ales. Food available in both the bar and restaurant *lunchtimes and evenings.* Vegetarians catered for. Outside seating.

Turk's Head Grove Street, Retford (01777 702742). Off town square. Vaux and Wards real ales. *Lunchtime food.* B & B. Disabled access.

Worksop

Leaving Forest Top Lock, the canal now wanders westwards before turning sharply south as it meets the noisy A1 road. The 7 miles of the canal beyond Worksop Town Lock are being progressively restored and the first phase, to Shireoaks Aqueduct over the River Ryton, was expected to be completed by December 1999. Within a further two years, navigation to the east portal of Norwood Tunnel should be possible.

Pubs and Restaurants

✕ 🍺 **Chequers Ranby** (01777 703329). Canalside. Boddingtons, Flowers, Marston's and three guest real ales. An extensive menu is available in the bar *all day, 7 days a week.* Vegetarian and children's menu. A large outside terrace overlooks the canal. Moorings.

🍺 **Canal Tavern** Canalside, Worksop (01909 481965). Boddingtons and three guest real ales. Bar meals *lunchtimes Mon-Sat.* Children welcome, beer garden. Quiz *Thur.* Moorings for patrons.

🍺 **Lock Tavern and Chevy's Bar** Cuckoo Wharf, Worksop (01909 501600). Set in the old warehouse and former depot manager's house.

🍺 **Fisherman's Arms** Church Walk, Worksop (01909 472806). 100yds south of Cuckoo Wharf. Children welcome. Folk club *once a fortnight, on Sun.* Quiz *Wed.*

🍺 **Mallard** Station Approach, Carlton Road, Worksop (01909 530757). An exciting selection of ever changing real ales from small breweries together with a comprehensive range of continental bottled beers. Outside seating and pub games. Real cider. Disabled access. *Open all day except Sun.*

🍺 **Greendale Oak** Norfolk Street, Worksop (01909 489680). Just off Westgate. Cosy, gas-lit, mid-terraced pub serving Tetleys and Stones real ales. Food *lunchtimes and evenings 17.00–19.30.* Outside seating.

🍺 **Shireoaks Inn** Westgate, Worksop (01909 472118). Once a row of cottages, now a welcoming hostelry dispensing Barnsley and guest real ales. Excellent value, home-cooked food available *lunchtimes and evenings.* Outside seating and pub games. No smoking area.

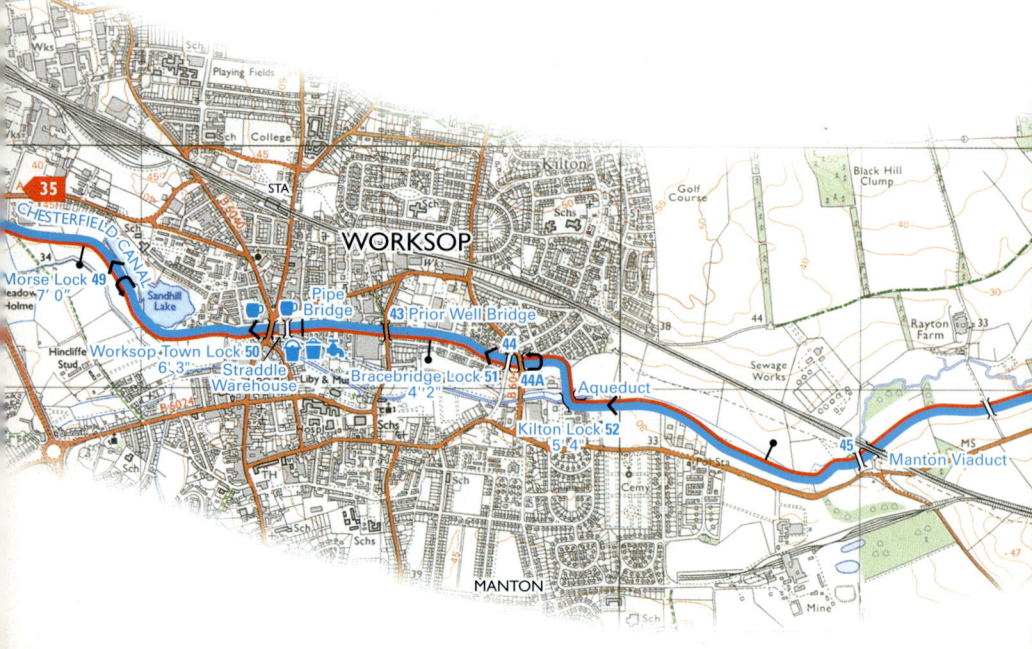

● **Ranby**

Notts. Tel. A small rambling village with a pub on the canal, the only one for miles in either direction.

Osberton Hall Built in 1806 by James Wyatt and enlarged and altered in 1853 (private).

● **Scofton**

Notts. This is the tiny estate village for Osberton Hall. The old stable block is impressive and is surmounted by a clock tower.

● **Worksop**

Notts. MD Wed, Sat. All services. Old buildings of note in Worksop are the Priory and its gatehouse.

Mr Straw's House 7 Blythe Grove, Worksop (01909 482380). When William and Walter Straw's father died in 1932, the brothers kept his house as a shrine and altered nothing. In 1991 William died and left the property, with a legacy of £1.5 million, to the National Trust. They have preserved this time capsule and opened it to visitors. *Open Apr–Oct, Tue–Sat 11.30-16.30.* Entrance by pre-booked time tickets only – telephone or write for tickets.

The Priory Near Prior Well Bridge. The church dates from the 12thC. Much rebuilding has taken place since then: in fact from 1970–2 the superstructure was added to, incorporating a new spire. Interesting paintings and monuments are inside the church and a gruesome relic from Sherwood Forest – a skull with the tip of an arrow embedded in it.

Pilgrim Fathers' Story Worksop Museum, Public Library, Memorial Avenue, Worksop (01909 501148.) *Open Mon, Tue, Wed & Fri 09.30–18.00, Thur & Sat 09.30–13.00. Closed B. Hols.* Free. Disabled access.

Tourist Information Centre Worksop Library, Memorial Avenue, Worksop (01909 501148).

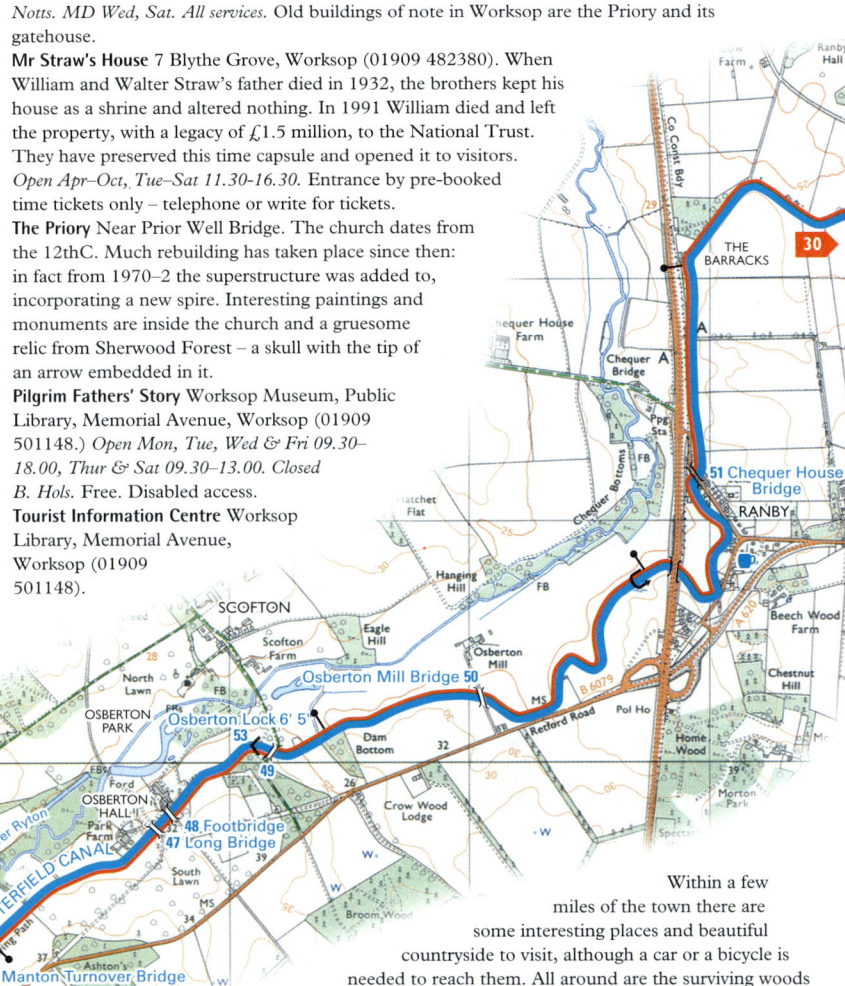

Within a few miles of the town there are some interesting places and beautiful countryside to visit, although a car or a bicycle is needed to reach them. All around are the surviving woods of Sherwood Forest, while to the south of the town is the area called the Dukeries, each of the adjacent estates of Thoresby, Clumber and Welbeck having been owned by a duke. Welbeck is now an army college, Thoresby Park is open to the public. Clumber House was demolished in 1938 but the Park, owned by the National Trust, is one of its most visited properties. Three miles west of Worksop is an outstanding building well worth visiting – the tiny Steetley Chapel – described as 'the most perfect and elaborate specimen of Norman architecture to be found anywhere in Europe'. *Open 09.30-16.30.* The quiet villages of north Nottinghamshire were home to the Pilgrim Fathers. The full story is told in Worksop museum which acts as a starting point for the Mayflower Trail leading out into the villages themselves.

Shireoaks

Beyond Worksop the waterway begins its steady ascent to the top pound at Norwood Tunnel: there are 31 locks over the next 7 miles making hard work for the boater and presenting an amazing challenge to the canal's original builders. At Shireoaks the navigation ducks under the re-constructed road bridge and passing the cricket field – a perfect replica of a county ground in miniature – it approaches the new lock, built to accommodate subsidence in the area. Crossing Shireoaks aqueduct, over the River Ryton, the navigation tunnels into a delightful ribbon of woodland and the locks begin in earnest. Nothing can prepare the boater for the magic of the next few miles for it is pure waterway witchcraft. Beyond Turnerwood Locks lies the charming collection of cottages ringing Turnerwood Basin and then, through the bridge, the first double lock. Amongst rolling farmland the canal wriggles its way onwards and steadily upwards through another double and then two treble locks. It is a truly awesome length of waterway and an amazing feat of early canal engineering. Back into woodland once more the boater glides through coppice to emerge in the cutting, approaching Norwood Tunnel, beside the Anston stone quarries: source of the stone used in the construction of the Houses of Parliament.

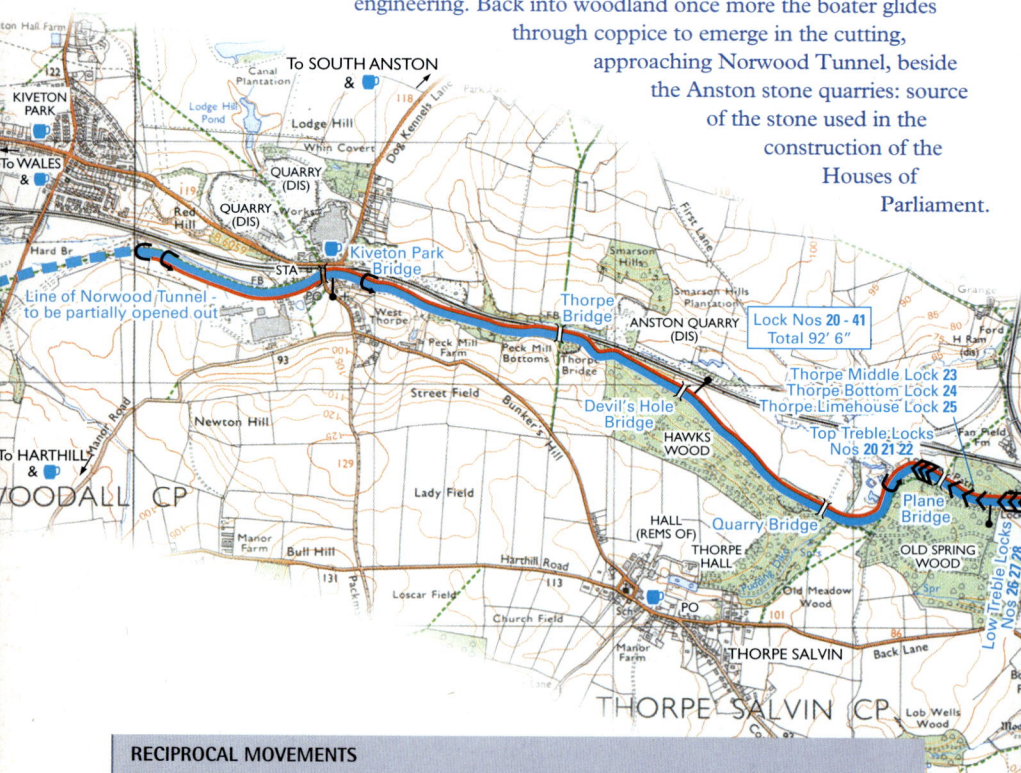

RECIPROCAL MOVEMENTS

Above John Varley's remarkable flights of locks are woods and stone quarries: areas where natural resources have been exploited in the developments of our age. Anston Quarries not only offered a ready source of stone for the locks and bridges along the canal, they were also the source of almost a quarter of a million tons of stone used to rebuild the Houses of Parliament when they burnt down during the 19thC. However the traffic has not been entirely one way. The small community of Shireoaks lost 24 young men in World War I (who are commemorated by a Calvary Cross) and exactly half that number in World War II. In their memory a clock was installed in the turret of St Luke's parish church with a double, three legged gravity escapement. The significance of this mechanism is that, not only will it resist outside influences – such as wind pressure on the hands – but that it is also a direct copy of Edmund Becket Denison's design for Big Ben.

Pubs and Restaurants

🍺 **Woodhouse Inn** Rhodesia, Worksop (01909 472747). Mansfield real ale. Beer garden and play area. Quiz *Thur.* Pool and snooker.

🍺 **The Station** Shireoaks (01909 472244). Canalside pub popular with the locals. Quiz night *Sun.* Sells gas.

🍺 **The Hewitt Arms** Shireoaks Park, Thorpe Lane, Shireoaks (01909 500979). 1/2 mile south west of the canal. A restrained conversion of the coach house and stables adjoining the Hall. A good range of real ales including Marston's and Morland can be enjoyed in stylish comfort overlooking the landscaped park. Meals are served *12.00–15.00 and 19.00–22.00 every day except Sun evenings.*

🍺 **The Parish Oven** Thorpe Salvin (01909 770685). A modern pub in the centre of the village.

🍺 **The Leeds Arms** South Anston (01909 567906). A busy local in the centre of South Anston. A choice of Morland and Whitbread real ales and food *lunchtimes and evenings.* Quiz night *Sat.* Disco *Thur.*

🍺 ✕ **Station Hotel** Kiverton Park Station (01909 773201). A pub for railway enthusiasts, furnished with memorabilia. John Smith's, Marston's and Stones real ales. Bar meals are served *lunchtimes and evenings except Sun.* Restaurant open *Tue–Sat*

19.30–20.00. Booking advisable at *weekends.* Children welcome. Quiz night *Tue.*

🍺 **The Beehive** Union Street, Harthill (01909 770205). A friendly village pub serving Tetley's and Marston's real ales and a good choice of food *lunchtimes and evenings (not Mon lunch except Bank Hols).* Quiz night *Tue.*

🍺 **The Saxon** Kiveton Park (01909 770517). North of Kiveton crossroads. Busy modern local.

🍺 **The Forge** Kiveton Park (01909 77045). On the main road, 1/2 mile west of the crossroads. Younger real ales in a town pub. Quiz nights, bingo.

🍺 ✕ **Lord Conyers Arms** The Square, Wales (01909 770258). Whitbread real ale in a town pub serving bar food *Mon–Sat lunchtimes only.* Restaurant *Thur, Fri & Sat 19.00–21.00. Sun lunch 12.00–14.15.* Live entertainment *Sat.*

🍺 **Duke of Leeds** Wales (01909 770301). A friendly pub opposite the church, formerly a coaching inn. A choice of four real ales and bar food *lunchtimes (except Mon & Tue) and evenings.*

🍺 **Lock-Keeper** Rhodesia, Worksop (01909 532565). A new family pub between Deep and Stret Locks serving Marston's and a guest real ale. Reasonably priced food *available all day, every day.* Vegetarians and children catered for. Canalside seating.

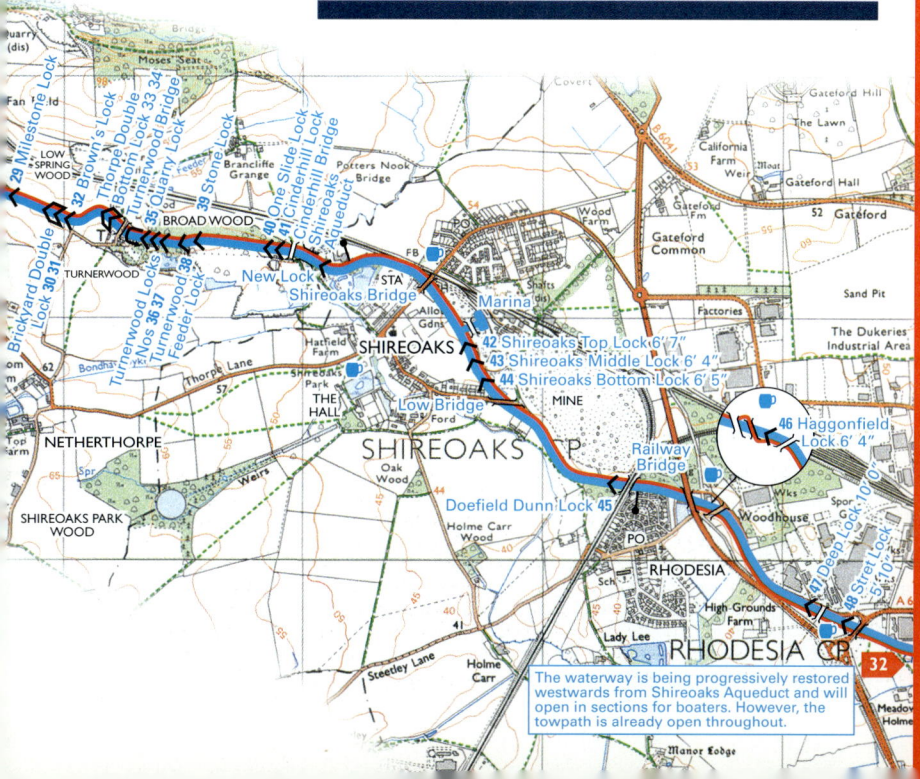

The waterway is being progressively restored westwards from Shireoaks Aqueduct and will open in sections for boaters. However, the towpath is already open throughout.

Rhodesia

Notts. PO, tel, stores (open Mon–Sat 08.00–20.00, Sun 09.00–14.00 & 18.00–20.00), fish and chips (closed Mon). A small settlement which is overshadowed by the A57 fly-over. Gas is available at the village store.

Shireoaks

Notts. PO (closed Wed), stores (open until late), butcher, garage, fish & chips, station. It is worth taking the time to explore this village whose splendid terrace of miners' cottages leads down the hill to the church. The village takes its name from a giant oak tree which cast its shade into Yorkshire, Derbyshire and Nottinghamshire and which was said to have measured 94 feet in circumference. The money for both the church and the cottages was given by the 5th Duke of Newcastle following the sinking of the pit. The presence of coal in the area brought work for up to 600 men and it is easy to imagine the impression that the newly-built colliers' cottages of Shireoaks Row must have made on the village. It is still possible to identify some of the original window casements and doors with their elaborate strap hinges, although many of the dwellings have cast history aside for more comfortable 20th-C fitments. The foundation stone of the church was laid in 1861 by Edward VII, then Prince of Wales. The quill pen which he used at the ceremony can still be seen in the church. Dedicated to St Luke, the building houses a beautiful altar, commemorating the Duke of Newcastle, and a painted ceiling. In 1975 the spire of the church had to be removed following subsidence caused by the mining in the area. A miner's lamp hangs above the pulpit as a poignant reminder of the industry which was the life-blood of the village until the closure of the pit in 1990. The village has twice won the best-kept village award. Just beyond Shireoaks Row stands the impressive half-ruined Jacobean Hall, built in 1612, whose coach-house has been sensitively converted into a pub. The 45 acres of land behind the hall were laid out as a water garden to include a lake, cascade and ornamental canal.

Thorpe Salvin

Derbyshire. Tel. A tiny village which has several times been winner of Britain in Bloom and had the onerous task of representing England in the European competition. The small nucleus of attractive stone houses is dominated by the now ruined Elizabethan Thorpe Hall and the church. A very fine Norman doorway, a chained bible and a font depicting the four seasons are some of the treasures which can be seen within.

South Anston

Derbyshire. PO, tel, stores, chemist, take-away. A sprawling settlement overlooked by the pretty church of St James with its elegant spire.

Harthill

Derbyshire. PO (closed Sat am), tel, stores, butcher, laundrette. An attractive village whose main street is described in Scott's *Ivanhoe*. Mentioned in the Domesday Book, the first church was established here in 1078 by the son-in-law of William the Conqueror. Its successor houses some fine wooden carvings and an imposing timber roof. It is here that the body of John Varley was buried in 1809.

Kiveton Park

Derbyshire. PO, tel, stores, chemist, butcher, bank, take-aways, station. Developed to serve the local colliery, Kiveton is a useful place for provisions.

Wales

Derbyshire. PO, tel, stores, garage. A mining community that now sits above the M1. The older area is set around the church. It is here that the body of Sir Thomas Hewitt, the somewhat eccentric owner of Hewitt Hall at Shireoaks, was eventually laid to rest. A confirmed atheist, Sir Thomas had begun to build an elaborate mausoleum at his home but died before it was completed. His servants tried to outwit the family's wishes to bury him at the church in Wales and one night filled the coffin with stones and set off with his body through the local woods at dead of night. Rumour has it that a strong wind blew out their torches and the servants were so frightened that they returned hastily to the hall with the body which was then buried according to the family's plan. Scratta Wood was eventually felled and burned following reputed hauntings! **Rother Valley Country Park** Wales Bar (0114 247 1452). One thousand acres of parkland catering for a wide variety of leisure pursuits on both land and water. There is an 18th-C working mill, craft centre, gift shop and cafeteria. For enquiries about leisure pursuits including boats, canoes, windsurfers and bicycles telephone 0114 247 1453. For access by bus telephone Busline on 01246 250450.

RIVER DERWENT AND THE POCKLINGTON CANAL

RIVER DERWENT

Environment Agency, Coverdale House, Amy Johnson Way, Clifton Moor, York YO3 4UZ (0113 244 0191).

MAXIMUM DIMENSIONS (at Barmby Lock)

Length: 62'
Beam: 16' 6"
Headroom: 10' 6"

A certificate must be purchased from the Barrage Control Centre if you are joining the Derwent, to certify that your craft complies with anti-pollution requirements. Navigation through or above Sutton Lock without riparian owners permission is a matter of contention.

MILEAGE

STAMFORD BRIDGE to:
Sutton Lock: 6$\frac{1}{2}$ miles

Junction with Pocklington Canal: 10$\frac{1}{2}$ miles, 1 lock
Bubwith: 15 miles, 1 lock
Wressle: 19 miles, 1 lock
RIVER OUSE: 22 miles, 2 locks

POCKLINGTON CANAL

MAXIMUM DIMENSIONS

Length: 57'
Beam: 14' 3"
Headroom: 8' 3"

MANAGER

01904 728229

MILEAGE

RIVER DERWENT to:
Melbourne: 5 miles
Bielby: 7 miles
CANAL HEAD: 9$\frac{1}{2}$ miles

RIVER DERWENT

Prior to 1702 the River Derwent was navigable to Stamford Bridge. A 'publick' act in that year allowed locks to be built to make the river navigable to Scarborough Mills, although works were never carried out above Yedingham, and little trade developed above Malton. Following the repeal of the 1702 Act in 1935, the navigation fell into disrepair, although pleasure craft continued to use sections of the river. New lower gates were fitted to Sutton Lock in 1972, and these are now owned by the Yorkshire Wildlife Trust (10 Toft Green, York YO1 1JT – 01904 659570). Consult them **before** making a passage through the lock, and inform the Enviroment Agency on 01757 638579. Entry into the lower part of the river from the River Ouse is by way of Barmby Barrage Lock, controlled by the Environment Agency.
The whole of the waterway covered by this book is a Site of Special Scientific Interest (SSSI), being considered one of the finest examples of a lowland river in the country. The seasonally flooded meadows around the lower reaches, known as the Derwent Ings, are of international importance for traditionally managed grassland communities and the species of wildfowl and wading birds supported.

THE POCKLINGTON CANAL

This canal was promoted in a bill of 1814 by merchants in Pocklington and was originally intended to join the River Ouse at Howden. However Earl Fitzwilliam, then owner of the Derwent Navigation, intervened before publication of the bill, and the canal was connected with the River Derwent. Coal, lime and fertiliser were brought in to Pocklington, and agricultural produce from the farmlands of the East Riding were taken out. However, the opening of the York & North Midland Railway in 1847 started the canal's demise, and traffic ceased in 1932. Restoration has been completed on structures as far as Coates Lock, although the canal is currently only navigable to Thornton Lock (the last turning place being the Melbourne Arm). The area surrounding Canal Head has also been put in good order. Virtually all of the route has been designated as an SSSI, and rich communities of aquatic plants and the invertebrates they support are well established in the disused section. Otters have also been recorded. The Pocklington Canal Amenity Society campaigns and works for its complete restoration.

Stamford Bridge

The presently navigable River Derwent leaves the western side of Stamford Bridge, and quickly passes under the road bridge to approach a large viaduct with a sturdy central iron span, built in 1846. Although no longer carrying a railway, it has been preserved as an ancient monument, and you can walk across it for a splendid view. Access is from the old station in Stamford Bridge (in High Catton Road). Beyond the viaduct the river flows into a shallow valley

amongst gentle rolling countryside, which persists until East Cottingwith. The village of Low Catton can be seen to the east, its Norman church standing quite close to the river.

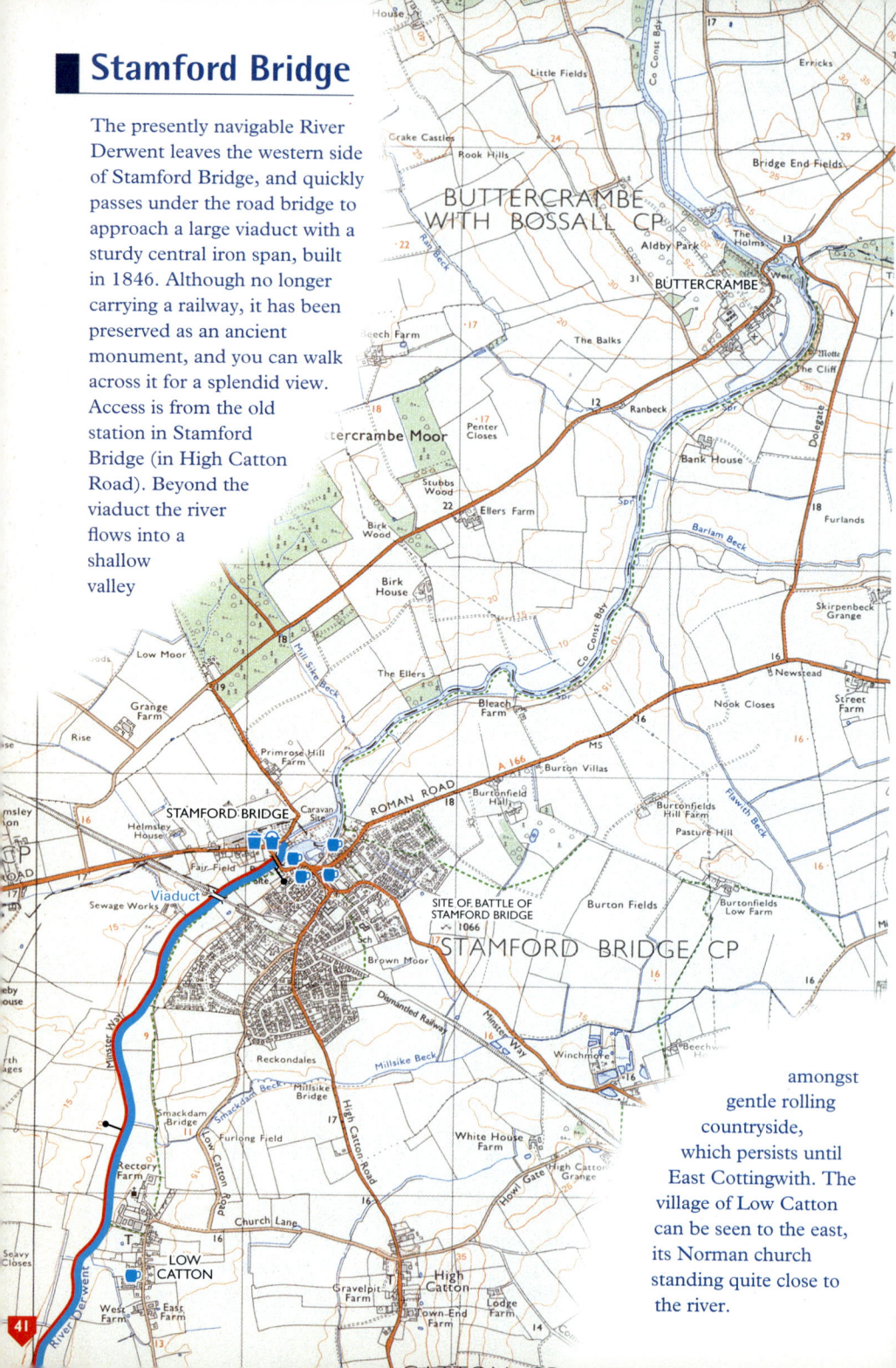

Stamford Bridge

N. Yorks. PO, tel, stores, garage, bank. An unremarkable but pleasant village centred to the east of the bridge, which was built in 1727 by William Etty. There are several small pleasant pubs to visit, and a picnic area immediately downstream of the road bridge, on the east bank. This is also a popular area for camping and caravanning.

Battle of Stamford Bridge, 1066 Taking place on the morning of 25 September, this battle was to mark the end of Scandinavian influence over the politics of England. Harald Hardrada had joined forces with the King's brother Tostig and together they had taken York. In response King Harold's army marched the 185 miles from London, in an astonishing six days, to take Hardrada's forces by surprise. Attacking across the river, they broke through the Viking lines and killed Hardrada. Harold then offered a truce, but this was rejected and the fighting continued until Tostig was also killed. With the now depleted English army in York, William of Normandy (William the Conqueror) seized his opportunity and landed unopposed on the south coast. The Battle of Hastings followed.

Low Catton

N. Yorks. PO box, tel. A plain village lying to the south east of All Saints church. Originally Norman, later additions include the north aisle and south doorway, both built in the 13thC. The font also dates from this time. The stained glass east window is worth a look. It depicts the crucifixion, dates from 1866, and is by Morris.

Pubs and Restaurants

The Swordsman The Square, Stamford Bridge (01759 371307). A large, rambling, comfortable and friendly riverside pub serving Samuel Smith's real ale, and substantial bar meals *lunchtimes and evenings in season.* Traditional *Sun* lunches and also vegetarian and children's menus. There is a large garden and during the season there is entertainment with traditional pub games and quiz nights.

The Stamford The Square, Stamford Bridge (01759 371338). Just up the road from the bridge. A pleasantly old-fashioned pub offering Tetley's and John Smith's real ale. Food.

The Bay Horse Main Street, Stamford Bridge (01759 371320). A handsome brick-built pub with a small garden, serving Tetley's and Camerons real ales and bar snacks at *lunchtime Mon–Sat during the summer months.*

Children are welcome at lunchtime, and there is a garden. Fish & chip shop next door.

The Corn Mill Main Street, Stamford Bridge (01759 371274). Tetley's real ale served in a large converted mill, with a waterwheel. Bar and restaurant meals served *lunchtimes and evenings* and restaurant meals, with carvery, *every L and weekend D.* Vegetarian menu available. Children are welcome and there is a riverside garden.

The Waterside Stamford Bridge. A pretty tea room offering light meals, cakes, ice cream and tea. Garden.

Gold Cup Inn Low Catton (01759 371354). Village pub with a pretty garden, serving John Smith's and Tetley's real ale and bar meals *lunchtimes and evenings (all day at weekends).* Restaurant meals *D only (and Sun L)* with vegetarian menu. Children are welcome.

AN ELECTION TAKES ITS TOLL

The Derwent Navigation was owned between 1782 and 1833 by Earl Fitzwilliam, and it became quite prosperous. But when, in 1807, the local electors did not return both of the Earl's nominees to Parliament, and voted instead for an independent, he gave vent to his displeasure by raising tolls on the river:

'Take Notice, That from and after the First Day of July next, you are hereby required to deliver ... to the Lock Keeper ... a full Account, in Writing, of all the Coals, Corn, Goods, Wares, Merchandize (sic), or Commodities, that shall be carried up or down the said River ... and to pay to the said Lock Keeper ... at Stamford Bridge, such sum of Money as shall be demanded, for every ton weight ... that shall be carried or conveyed in any such Boat, barge or Vessel, up the said River Derwent ... or down the said River Derwent ... not exceeding Eight Shillings ... *Dated this 16th Day of June, 1807*'

When the independent's election to Parliament was later declared to be invalid, he was replaced by the Earl's nominee. Tolls were then brought back to their original rates.

Elvington

Discreetly hiding away in its shallow valley, the River Derwent proceeds virtually due south, gently meandering and avoiding all settlements, which have sensibly been kept well away from the flood plain. The countryside is pleasantly old-fashioned, being divided into many small fields, each separated by a substantial hedge. The meadow known as the Mask, on the eastern bank, is particularly pretty. Hedges here are rich with hawthorn, crab apple, dog rose and oak.

● **Kexby**
N. Yorks. There is nothing much of note in this village. The church of St Paul, constructed in 1852, lies to the west of the river. The main road now bypasses the original bridge, which dates from the 17thC.

● **Elvington**
N. Yorks. PO, tel, stores. There are moorings below Sutton Lock, so you can leave your boat here and walk up to the village, which is particularly pretty around the green. Holy Trinity church, built in 1877, is well worth a look. It has a large nave and aisle, a substantial square tower with a clock, and a timber bell-stage. Sutton Bridge was built around 1700: just downstream is the lock, which was constructed in 1878 and more recently restored in memory of E.L. who was, apparently, 'a true gentlemen'. The water abstraction plant above the village, and another at Barmby on the Marsh, take as much as 20 per cent of Yorkshire's water supply from the river. **Yorkshire Air Museum** Halifax Way, Elvington (01904 608595). About 2 miles north west of Elvington, off the B1228. An airfield which captures the atmosphere of World War II, with a Halifax and a Mosquito to see, along with the control room and a NAAFI restaurant. Also Lightning, Mirage and Hunter fighters, the Buccaneer bomber and a Victor tanker. *Open Jan-Mar, daily 11.00-15.00; Apr-Dec, Mon-Fri 10.30-16.00, Sat & Sun 10.30-17.00.* Charge.

● **Sutton-upon-Derwent**
N. Yorks. (PO at the Sutton Arms). The church of St Michael and All Angels stands above the lock on the east bank, and dates from the early Norman period. Indeed the organ arch, discovered in 1927, is the original arch of a church without aisles. The arches of the arcades are also Norman. Other details, and the aisle windows, date from the 14thC. The substantial remains of an 11th-C cross shaft is still to be seen, with carved beasts heads, the Virgin and child and other Viking work. The rest of the village is scattered away from the river.

● **The Ings**
By the river, and extending downstream past Wheldrake Ings Nature Reserve, these areas are a showpiece for local traditional farming methods – flooding in winter, never ploughed and never treated with artificial fertilisers.

NAVIGATIONAL NOTES

Please refer to the notes on page 37 **before** making a passage through Sutton Lock. Only one set of paddles on the downstream gates were operable in August 1999.

Pubs and Restaurants

🍺 **Grey Horse Inn** Main Street, Elvington (01904 608335). A cosy and friendly village pub serving generous helpings of food *lunchtimes and evenings daily (except Tue evenings)*, with vegetarian choices. John Smith's, Courage and a guest real ale. Children are welcome. Garden.

🍺 **St Vincent Arms** Main Street, Sutton-upon-Derwent (01904 608349). A comfortable village pub serving Fuller's and Adnams real ale and meals *lunchtimes and evenings*, with vegetarian choices at *weekends*. Children are welcome. Garden.

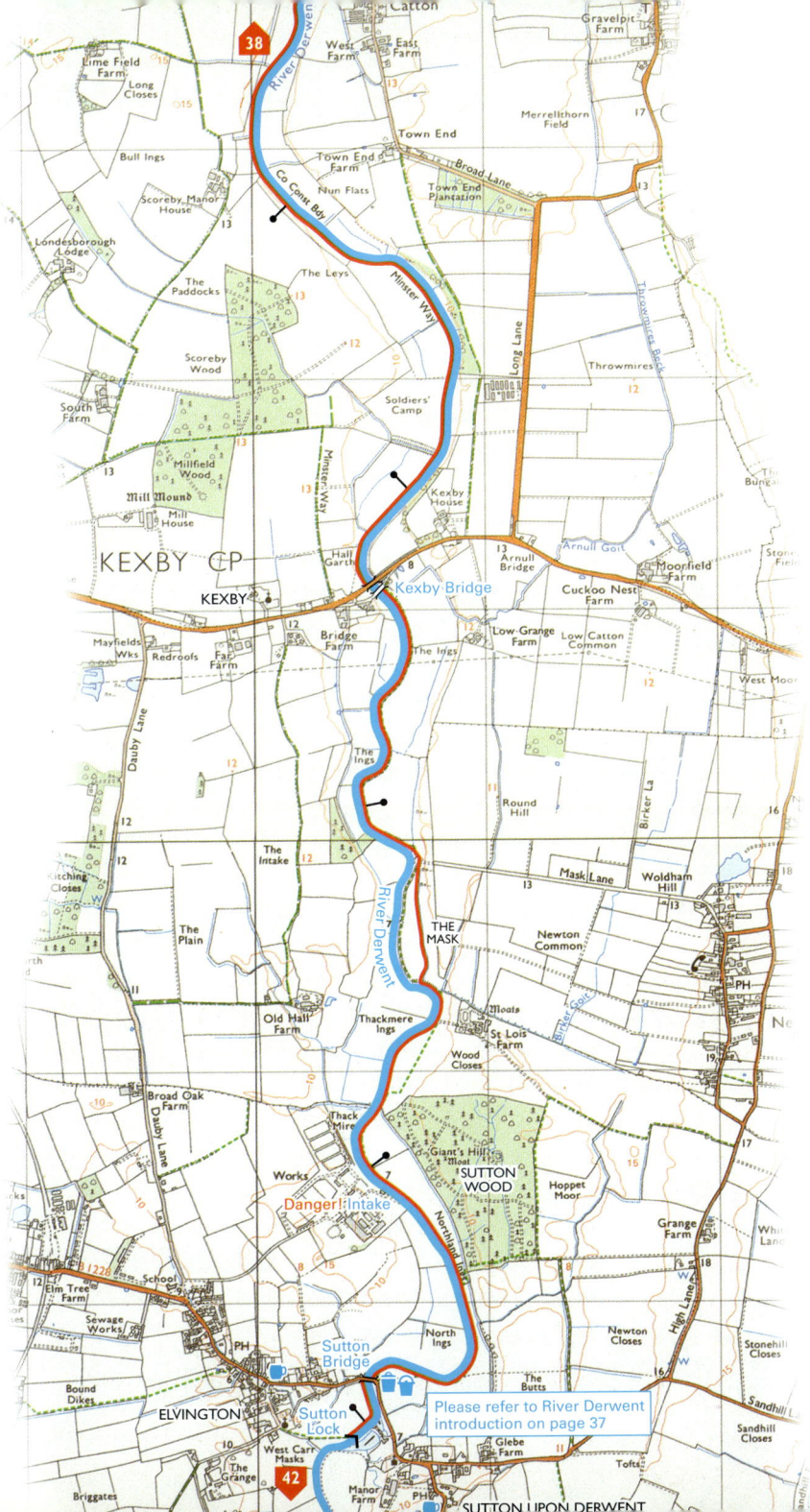

38

Catton

Gravelpit Farm

Lime Field Farm

Long Closes

West Farm

Eass Farm

Merrellthorn Field

17

Bull Ings

Town End Farm

Town End

Broad Lane

Nun Flats

Town End Plantation

13

Scoreby Manor House

Co Const Bdy

13

Londesborough Lodge

The Paddocks

The Leys

Minster Way

Throwmires Beck

Scoreby Wood

Soldiers' Camp

Throwmires

12

South Farm

13

Millfield Wood

Minster Way

Long Lane

Kexby House

Mill Mound

Mill House

13

Bungalow

KEXBY CP

Hall Garth

13

Arnull Bridge

Arnull Goit

Moorfield Farm

Stone Field

KEXBY

Kexby Bridge

Cuckoo Nest Farm

Mayfields Wks

Redroofs

Bridge Farm

The Ings

Low Grange Farm

Low Catton Common

Far Farm

12

West Moor

Dauby Lane

The Ings

12

The Ings

Round Hill

11

Birker La

16

Kitching Closes

12

The Intake

Mask Lane

Woldham Hill

13

18

The Plain

River Derwent

THE MASK

Newton Common

PH

Old Hall Farm

Thackmere Ings

Moats

St Lois Farm

Birker Goit

Ne

11

Wood Closes

19

Broad Oak Farm

Thack Mire

Giant's Hill Moat

SUTTON WOOD

Hoppet Moor

17

Dauby Lane

Works

Danger! Intake

7

Northhill Lane

Grange Farm

White Lane

15

8

18

Elm Tree Farm

School

B1228

North Ings

Newton Closes

High Lane

Stonehill Closes

Sewage Works

PH

Sutton Bridge

Sutton Lock

North Ings

The Butts

16

Sandhill L

Bound Dikes

ELVINGTON

Please refer to River Derwent introduction on page 37

Glebe Farm

11

Sandhill Closes

42

The Grange

West Carr Masks

Manor Farm

PH

Tofts

Briggates

SUTTON UPON DERWENT

Please refer to River Derwent introduction on page 37

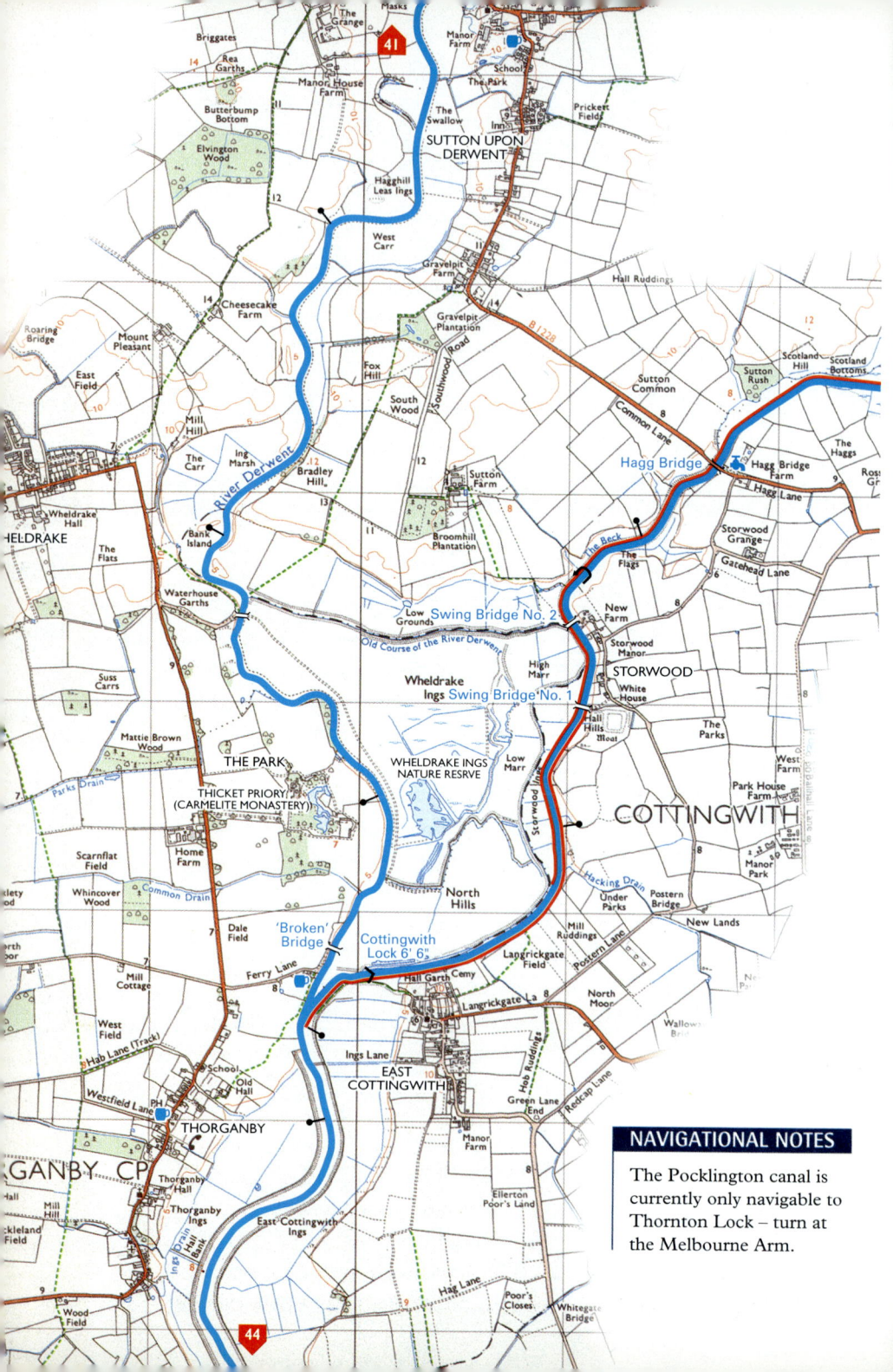

41

Masks

The Grange

Briggates

Rea Garths

Butterbump Bottom

Manor House Farm

Manor Farm

School

The Park

The Swallow

Pricket Field

Inn

SUTTON UPON DERWENT

Elvington Wood

Hagghill Leas Ings

West Carr

Gravelpit Farm

Hall Ruddings

B1228

Roaring Bridge

Mount Pleasant

Cheesecake Farm

Southwood Road

Gravelpit Plantation

Scotland Hill

Scotland Bottoms

East Field

Fox Hill

South Wood

Sutton Common

Sutton Rush

The Haggs

Ros Gr

Mill Hill

The Carr

Ing Marsh

Bradley Hill

Sutton Farm

Common Lane

Hagg Bridge

Hagg Bridge Farm

Hagg Lane

River Derwent

WHELDRAKE

Wheldrake Hall

The Flats

Bank Island

Broomhill Plantation

The Beck

The Flags

Storwood Grange

Gatehead Lane

Waterhouse Garths

Low Grounds

Swing Bridge No. 2

Old Course of the River Derwent

New Farm

Storwood Manor

Suss Carrs

Wheldrake Ings

Swing Bridge No. 1

High Marr

Low Marr

STORWOOD

White House

Hall Hills Moat

The Parks

West Farm

Mattie Brown Wood

Parks Drain

THE PARK

THICKET PRIORY (CARMELITE MONASTERY)

WHELDRAKE INGS NATURE RESRVE

North Hills

Storwood

COTTINGWITH

Park House Farm

Manor Park

Scarnflat Field

Home Farm

Common Drain

Whincover Wood

Dale Field

'Broken' Bridge

Cottingwith Lock 6' 6"

Ferry Lane

Hall Garth

Langrickgate Field

Mill Ruddings

Hacking Drain

Under Parks

Postern Bridge

Postern Lane

New Lands

West Field

Mill Cottage

Cemy

Langrickgate La.

North Moor

Wallow Bri

Hab Lane (Track)

School

Old Hall

Ings Lane

EAST COTTINGWITH

Hob Ruddings

Redcap Lane

Westfield Lane

PH

THORGANBY

Green Lane End

Manor Farm

GANBY CP

Thorganby Hall

Thorganby Ings

Hall Bank

East Cottingwith Ings

Ellerton Poor's Land

Hall

Mill Hill

ckland Field

Ings Drain

Wood Field

Hag Lane

Poor's Closes

Whitegate Bridge

44

NAVIGATIONAL NOTES

The Pocklington canal is currently only navigable to Thornton Lock – turn at the Melbourne Arm.

East Cottingwith

Just beyond a tiny and hardly recognisable riverside pub the the river splits: the Beck heads north east and is joined by the Pocklington Canal at Cottingwith Lock. The towpath can be picked up to the north of East Cottingwith, via the path (Cemetery Lane) by the village's old cemetery. Continuing through the flat farmland the canal reaches Melbourne, where there is an arm with services and moorings. The canal beyond here has been restored as far as Coates Lock, although it is not currently navigable above Thornton Lock, due to silting. Walk along the remaining one-and-a-half miles to Canal Head, to enjoy the scenery and view the restoration work.

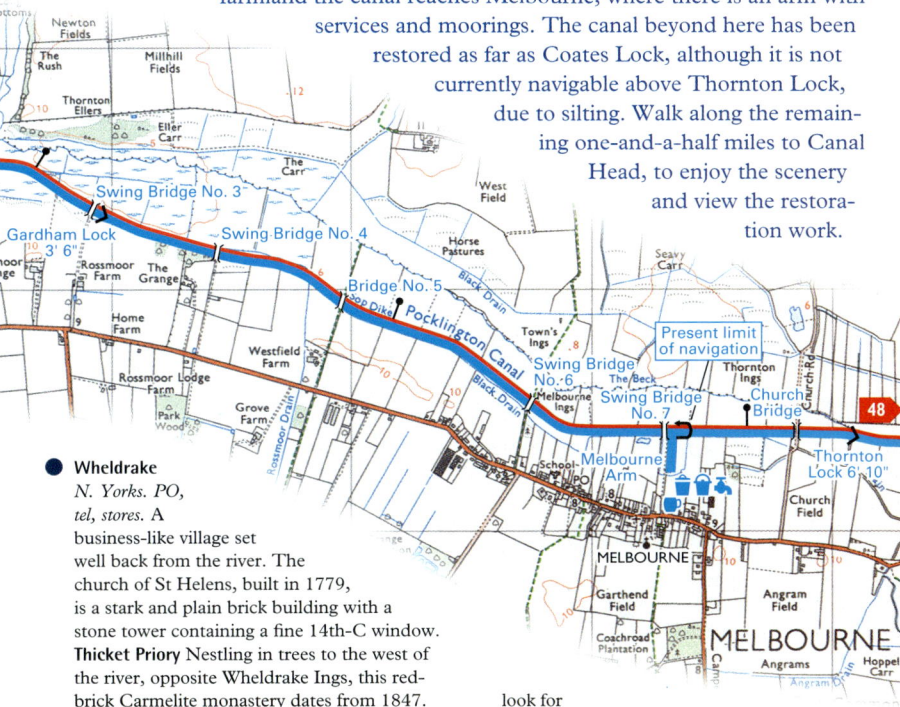

Wheldrake
N. Yorks. PO, tel, stores. A business-like village set well back from the river. The church of St Helens, built in 1779, is a stark and plain brick building with a stone tower containing a fine 14th-C window. **Thicket Priory** Nestling in trees to the west of the river, opposite Wheldrake Ings, this red-brick Carmelite monastery dates from 1847.

Thorganby
N. Yorks. PO box, tel. A pleasant village. The church of St Helens is brick-built with a stone tower, the base of which dates from the 12thC. The church registers date from 1653.

East Cottingwith
E. Riding. PO box, tel. A simple red-brick village built just above the flood plain of the river. The handsome church of St Mary dates from 1780:

look for the plaque on the outside wall dedicated to Robert Grey, full of lines of type which don't quite fit.

Melbourne
E. Riding. PO, tel, stores. Linked to the canal by an arm, the village is enlivened by handsome Georgian houses and a delightful corrugated-iron church, dating from 1882.

Pubs and Restaurants

The Ferry Boat Inn Riverside garden with willow trees and a jetty.

The Jefferson Arms Main Street, Thorganby (01904 448316). Black Sheep and John Smith's real ale are served in this relaxed pub, where, alongside the bar and restaurant areas, there is a lovely sitting room. The food is excellent and unusual, well-served and in the correct proportions. It is available *lunchtimes and evenings (not Mon)*, with excellent vegetarian choices. Children are welcome and there is a conservatory set aside for families. Garden, barbecue area, pond. B & B.

✕ Cross Keys Melbourne. Three real ales and excellent food *lunchtimes and evenings* in a bright and cheerful village pub.

Bubwith

Firmly enclosed by floodbanks, the River Derwent, more substantial now, continues its business-like progress towards its junction with the Ouse. The countryside is quite flat, with the few buildings which are to be seen providing landmarks and an odd group of trees here and there giving a little colour. Just one road crosses on this section: the A163 between North Duffield and Bubwith.

Ellerton

E. Riding. PO box, tel. A small village of old and new brick houses, with a pretty chapel and a duckpond. A windmill, standing separately to the east, has been converted into a dwelling. At the far west end of the village is the site of a priory, but nothing now remains. The church of St Mary, built in 1848, stands nearby, once abandoned but now being expertly restored.

Aughton

E. Riding. PO, tel. At the western end of this small farming village, beyond the substantial remains of a motte and bailey, is the splendid church of All Saints. Before you enter, it is worth having a good look from the outside: the tower slopes unreasonably and the chancel appears to have been sliced in half through a doorway, which is now bricked up. The Perpendicular tower has fine gargoyles and sinuous carvings of newt-like creatures crawling over the wall. These are the sign of the Aske family, who have long associations with the village. On the south side there is a sundial. The chancel arch is Norman, as is the south doorway. Brasses of Richard Aske and his wife date from 1466. Robert Aske, leader of the Pilgrimage of Grace, and executed in 1536, was born in the village.

Bubwith

E. Riding. PO, tel, stores. A pleasant village with several attractive Georgian houses facing the street, which is just a short walk along from the bridge, built in 1793. The large church of All Saints is tucked away right by the river. It is Norman in origin, with a chancel arch topped by a Norman gable end. The fine tower is Perpendicular. Fragments of Norman work can be seen built into the church, including a tiny winged figure, dating from circa 1200.

Pubs and Restaurants

Boot & Shoe Inn Ellerton (01757 288346). A pretty country pub near the chapel, serving Old Mill and John Smith's real ale. Bar meals are available *evenings Wed–Sat, with a traditional Sunday lunch also served.* There is a garden.

White Swan Bubwith (01757 288209). This pleasant village pub serves Tetley's, John Smith's and guest real ales. Bar meals are served *lunchtimes and evenings (not Thurs lunchtime)* with vegetarian choice and a children's menu. Children are welcome, there is a garden, and entertainment *every Sun evening* with country and Western music. B & B.

A HALF-PRICE OFFER ON KELP AND LING – BUT FEW TAKERS

Much of the material used to construct the York & North Midland Railway's York & Scarborough line, opened in 1845, was carried on the Derwent – a last flush of trade on the river before an inevitable decline. Drastic toll cutting followed, but to little effect:

'On Coal, Slack and Cinders – 4d per Ton, *instead of 10d*

On Flour and Shelling – 4d per 20 Stone, *instead of 6d*

On Bones, Cobbles, Flints, Horns, Shoddy, Guano, Nitrate of Sods – 1s 6d per Ton, *instead of 2s 6d*

On Carrots, Potatoes, Fullers Earth, Kelp, Ling, Oil-Cake, Pipe-Clay – 1s 6d per Ton, *instead of 3s*

On Alum, Copperas, Fish, Iron of all descriptions, Woad, Chicory – 2s per Ton, *instead of 3s*'

The 70 or so barges which worked to Malton in 1855 had reduced to a single craft by 1894. Between 1921 and 1935 the London & North Eastern Railway took responsibility for the navigation, and administered its ultimate commercial decline.

Barmby on the Marsh

A few moored boats mark the presence of the pub at Breighton Ferry. Of course boating is a pleasure reserved just for the summer months, as during winter the situation can change radically, and high flood banks on the lower reaches of both the Derwent and the Ouse are a constant reminder of the potential power of these rivers. The Derwent finally enters the Ouse at the Barmby Tidal Barrage. There are moorings (available *daylight hours only*) here, so it is worthwhile stopping to explore. Boaters can either head upstream (right) *with the tide* towards York, or downstream (left) towards the North Sea, given a suitable craft.

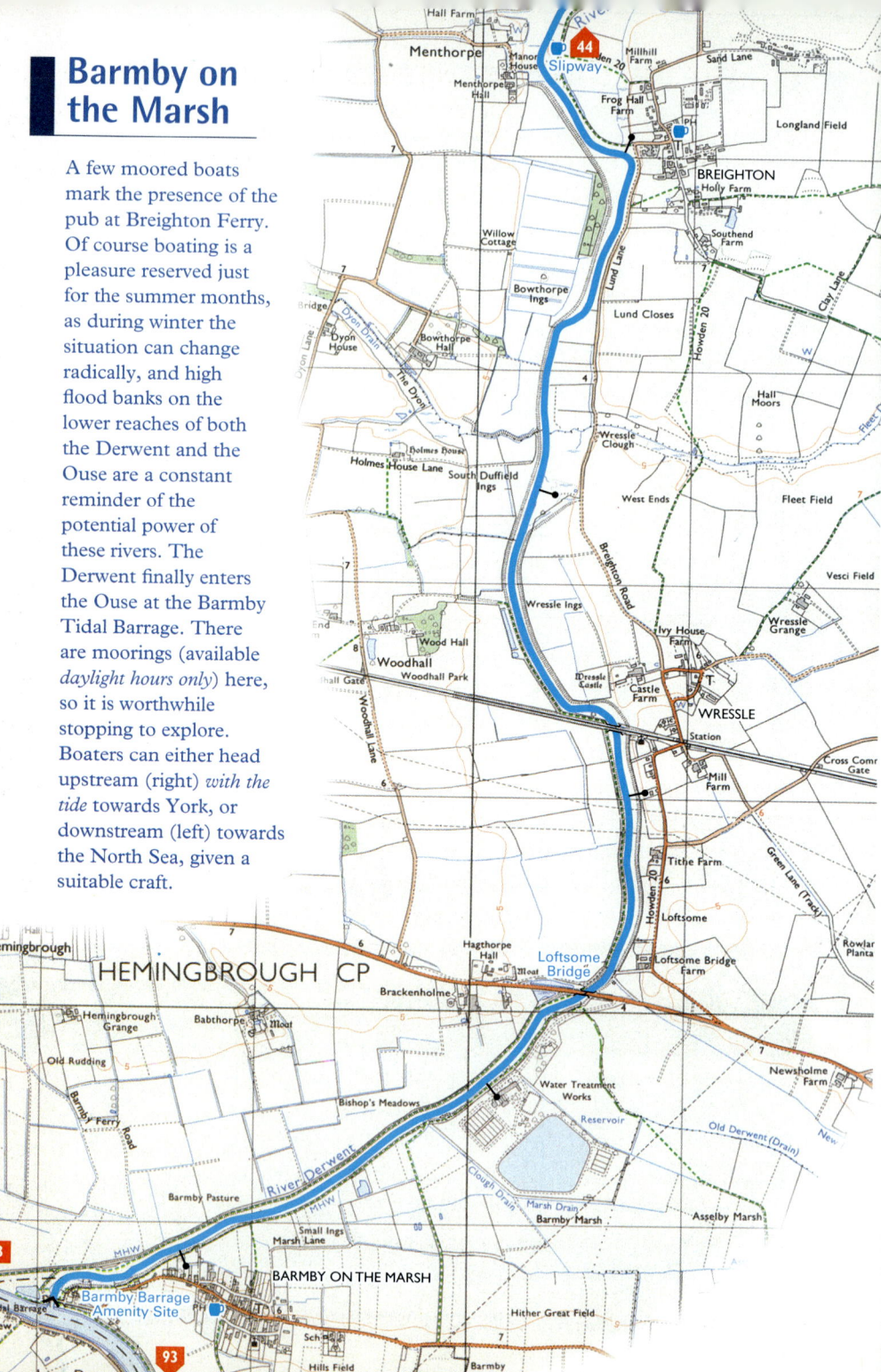

NAVIGATIONAL NOTES

Entry to or exit from the River Derwent is through the lock at Barmby. Telephone and check your passage on 01757 638579, or call on VHF channel 74. The maximum craft size is 62' x 16' 6". A certificate must be purchased from the Barrage Control Centre if you are joining the Derwent, to certify that your craft complies with anti-pollution requirements.

● **Breighton**
E. Riding. PO box, tel. A small, quiet agricultural settlement.
The Real Aeroplane Museum
The Aerodrome, Sand Lane, Breighton (01757 289065). Situated at the end of a bumpy, muddy track (don't be put off) this enthusiastic working museum, airfield and runway has a splendid collection of aircraft, including a Supermarine Spitfire PR11, a Hawker Hurricane Mk12, a Messerschmitt Bf 109 and many others. There are plenty of exciting events during the summer where you will see, weather permitting, these planes, or others, in the air! Refreshments. *Open Sat & Sun 10.30-16.00.* Charge.

● **Wressle**
E. Riding. PO box, tel. A farming village scattered either side of the station and level crossing. Standing prominently to the north west, by the river, are the impressive towers of Wressle Castle, built for Sir Thomas Percy, Earl of Northumberland, around 1380. Beautifully constructed from fine stone, two of the four original towers still remain containing fragments of rooms, spectacular windows, fine fireplaces and, at the top, a stone crucifix. You can admire the remains of the castle from the river or the road, *but there is no public access.* Just to the south, over the railway crossing, is the handsome church of

St John of Beverley. This was built wholly of brick in 1799. There is a pretty chapel house just down the road.

● **Barmby Tidal Barrage**
Barmby on the Marsh, Goole (01757 638579). Constructed between 1972-4 at a cost of £750,000, the barrage excludes the tide from the River Derwent, thus allowing more water to be extracted for domestic supply. The National Rivers Authority has, however, been quick to grasp the amenity value of the site, and there are excellent leisure facilities. Bird watching can be conducted from the wetland hide, which is *open daily 08.00-20.00.* Here you can expect to see the usual waders, plus herons, kingfishers, mallard, teal and swans, amongst others. Coarse fishing is free at the site and specially constructed platforms provide angling facilities for the disabled. There are several waterside picnic areas. The Trans Pennine Trail, a walking and cycling route from Liverpool to Hull, crosses the barrage. There are toilets, and facilities for wheelchair users.

● **Barmby on the Marsh**
E. Riding. PO box, tel. A straggling red-brick village with some fine Georgian houses, hemmed in by the Rivers Ouse and Derwent. St Helens church was built in the 18thC, and has a handsome brick tower, with some medieval work in the nave.

Pubs and Restaurants

● ✕ **The Breighton Ferry** Breighton (01757 288407). In a fine riverside position, this homely pub serves bar meals, as well as more elaborate restaurant meals in the Wheelhouse. Moorings are maintained, there is launching for day boats, and fishing rights are held. Children will enjoy the play-things in the large garden. Camping and caravanning.

● ✕ **Olde Poachers Inne** Breighton (01757 288849). A lively pub tucked away in the village centre, serving bar meals and restaurant meals with a carvery for *Sun lunchtime,* including vegetarian meals. Children are welcome, and there is a garden. Entertainment with quiz nights.

✕ ♈ **Loftsome Bridge Coaching House** Loftsome Bridge Farm, South of Wressle (01757 630070). A modern riverside hotel and restaurant with a bar. Restaurant meals available *Mon–Sat evenings and Sun lunchtimes* with vegetarian choices. Children are welcome *for Sun lunchtime meals only.* B & B.

● **King's Head** Barmby on the Marsh (01757 638357). A comfortable and friendly village pub serving John Smith's and Tetley's real ale. Meals are served *lunchtimes and evenings every day,* children are welcome, and there is a garden.

Canal Head, Pocklington Canal

This last section of the Pocklington Canal is really very attractive, flanked on the east side by overhanging bushes and trees, and on the west by a low towpath hedge, broken occasionally by a rambling farm with grazing animals. The canal beyond Coates Lock is currently being restored: when this remaining section of the waterway is open, it will provide a worthy addition to the network (subject to a satisfactory agreement between British Waterways and English Nature). As the waterway turns towards Pocklington, the Bielby Arm, which would have once served the village and an old mill, is passed. To the north are the Wolds, low hills forming the horizon as the final locks are climbed and Canal Head is reached. The basin area here has been restored, and there are picnic tables overlooked by a canal warehouse, now tastefully converted into dwellings. A busy main road separates the basin from the Wellington Oak pub, where there is a post box.

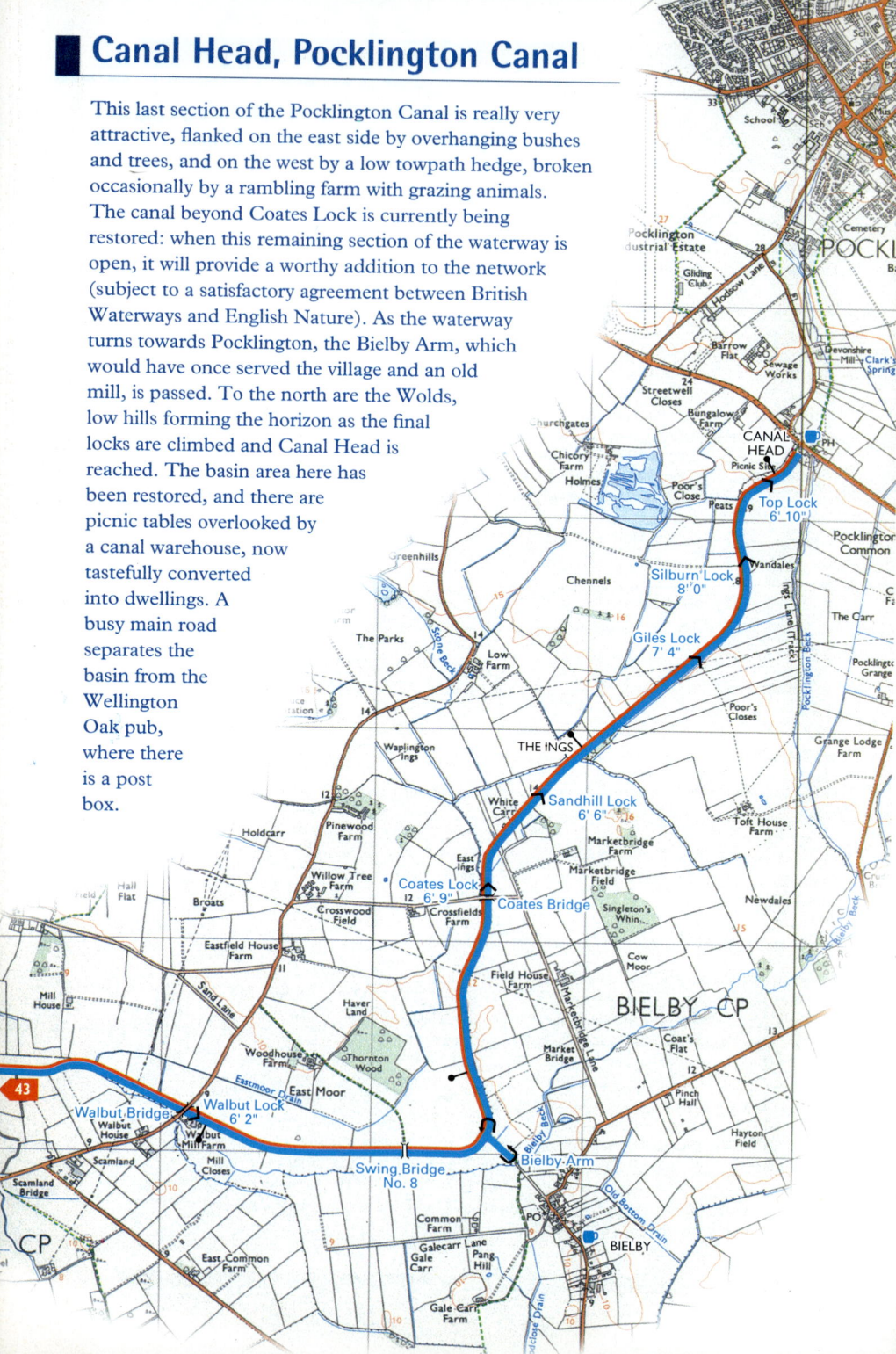

NAVIGATIONAL NOTES

This section is unnavigable at present.

● **Bielby**

E. Riding. PO, tel. Quiet and attractive. The little church of St Giles dates from 1792, but has some far more ancient features. The Wesleyan chapel on the other side of the road dates from 1837, and is now a house, with an attractive sundial on the wall.

● **Pocklington**

E. Riding. PO, tel, stores. A mile to the north of Canal Head, but a worthwhile walk by road or footpath to explore this charming East Riding Town. Prominent is the tall battlemented tower of All Saints church, an endearing mixture of early English and Perpendicular styles, with Norman fragments. By the pulpit is an engraved slab dating from the 13thC, but re-used to record the death of Margaret Easingwold, Prioress of Wilberfoss Priory in 1512. Kept inside is a churchyard cross dating from the 14thC: the crucifixion is depicted on one side, with the Virgin on the reverse. Readers of the inscription are asked to pray for John Sotheby. The Grammar School was founded in 1514 and proudly records the attendance of the philanthropist William Wilberforce (1759–1833), who was born in Hull. He led the parliamentary campaign against the slave trade, which was finally abolished in 1807.

Burnby Hall Gardens and Museum Trust Pocklington (01759 302068). On the way into Pocklington from Canal Head. The gardens contain the finest collection of water lilies in Europe, with 80 varieties to be seen. The gardens and museum are open *early Apr–end Sep, daily 10.00–17.30*. There is a café on site. Admission charge (parties of over 20 people *should telephone to book* and will get a discount).

Pubs and Restaurants

💬 ✗ **College Arms** Main Street, Bielby (01759 318361). A pleasant village pub with a garden and children's play area. Tetley's real ale and restaurant meals *lunchtimes and evenings at weekends and weekday evenings (not Mon)*, with a vegetarian menu. Children are welcome.

💬 ✗ **Wellington Oak** Canal Head (01759 303854). A smart and pleasant brick and timber pub serving Tetley's and the occasional guest real ale. Bar and à la carte restaurant meals available *lunchtimes and evenings every day*, with vegetarian choices. Children are welcome and there is a garden.

MISSING THE BOAT

What is now called the canal age was the short period from 1760 to 1840 – 80 years during which the population of England and Wales rose from 6^{1}/$_{2}$ million to 16 million. In 1760 Josiah Wedgwood founded his pottery works at Etruria, Stoke-on-Trent, and Clive left India. In 1840 the penny post was established. Ideas for building the Pocklington Canal were first mooted in the 1770s: a public meeting was called, and agreed the canal would be a 'great utility'. In 1813 Lord Fitzwilliam, owner of the River Derwent Navigation, asked George Leather to make a survey, and this finally appeared in 1814. Subscriptions were opened and an Act of Parliament to enable the selling of shares was passed in 1815. Construction work began in August 1816, when it was agreed to 'let by ticket the cutting of the canal', and the 9^{1}/$_{2}$ mile route was finally completed in 1818, remarkably at less than the estimated cost. A mere 29 years after the initial celebrations it began its inevitable decline in the face of railway competition, slowly falling into disuse. The last commercial traffic used the canal in 1932.

St Botolph's Church, from the River Witham (see page 70)

FOSSDYKE & WITHAM NAVIGATIONS

MAXIMUM DIMENSIONS

Fossdyke Navigation (Torksey to Lincoln)
Length: 75'
Beam: 15' 3"
Headroom: 12'

Witham Navigation (Lincoln to Boston)
Length: 75'
Beam: 15' 3"
Headroom: 9' 2"

MANAGER

01636 704481

MILEAGE

TORKSEY to
Saxilby: 5½ miles
Brayford Pool, Lincoln: 11 miles
Bardney: 20½ miles
Southrey: 23¼ miles
Kirkstead: 26¾ miles
Dogdyke: 31¾ miles
Anton's Gowt: 40¼ miles

BOSTON Grand Sluice: 42¾ miles

Locks: 3

The Fossdyke Navigation was built in about 120 AD by the Romans, and is the oldest artificially constructed waterway in the country which is still navigable. It was designed to connect the River Witham (made navigable by the Romans) to the Trent and the Humber. The two navigations were used by the Danes when they invaded England, and later by the Normans to carry stone to build Lincoln Cathedral. Subsequently the Fossdyke and the Witham navigations became the responsibility of various riparian landowners, and of the church. They gradually deteriorated and by the beginning of the 17thC were virtually impassable. But King James I transferred the Fossdyke to the Corporation of Lincoln, and from that time conditions improved. Acts of Parliament were passed in 1753 and 1762 for straightening and dredging both navigations, and in 1766 the Grand Sluice at Boston was built, to protect the Witham from the damaging effects of tides and floods. In the 18thC and 19thC further improvements were made, many related to the extensive drainage systems carried out throughout the Fenlands. Thus over a period of centuries the two navigations came to assume the wide, straight course that is so characteristic of them today.

In 1846 the navigations were leased to the Great Northern Railway Company, and immediately their revenue began to fall. Railway competition continued, and by the end of the 19thC both navigations were running at a loss. After a period of dormancy the Witham & Fossdyke navigations became established cruising waterways, as pleasure boats replaced the last surviving commercial operators.

Today their isolation and total lack of development attracts many, while their survival preserves the pleasures of visiting Lincoln by boat; also Boston is one of the vital links between the inland waterway system and the open sea.

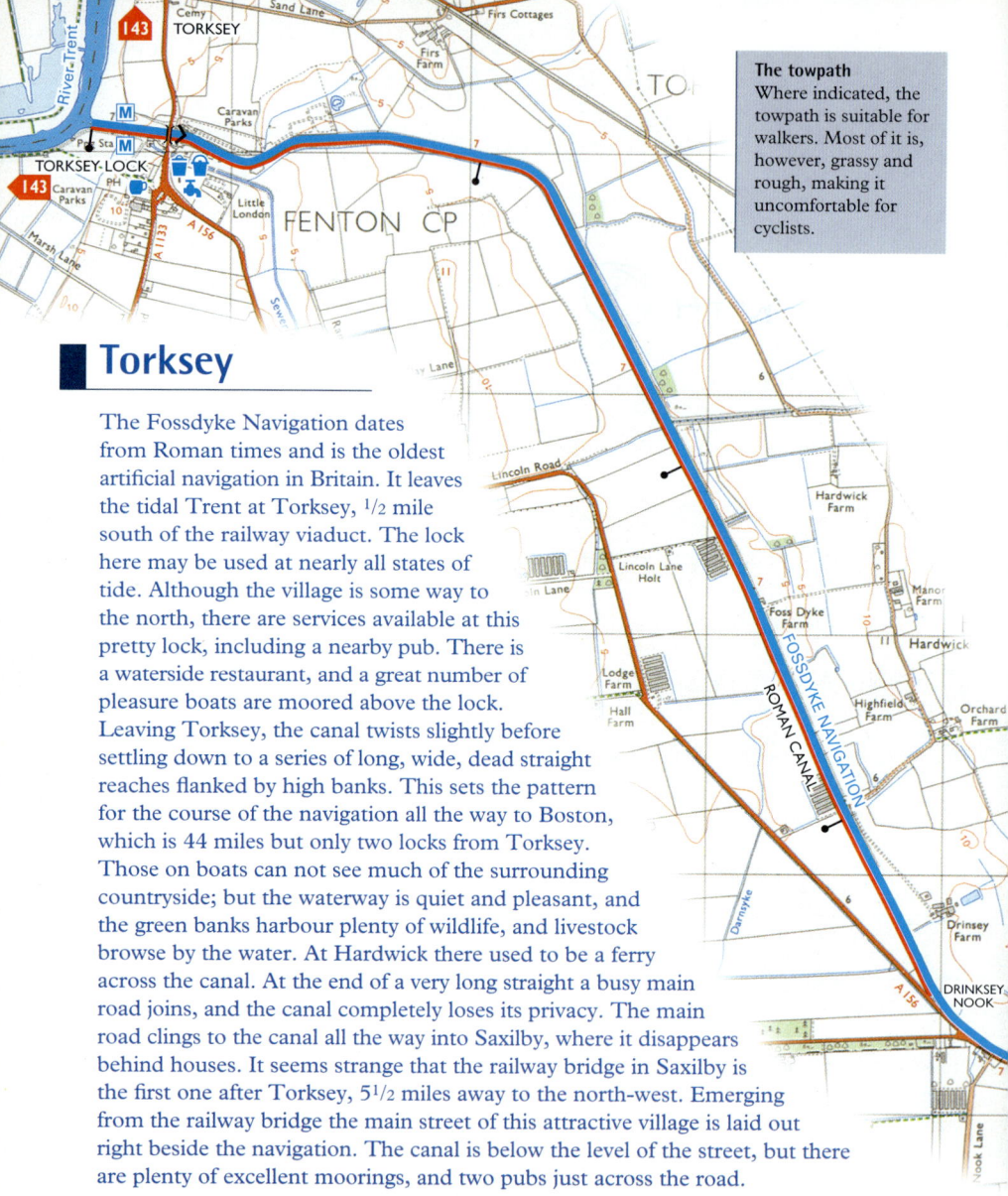

143

The towpath
Where indicated, the towpath is suitable for walkers. Most of it is, however, grassy and rough, making it uncomfortable for cyclists.

Torksey

The Fossdyke Navigation dates from Roman times and is the oldest artificial navigation in Britain. It leaves the tidal Trent at Torksey, 1/2 mile south of the railway viaduct. The lock here may be used at nearly all states of tide. Although the village is some way to the north, there are services available at this pretty lock, including a nearby pub. There is a waterside restaurant, and a great number of pleasure boats are moored above the lock. Leaving Torksey, the canal twists slightly before settling down to a series of long, wide, dead straight reaches flanked by high banks. This sets the pattern for the course of the navigation all the way to Boston, which is 44 miles but only two locks from Torksey. Those on boats can not see much of the surrounding countryside; but the waterway is quiet and pleasant, and the green banks harbour plenty of wildlife, and livestock browse by the water. At Hardwick there used to be a ferry across the canal. At the end of a very long straight a busy main road joins, and the canal completely loses its privacy. The main road clings to the canal all the way into Saxilby, where it disappears behind houses. It seems strange that the railway bridge in Saxilby is the first one after Torksey, 5 1/2 miles away to the north-west. Emerging from the railway bridge the main street of this attractive village is laid out right beside the navigation. The canal is below the level of the street, but there are plenty of excellent moorings, and two pubs just across the road.

NAVIGATIONAL NOTES

1 Torksey Lock may be self-operated during daylight hours outside normal working hours, but you must check the gauge board to ensure a sufficient depth of water over the sill. The lock keeper can be contacted on 01427 718202, VHF Channel 74. The lock may be used at nearly all states of the tide.

2 See Navigational Note 5, page 152. This also applies to Torksey Lock.

3 During the winter months these navigations perform a vital drainage function. Bear in mind that *water levels can change rapidly*.

4 Commercial river traffic operates on VHF channel 6 upsteam of Keadby Bridge on the River Trent. It is useful for VHF users to monitor this channel to establish the where-abouts of large craft on the river.

Pubs and Restaurants

🛥 **White Swan** Torksey Lock (01427 718225). Near the lock. John Smith's and Worthington real ales are served, along with food *lunchtimes and evenings*. Children are welcome, and there is a play area and garden, with moorings. Also caravan and camping site.

✗ 🍷 **Wheelhouse Restaurant** By Torksey Lock (01427 718301). A riverside restaurant, right by the moorings, serving English food. Families are welcome, and it is all non-smoking. *L & D (closed Mon)*.

🛥 ✗ **Hume Arms Hotel** Main Street, Torksey (01427 718613). Situated 300yds from the junction of the Fossdyke & Trent navigations. A la carte menu with fish specialities, *Sunday* carvery and a vegetarian menu served *lunchtime every day*. Garden. Children's room. B & B.

🛥 **Carpenters Arms** Fenton (01427 718633). Marston's real ale and restaurant and bar meals *lunchtimes and evenings (not Mon)*, plus vegetarian choices, in a recently refurbished pub. Children welcome, garden.

🛥 **Pikehouse** Gainsborough Road, 5 minutes walk from Saxilby (01522 702202).

Restaurant and bar meals *all day*, with vegetarian choices. Children are welcome. Garden.

🛥 ✗ **Bridge Inn** Gainsborough Road, Saxilby (01522 702266). A traditional pub near the Fossdyke, with moorings, a large garden, patio and play area. Real ales are served, along with steak and seafood *lunchtimes and evenings*. *Closed Mon.*

🛥 **Anglers Hotel** High Street, Saxilby (01522 702200). Home, Theakston's and a guest real ale in a refurbished local, with plenty of pub games. Children welcome. Stores nearby.

🛥 **Ship Inn** Bridge Street, Saxilby (01522 702259). Canalside. John Smith's real ale. Bar meals available *every lunchtime, and evenings Thu-Sat, with a traditional Sun lunch*. There are vegetarian options, and children are welcome. Outside seating.

🛥 ✗ **Sun Inn** Bridge Street, Saxilby (01522 702326). A canalside pub serving Whitbread real ale, along with bar meals *lunchtimes Mon-Sat, with Sunday lunch, and evening meals in summer (not Fri or Sun)*, with vegetarian choices. Children are welcome, and there is a garden. Live music Fri & Sun. B & B.

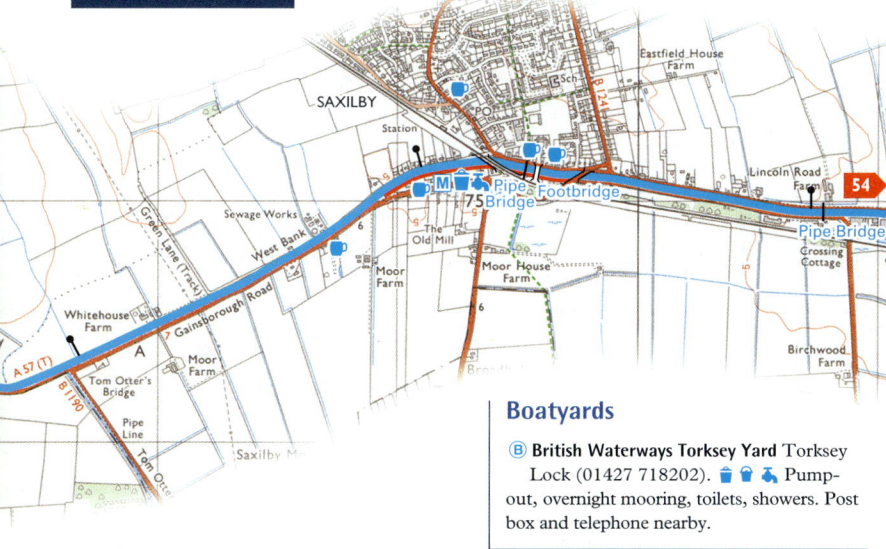

Boatyards

Ⓑ **British Waterways Torksey Yard** Torksey Lock (01427 718202). 🚽 🚻 🔧 Pump-out, overnight mooring, toilets, showers. Post box and telephone nearby.

● **Torksey**
Lincs. PO, tel. Once an important Roman port, this was also a thriving settlement in the Middle Ages. It is now a small riverside village, a short walk north of the settlement centred upon the lock.

● **Saxilby**
Lincs. PO, tel, stores, garage, bank, station, fish & chips. The presence of the Fossdyke has clearly determined much of the layout of the village, although the siting of the church over

half-a-mile to the north has obviously provided another focal point, and as a result Saxilby extends between the two. All the buildings in the main street actually face the waterway, and a line of attractive cherry trees completes the scene. The church of St Boltolph is pretty, having an interesting mélange of building styles that may be the result of the west tower being at one time free-standing.

Lincoln

As the road finally moves away from the navigation, the Gainsborough–Lincoln railway line moves in to take its place on the other bank, although separated from the canal for much of the way by a low hedge. After a few industrial works on the way out of Saxilby, the canal is entirely in countryside, green and flat. There then follows a fascinating stretch of waterway. The approach of Lincoln is marked by the magnificent towers of the cathedral on the hill.

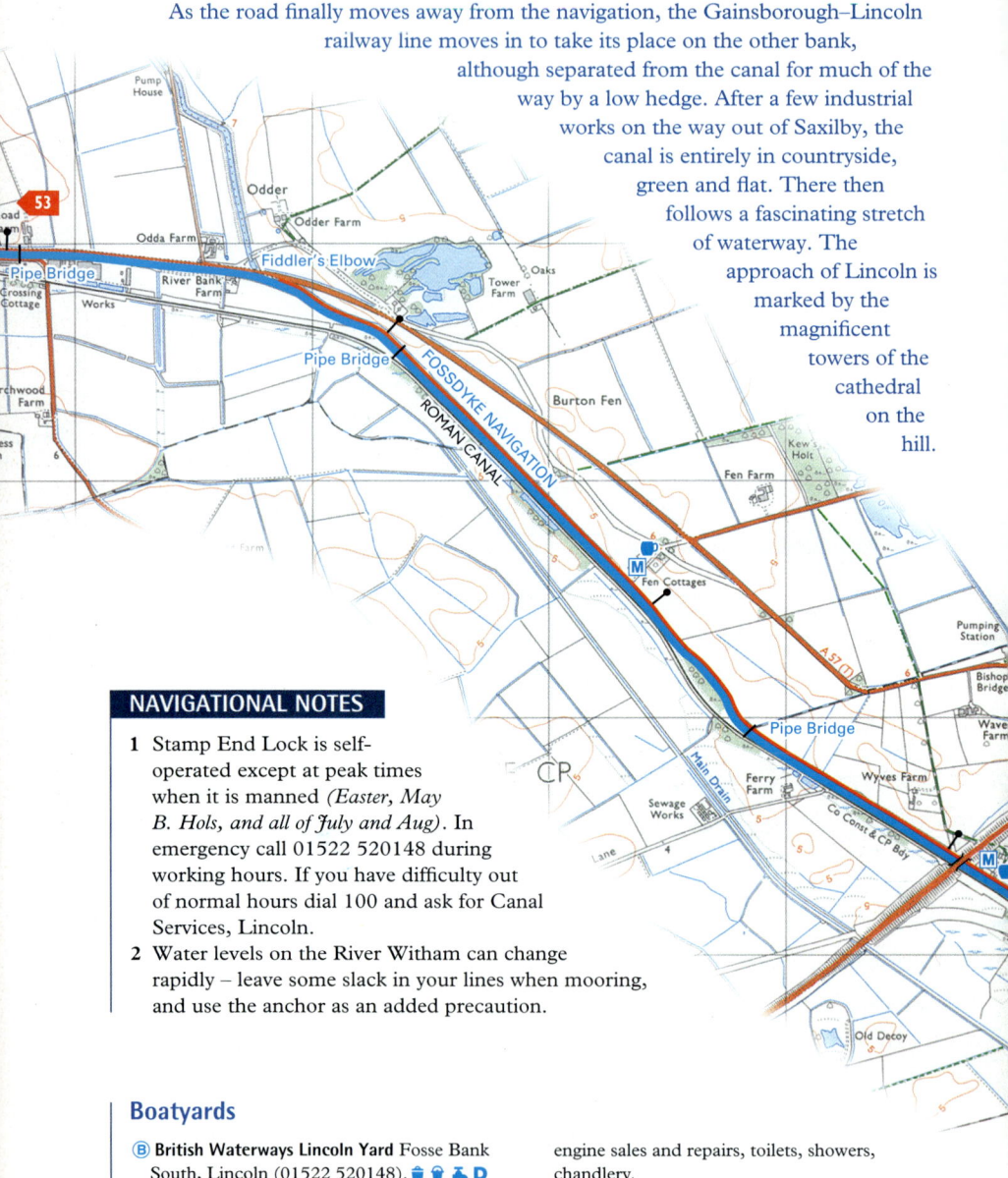

NAVIGATIONAL NOTES

1 Stamp End Lock is self-operated except at peak times when it is manned *(Easter, May B. Hols, and all of July and Aug)*. In emergency call 01522 520148 during working hours. If you have difficulty out of normal hours dial 100 and ask for Canal Services, Lincoln.

2 Water levels on the River Witham can change rapidly – leave some slack in your lines when mooring, and use the anchor as an added precaution.

Boatyards

Ⓑ **British Waterways Lincoln Yard** Fosse Bank South, Lincoln (01522 520148). 🚽 🚿 ♿ **D** Public telephone, toilets and showers.

Ⓑ **Lincoln Marina, James Kendall & Co** Brayford Pool, Lincoln (01522 526896). 🚽 ♿ **D** Gas, overnight and long-term mooring, winter storage, slipway, crane, dry dock, chandlery, boat and

engine sales and repairs, toilets, showers, chandlery.

Ⓑ **Brayford Trust** Lincoln (01522 521452). 🚽 🚿 ♿ (**D** nearby) Pump-out, overnight and long-term mooring, small slipway, telephone nearby, toilets, showers, café, chandlery, launderette.

Passing the isolated Pyewipe pub on the canal bank, the Fossdyke bends briefly as it reaches Lincoln Racecourse, which is edged by trees. Then a long line of moored pleasure boats leads to a new road bridge. Beyond this the navigation widens out dramatically into the vast expanse of water known as Brayford Pool. There is a boatyard here, and boat clubs. Continuing straight through the pool, the River Witham can be seen flowing in as an unnavigable stream at the south corner, and from here onwards (eastward) the Fossdyke Canal is replaced by the Witham Navigation. Leaving Brayford Pool, the concrete bridge is passed; here the channel becomes extremely narrow and goes straight through the heart of old Lincoln, passing through the famous and well-named Glory Hole, with an ancient half-timbered building astride the navigation. The arch dates from around 1160, and was once called the Murder Hole. The houses on the bridge date from around 1540. East of the Glory Hole the navigation continues its narrow course along a pleasantly landscaped stretch before the channel widens out, passing the old flour mills that once used barges for shipping the grain. Further on are Stamp End Lock and sluices. The top gate has no paddles, being simply raised *à la guillotine* into a steel framework to let the water rush in and boats pass underneath. Beyond the next railway bridge is another, larger bridge (with moorings): you are then in an uncluttered, flat landscape, wondering at the difference between the Fossdyke Canal and the River Witham. To the west is Lincoln Cathedral, standing proudly on the hill above the town.

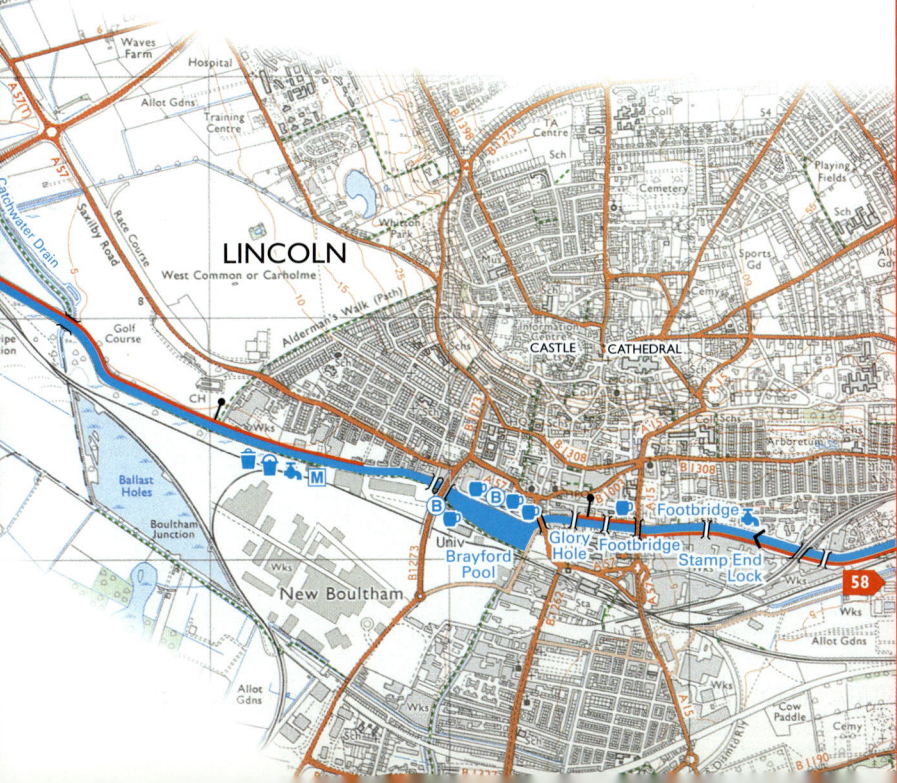

Brayford Pool

This expanse of water separates old Lincoln from industrial Victorian Lincoln. It joins the Fossdyke Canal to the Witham Navigation, and provides the navigator with a welcome relief from the long straight stretches of water either side of Lincoln. The modern building on the south bank is the campus of the University of Lincolnshire, opened by H M Queen on 11th October 1996. The annual Mayor's Regatta, held on Brayford Pool *in June*, is becoming a major event.

Lincoln

All services. Lincoln is a fine city, with a vast amount for the visitor to see. Once the Celtic settlement of Lindon, it became Lindum Colonia, a Roman town; and many Roman remains have been discovered. Plenty of these traces can be seen around the town. The old part of Lincoln is of course grouped around the cathedral, which sits on a hill to the north of the river, overawing the city and the surrounding countryside for miles. There are some splendid rows of houses in the Close and just outside it, where the steep and narrow cobbled streets have remained unchanged for centuries, and motor traffic can hardly penetrate.

Lincoln Cathedral (01522 544544). This splendid building dominates the city and should certainly be seen by visitors to Lincoln. The original Norman cathedral was begun in about 1074, but a fire and an earth tremor in the next century made two extensive restorations necessary. The present triple-towered building is the result of rebuilding in Early English style begun in 1192 by St Hugh of Avalon after the second disaster, although the magnificent central tower (271 feet high) was not finished until 1311. The vast interior contains an abundance of fine stone monuments and wood carvings, and in the Cathedral Treasury is one of the original copies of the Magna Carta. *Open Jun-Aug, Mon-Sat 07.15-20.00 (Sun 18.00); Sep-May, Mon-Sat 07.15-18.00 (Sun 17.00).* Café and shop on site. No charge but a donation is appreciated.

Lincoln Castle Castle Hill (01522 511068). Built as a stronghold for William the Conqueror in 1068, it stands on the crest of the hill close to the cathedral, where 166 houses were demolished to make the necessary space. Over 6 acres of lawns and trees are enclosed by the thick walls, the two towers and the Cobb Hall – a 14th-C addition. The Observatory Tower and the old keep were built on separate mounds on the south side of the castle. The keep is now a mere shell, but the Observatory Tower is in good repair and there is an excellent view of the surrounding area from the top. Cobb Hall, a lower battlemented tower, was built in the north east corner of the castle and was a place of imprisonment and execution. *Open all year Mon-Sat 09.30-17.30, Sun 11.30-17.30, closing in winter at 16.00.* Café for refreshments. Charge.

Tourist Information Centre Castle Hill, Lincoln (01522 529828). Friendly and helpful. Guided walks are run *Easter, Whitsun, Spring and August B. Hols; daily July & Aug; weekends Sep & Oct.*

BOAT TRIPS

Cathedral City Cruises c/o Brayford Trust, Brayford Wharf North, Lincoln (01522 546853, evenings 01777 816910 or 0850 000703). *MV City of Lincoln* cruises daily *Easter-Oct, 11.00, 12.00. 13.30, 15.00 & 16.00* to the Pyewipe Inn. Also private charter. *The Belle* Conducts *hourly cruises in season 11.00-15.00* from near the Witch & Wardrobe pub, Lincoln.

FLYING AROUND LINCOLNSHIRE

Finding yourself with some time to spare on the Fossdyke & Witham, you might like to make an excursion to see some of the county's RAF airfields. East of Tattershall Bridge is the Battle of Britain Memorial Flight Centre, where a Lancaster bomber, five Spitfires, a Hurricane and a Dakota are maintained at RAF Coningsby. These aircraft are not empty airframes filling a museum, but are fully maintained airworthy examples. You can visit *10.00-17.00 on weekdays.*

South of Lincoln is RAF Waddington, and here you can watch the activity from a public viewing area alongside the A15 road. This airfield came into service in 1916 as a training station for the Royal Flying Corps. It closed down in 1918 but re-opened in 1926, becoming a base for Hampdens, which attacked enemy shipping in the channel during the early part of World War II. The indomitable Lancaster first entered service at this base, on Christmas Eve 1941, flown by 44 Squadron. The long runway was built in 1953, assuring the airfield's future, and today AWACs (airborne early warning and control aircraft), with their prominent radar dishes mounted in front of the tail fin, and Nimrods, fly from here.

Lincoln Cathedral

Pubs and Restaurants

The Woodcocks Saxilby Road, Burton Fen (01522 703460). A stylish comfortable pub, serving Marston's and guest real ales. Bar meals from a wide ranging menu are available in a vast eating area *daily 11.30–22.00*, with vegetarian menu. There is both an indoor and outdoor play area for children. Garden. Regular entertainment with theme nights.

Pyewipe Inn and Restaurant Fossebank, Saxilby Road. (01522 528708). Two miles west of Lincoln. A comfortable and isolated pub dating from circa 1780, with moorings, and a terrace overlooking the Fossdyke. Bass, Fuller's, Greene King, Tetley's and Wadworth's real ales, plus an extensive home-cooked menu and à la carte restaurant. Excellent vegetarian choices.

The Hogshead Lincoln Marina, Brayford (01522 526090). Well situated, with a riverside garden and a terrace upstairs, this fine new pub serves a choice of ten real ales, such as Bateman's and Flowers. Meals are served *all day every day*, with vegetarian choices. Children are welcome. Quiz night is *Sunday*.

The Barge on the Brayford Brayford Wharf North, Lincoln (01522 511448). A fine floating restaurant specialising in fresh fish and continental cuisine, and serving Mansfield real ale. Meals available *lunchtimes and evenings every day*, with vegetarian options. Children welcome. There is a sun terrace for warm days.

Royal William IV Brayford Head, Lincoln (01522 528159) At the north east corner of Brayford Pool. A stylish old pub which is *open all day.* Serving John Smith's real ale and food *lunchtimes and evenings every day,* with a vegetarian and children's menu. Outside seating.

Witch and Wardrobe Waterside North, Lincoln (01522 538114) A smart new pub serving Mansfield real ale and food *lunchtimes daily,* with a vegetarian menu. Children welcome at mealtimes. Large garden and regular entertainment.

Green Dragon Broadgate, Lincoln (01522 524950). By the main road bridge, 300yds east of the Glory Hole. This pub beside the River Witham was once a 14th-C merchants house, known as the Great Garrett. These days it serves Everards real ale and bar meals *lunchtimes only (not Sat),* with vegetarian choices. Children welcome *at meal times only.* Regular entertainment.

Stokes High Bridge Restaurant High Street, above the Glory Hole, Lincoln (01522 512534). Serves fine tea and coffee *09.00– 11.00,* and meals *11.30–16.40. Closed Sun.* Vegetarian menu available.(*lunchtime only*).

Number One Restaurant Brayford Side North, Lincoln (01522 560780). Brasserie serving *lunchtimes and evenings every day,* with vegetarians catered for. Children welcome. Fully licensed.

Washingborough

Leaving Lincoln, the River Witham heads due east in a series of straight, wide reaches through landscape little different to that seen from the Fossdyke, following the bottom of a wide valley. To the west, the towers of Lincoln Cathedral remain visible from the river for about 10 miles to the east. Overhead, AWACs (airborne early warning and control aircraft) fly lazily away on their missions, having taken off from a nearby air-field. There are several villages on the hills overlooking the Witham; to the south is Washingborough, all trees and chimneys, while opposite is Greetwell Hall and its little stone church. Further east is the unappealing sprawl of Cherry Willingham, and then Fiskerton. There is an overnight stop jetty at Washingborough.

● **Washingborough**

Lincs. PO, tel, stores, garage. The centre of this village on the south side of the Witham valley is quite pretty. There are some attractive stone terraced cottages, and many trees around the church of St John Evangelist, which contains an ornate Georgian chandelier, thought to have originated in Brighton. This has now become a smart commuter village.

● **Fiskerton**

Lincs. PO, tel, stores, garage. The name of this village comes from 'fisher's town', since in the old days it was a fishing village, where boats could sail right up to the church on the tide. Later, the Fens here were drained and the river diverted into its present straight course. Since then Fiskerton has stood back from the water. When the river breached its banks in 1962 however, the water once again reached the church. St Clement's itself is curious, as its Perpendicular west tower was built around the only circular tower in Lincolnshire. The rest of the building is a rich mélange of styles and parts, perhaps from the monastic houses at Bardney or Tupholme. The village itself is now full of new housing.

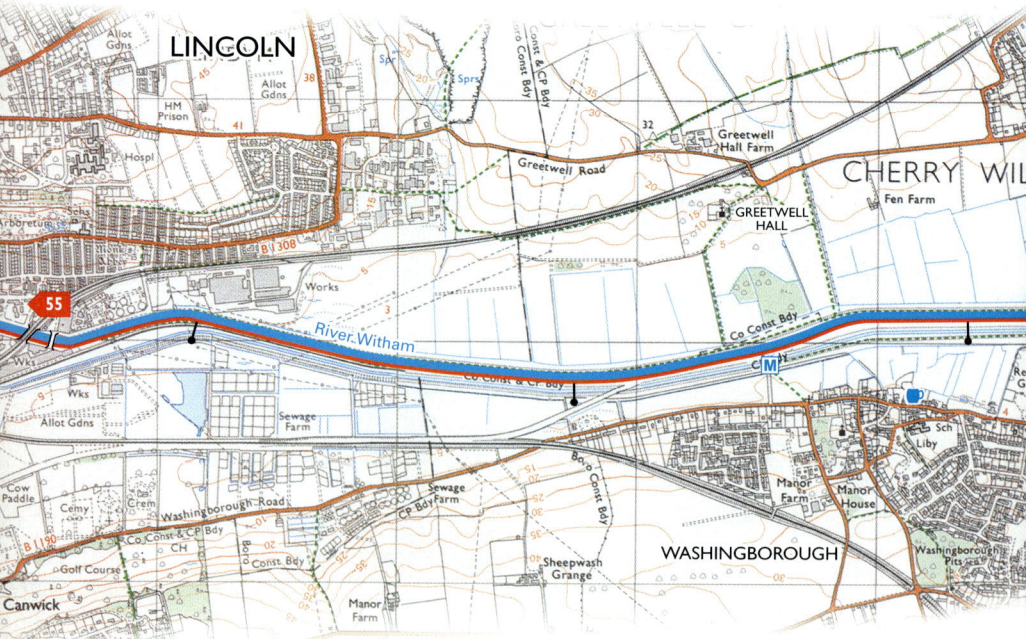

Traditional canal boat decoration

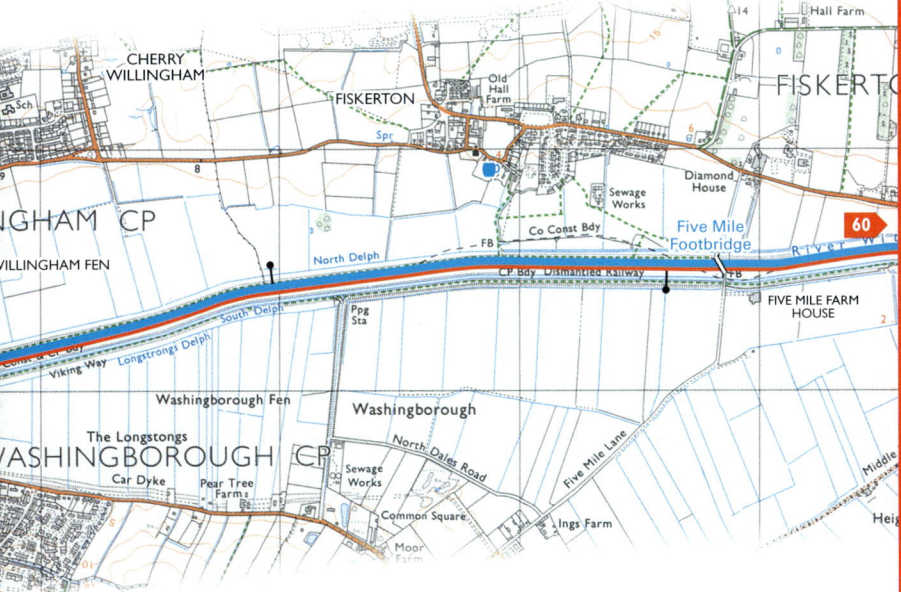

Pubs and Restaurants

Royal Oak Main Road, Washingborough (01522 794412) A friendly village pub serving Eldridge Pope, Marston's and Tetley's real ales. Food is available *lunchtimes Thur–Sun and evenings (not Wed)*. There are vegetarian choices, children are welcome, and there is a garden. Quiz night is *Sun*, and there are bands once a month, on *Fri*.

Carpenter's Arms High Street, Fiskerton (01522 751806). A black-and-white village pub serving Ruddles real ale, and food *lunchtimes and evenings every day*, with vegetarian choices. Children are welcome.

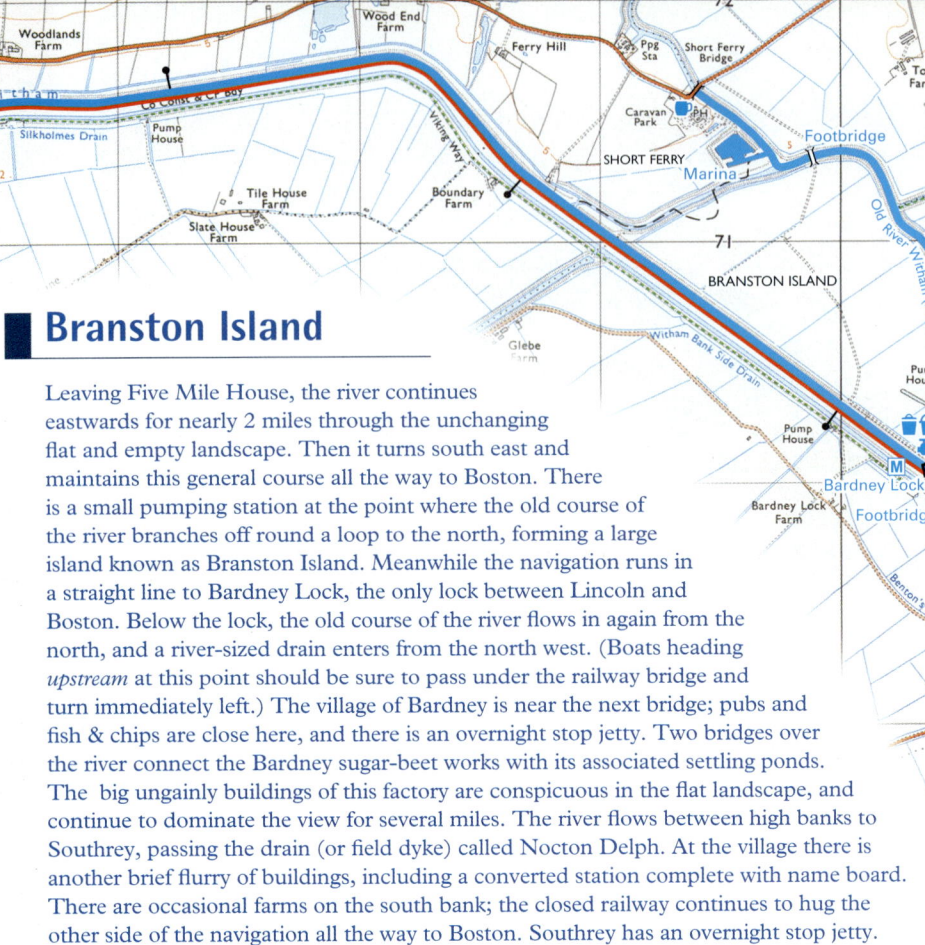

Branston Island

Leaving Five Mile House, the river continues eastwards for nearly 2 miles through the unchanging flat and empty landscape. Then it turns south east and maintains this general course all the way to Boston. There is a small pumping station at the point where the old course of the river branches off round a loop to the north, forming a large island known as Branston Island. Meanwhile the navigation runs in a straight line to Bardney Lock, the only lock between Lincoln and Boston. Below the lock, the old course of the river flows in again from the north, and a river-sized drain enters from the north west. (Boats heading *upstream* at this point should be sure to pass under the railway bridge and turn immediately left.) The village of Bardney is near the next bridge; pubs and fish & chips are close here, and there is an overnight stop jetty. Two bridges over the river connect the Bardney sugar-beet works with its associated settling ponds. The big ungainly buildings of this factory are conspicuous in the flat landscape, and continue to dominate the view for several miles. The river flows between high banks to Southrey, passing the drain (or field dyke) called Nocton Delph. At the village there is another brief flurry of buildings, including a converted station complete with name board. There are occasional farms on the south bank; the closed railway continues to hug the other side of the navigation all the way to Boston. Southrey has an overnight stop jetty.

Pubs and Restaurants

Tyrwhitt Arms Short Ferry (01526 398460). Between Bardney and Fiskerton. A large sociable pub serving Ward's real ale. *Lunchtime* bar snacks and restaurant *open every evening*, with vegetarian options. Children's room, garden, and regular entertainment. Caravan site. Access for boats is north from Bardney Lock up the old course of the Witham.

Bards Wragby Road, Bardney (01526 398376). John Smith's and a guest real ale are served, along with bar meals *lunchtimes and evenings*, with vegetarian choices. Children welcome, and there is outside seating.

Black Horse Bardney. A friendly village pub. Garden with a play area.

Nags Head Abbey Road, Bardney (01526 398402). A fine red-brick ale house dated 1897 right in the village centre, serving Greene King and a guest real ale. Bar meals served *lunchtimes Sat & Sun*, with bar snacks *at other times*. Children welcome.

Gypsy Queen Station Road, Bardney (01526 397188). A basic but friendly pub serving John Smith's, Wood's and a guest real ale. Children are welcome, and there is a garden.

The Tavern Bardney (01526 398313). This pub, by the old station, was closed for a while, but now has new owners. *Fish & chips* nearby.

The Riverside Inn Southrey (01526 398374). A spacious and pretty pub serving Theakston's and a guest real ale. Restaurant and bar meals are served *Tue, Sat & Sun lunchtimes, and Tue-Sat evenings*, with a vegetarian menu. Children welcome, and there is a garden. B & B.

Whitehorse Inn Dunston Fen (01526 398341). A wonderfully remote, but welcoming, pub offering a couple of changing real ales, along with food *lunchtimes and evenings every day in summer (restricted in winter)*. There are vegetarian choices, children are welcome, and there is a garden. Showers.

● **Bardney**

Lincs. PO, tel, stores, garage, banks. A small village to the east of the river, on a slight rise, Bardney is attractive, with the mellow 15th-C church of St Lawrence and a pleasant village green. Inside the church is an incised slab to Abbot Richard Horncastle, 1508, taken from the abbey, together with many minor architectural features from the same source. The parish almshouses by the green were built in 1712. The remains of the Benedictine abbey lie the north of the village. It was founded late in the 7thC and subsequently over-run by the Danes. Re-established in 1087 by Gilbert of Ghent as a cell of Charroux, the abbey buildings were begun again in 1115. The whole site was excavated 1909–14, and reported on by Sir Harold Brakspear in 1922. Much of what was found then has once again disappeared. Bardney has become well known in recent years as the scene of music festivals; in fact the site is to the south east of the village, towards Southrey.

● **Southrey**

Lincs. PO box, tel. A small village of little intrinsic interest, but with reasonable river access. The little white wooden church of St John the Divine, with its belfry, is delightful. It was built by the villagers in 1898. A mile to the north, in undulating country-side, are the ruins of Tupholme Abbey, founded in 1160. Alas the railway is no more, although the platform and name board survive.

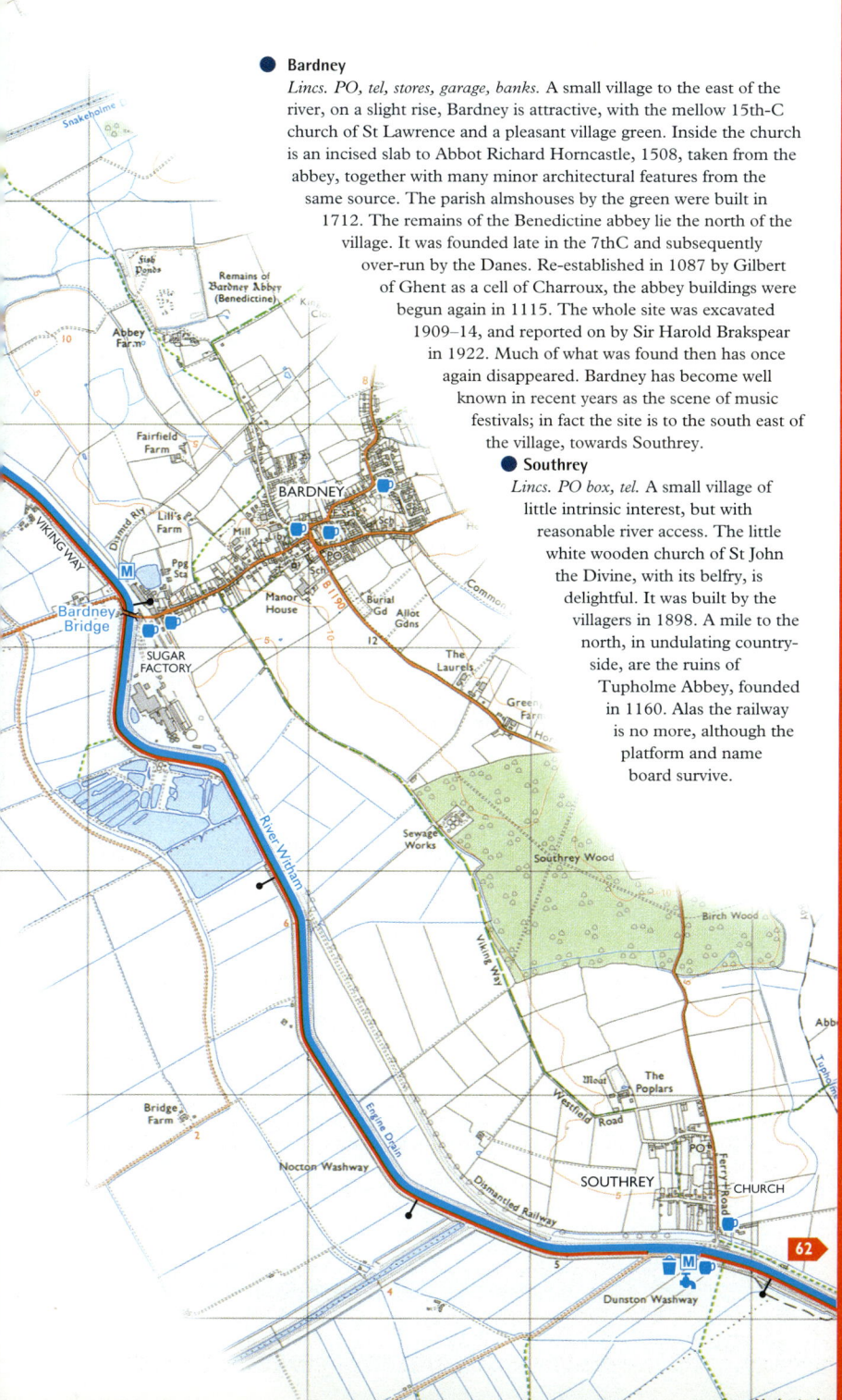

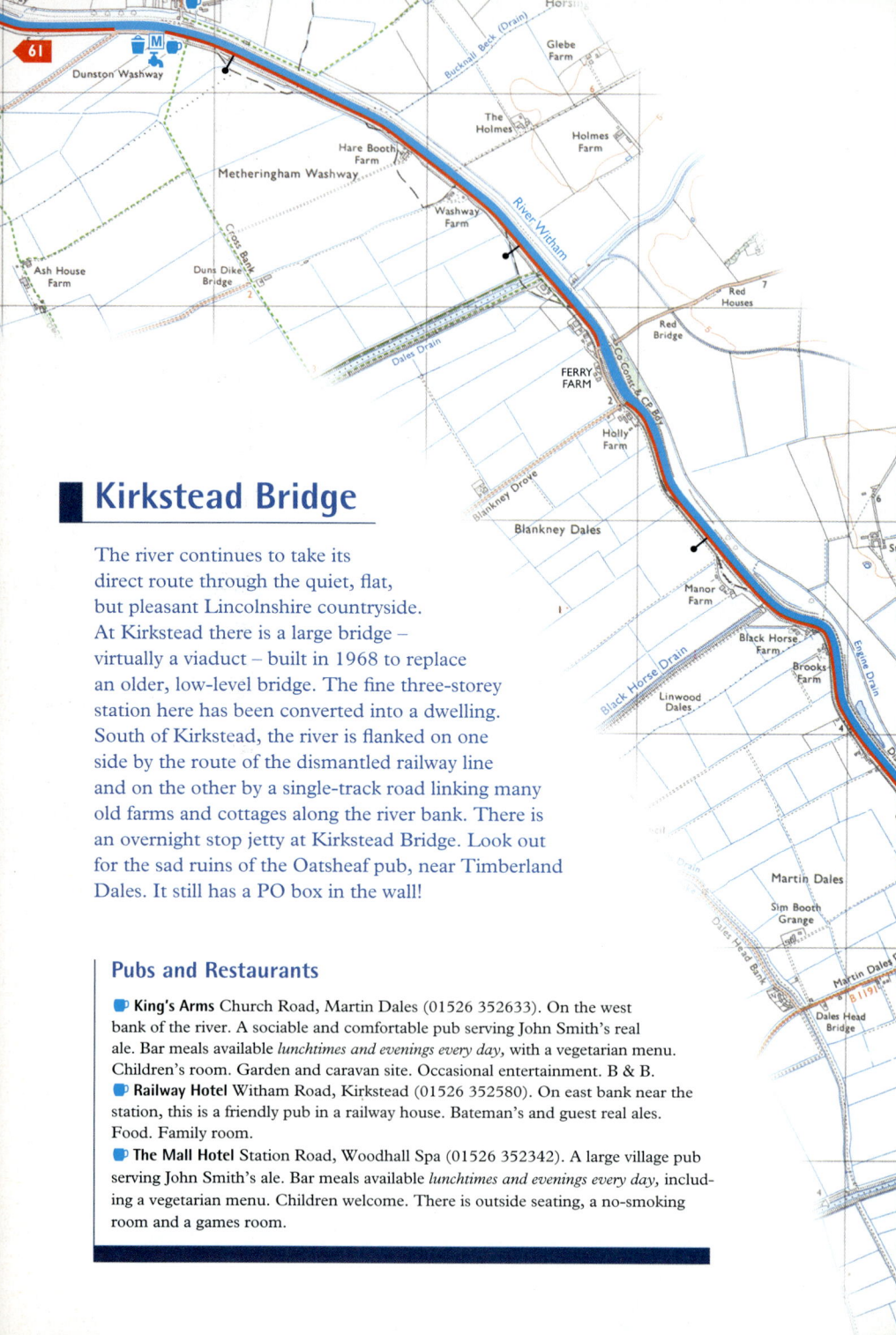

Dunston Washway

Horsing

Glebe Farm

Bucknall Beck (Drain)

The Holmes

Holmes Farm

Hare Booth Farm

Metheringham Washway

Washway Farm

River Witham

Cross Bank

Duns Dike Bridge

Ash House Farm

Dales Drain

Red Houses

Red Bridge

Lo Comm & CP Bdy

FERRY FARM

Holly Farm

Blankney Drove

Blankney Dales

Stixs G

Manor Farm

Black Horse Farm

Brooks Farm

Linwood Dales

Black Horse Drain

Engine Drain

Martin Dales

Sim Booth Grange

Dales Head Bank

Martin Dales Dr

B 1191

Dales Head Bridge

Dales Br Farm

Kirkstead Bridge

The river continues to take its
direct route through the quiet, flat,
but pleasant Lincolnshire countryside.
At Kirkstead there is a large bridge –
virtually a viaduct – built in 1968 to replace
an older, low-level bridge. The fine three-storey
station here has been converted into a dwelling.
South of Kirkstead, the river is flanked on one
side by the route of the dismantled railway line
and on the other by a single-track road linking many
old farms and cottages along the river bank. There is
an overnight stop jetty at Kirkstead Bridge. Look out
for the sad ruins of the Oatsheaf pub, near Timberland
Dales. It still has a PO box in the wall!

Pubs and Restaurants

King's Arms Church Road, Martin Dales (01526 352633). On the west
bank of the river. A sociable and comfortable pub serving John Smith's real
ale. Bar meals available *lunchtimes and evenings every day,* with a vegetarian menu.
Children's room. Garden and caravan site. Occasional entertainment. B & B.

Railway Hotel Witham Road, Kirkstead (01526 352580). On east bank near the
station, this is a friendly pub in a railway house. Bateman's and guest real ales.
Food. Family room.

The Mall Hotel Station Road, Woodhall Spa (01526 352342). A large village pub
serving John Smith's ale. Bar meals available *lunchtimes and evenings every day,* including a vegetarian menu. Children welcome. There is outside seating, a no-smoking
room and a games room.

● **Kirkstead Abbey** ³/4 mile east of Kirkstead Bridge. A solitary finger of masonry about 30 feet high is all that remains of the enormous Cistercian monastery known as Kirkstead Abbey, which was founded in 1139, and moved here in 1187. The trained eye can recognise the former fishponds attached to the monastery ground.

St Leonard's Church Kirkstead. Originally an extramural chapel of the abbey, it was built in the mid 13thC and survives largely intact as one of the finest examples of its kind. Beautifully decorated, it was sensitively restored in 1913–14. The 13th-C wooden screen is one of the oldest in the country, and an effigy of a knight, dating from circa 1250, must also be one of the earliest in the country. The church is just a few hundred yards north east of the bridge.

● **Woodhall Spa**

Lincs. PO, tel, stores, garage, bank, cinema. A resort town in the woods a mile north east of Kirkstead Bridge, and which would not look out of place on the south coast. Perhaps you will

notice also that the town sign features a fine railway engine, although regrettably the line to Woodhall Spa is no more. In 1811, while drilling for coal, iodine mineral water was found at a depth of 511 feet. An inn was built beside the shaft, and a new well was sunk in 1824. The town then grew and it still has the characteristic Victorian atmosphere of many English spa towns. There is a very popular and curious Kinema, complete with Compton organ, tucked away in the woods near to the spa building. It was built in the 1920s, and is unusual in that it uses back-projection (telephone 01526 352166 for programme details). One-and-a-half miles north east of the town is the Wellington Monument, by Waterloo Wood, which was planted from acorns 'sown immediately after the memorable Battle of Waterloo'.

The Cottage Museum Iddesleigh Road (see below). Contains a variety of historical information about the town, and also has a Dambusters exhibition – the bombers flew from an airfield near here. *Open Easter to early Oct, Mon–Sat 10.00–17.00 and Sun 11.00–17.00.* Charge.

Tourist Information Centre Seasonal at the Cottage Museum, Iddesleigh Road, Woodhall Spa (01526 353775). Out of season contact Louth Tourist Information Centre on 01507 609289 for a helpful and informative service.

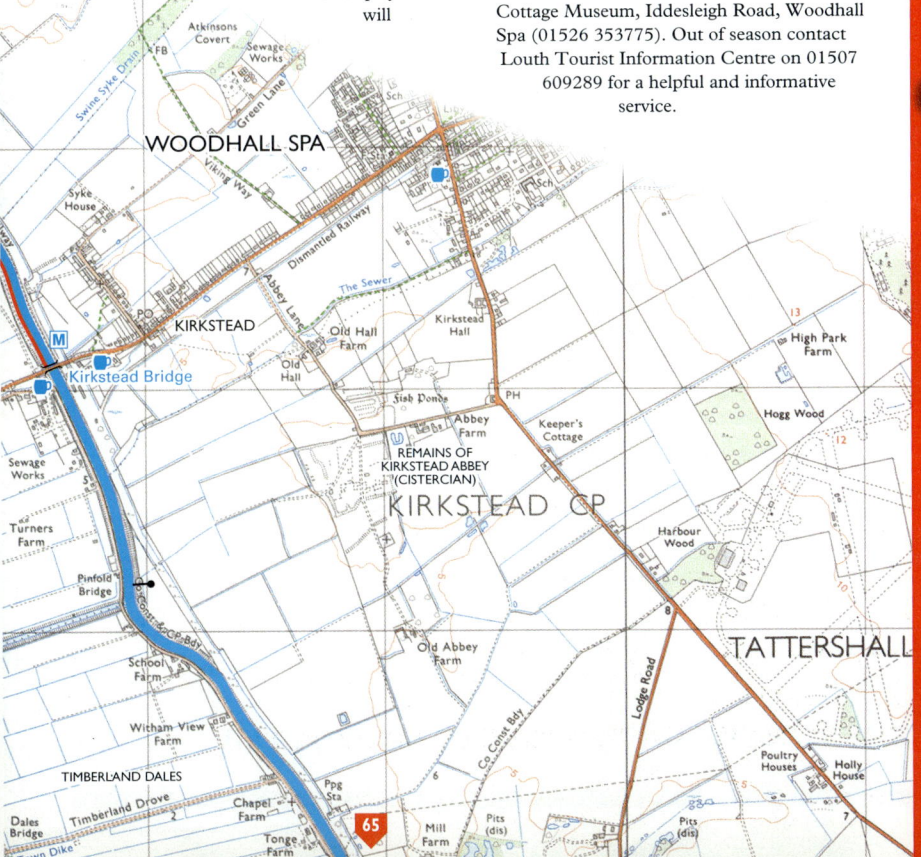

Dogdyke

The river continues southward, now on a pretty and winding course which provides a pleasant contrast to the former straight navigation. Along the Kesteven bank are a number of farm cottages served by a minor road. The old junction with the Horncastle Canal can still just be seen as a slight dent in the east bank. Less than a mile from Tattershall Bridge is Dogdyke, just a short way beyond the old steam pump. It is an attractive place with a marina, a restaurant and a riverside pub. Coningsby Airfield is close by: one end of the runway is near the river, so navigators may find aircraft screaming over them at a height of perhaps 100 feet. This can be disconcerting on an otherwise quiet summer's afternoon. South of Dogdyke there is a small landing stage on the west bank; this marks a caravan site with facilities useful to those on boats (shop, shower, gas, ♨ etc). Beyond it are the houses of Chapel Hill, where the Kyme Eau or Sleaford Navigation joins (see below). Beyond here the river becomes straight and wide once again, with piling to protect and strengthen the bank on one side, and reeds on the other. Boston Stump, the tower of the church, can be seen from here, some 9 miles away beneath breezy open skies. There is an overnight stop jetty at Tattershall Bridge.

Tales of the River Bank Visitor Centre Telephone Sleaford TIC for opening times (01529 414294). An exhibition explaining how the fen was formed, how it is drained, and how it is used.

Timberland Pumping Station Telephone Sleaford TIC for opening times (01529 414294). This pumping station was built in 1839 to drain 2500 acres of Timberland and Thorpe Tilney Fens It is a splendid working example, and once featured a scoop wheel over 26 feet in diameter, lifting water from Walton Delph into the River Witham. The present pump was installed by Gwynnes of London in 1924.

Tattershall Castle (01526 342543). One mile north east of Tattershall Bridge. The original castle was built by Sir Robert de Tateshall in 1231, but was rebuilt in brick in the 15thC for Ralph Cromwell, Treasurer of England 1434–5. Only the keep of this superb building remains, where stone was used sparingly for some windows and door frames. It is 110 feet high, and the bricks, 322,000 of them, were supplied from Edlington Moor, 9 miles to the north. The derelict Horncastle Canal at one time fed the moat at Tattershall Castle. It is now in the care of the National Trust. *Open Apr–Oct, Sat–Wed 10.30–17.00; Nov–Dec weekends only, 12.00-16.00. Closed Jan–Mar.* Charge.

Horncastle Canal This navigation, 10 miles long, was built 1792–1802 to serve the small country town of Horncastle. It left the River Witham 1/2 mile upstream of Tattershall Bridge, but now an embankment has been built over the junction in the cause of flood prevention, so those travelling on

the river must look carefully to discover any trace of the junction. The remains of the first lock are about 300yds from the river. Nearer Horncastle parts of the canal are still in water, and the town basin survives. It was abandoned in 1885.

Tourist Information Centre Trinity Centre, Spilsby Road, Horncastle (01507 526636). Out of season, contact Louth TIC (01507 609289) for a helpful and friendly service.

● **Dogdyke**
Lincs. PO box, tel. 'A ditch where docks grow', and now a riverside settlement close to a signpost which indicates 2¹/2 miles to New York and 12 miles to Boston – nice for a photograph.

Dogdyke Pumping Station Between Tattershall Bridge and Dogdyke (01526 342230). An 1855 steam beam-engine and scoop-wheel. *Open first Sun in each month Easter–Oct 13.30–17.00.* Charge.

● **Chapel Hill**
Lincs. PO box, tel, stores, garage. A pleasantly compact and tiny village at the entrance of Kyme Eau into the Witham.

Kyme Eau Secretary: Steven Hayes, 10 Chelmer Close, North Hykham Lincs LN6 8TH (01522 689460). Now navigable through Kyme Lock (BW key needed) for over 4 miles to Cobblers Lock, where it is possible to wind. Maximum dimensions are 72' x 14' 6", with headroom of 6' 6". Progress can be slow on this navigatiion. From *Oct–Mar* the gates at Kyme Eau Lower Lock are chained back for flood prevention reasons, and navigation is difficult in winter. Full restoration to Sleaford is planned.

Boatyards

Ⓑ **Belle Isle Marina** Dogdyke (01526 342124). 🚽 ♨ Overnight and long-term mooring, winter storage, slipway, crane, boat and engine sales and repairs, telephone, toilets, showers.

🛥 ✗ **Orchard Caravan Park** Chapel Hill (01526 342414). 🚽 ♨ Overnight mooring, swimming pool, toilets, showers, bar, and bar meals *lunchtimes and evenings.*

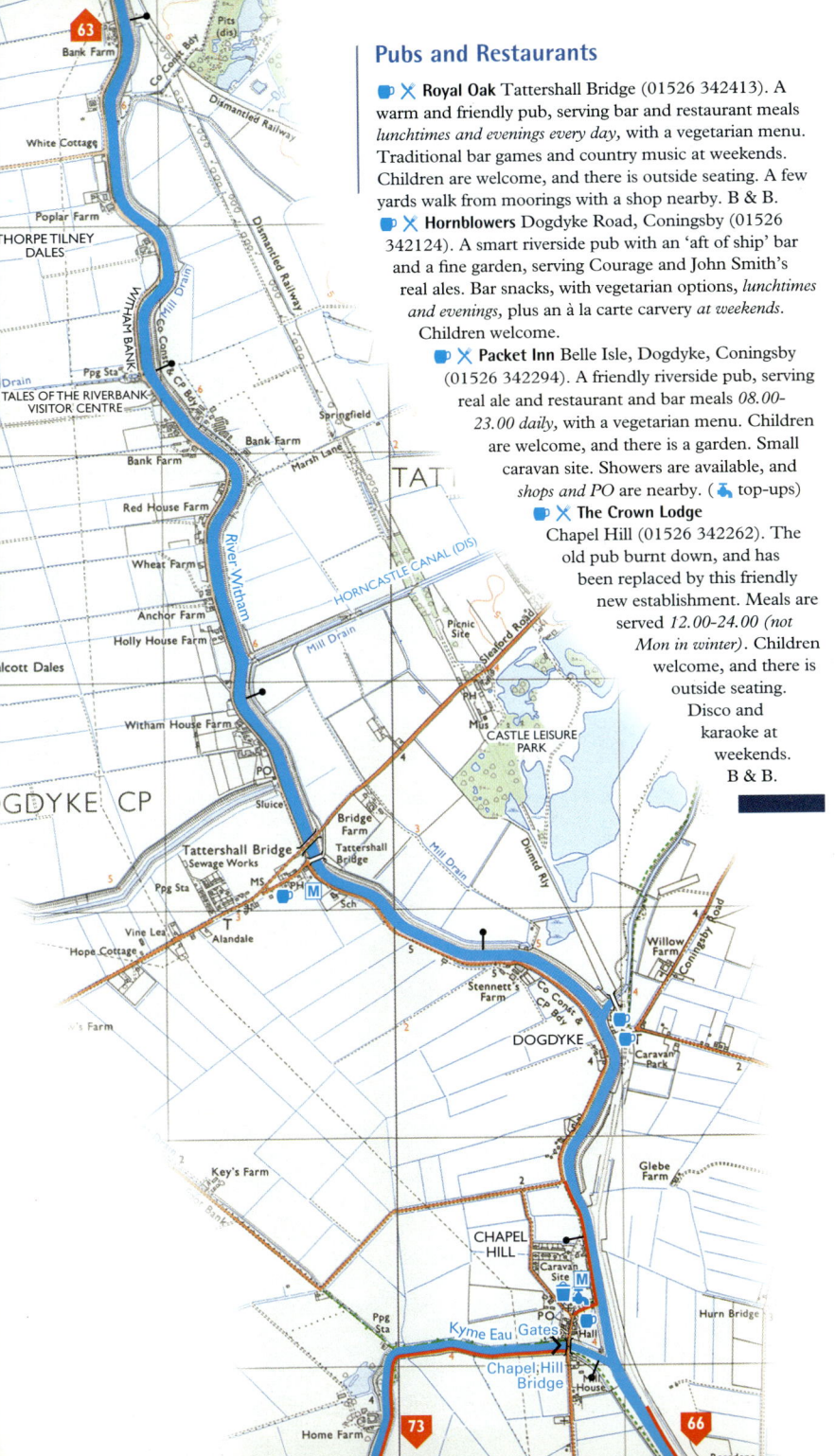

Pubs and Restaurants

🍽 ✕ **Royal Oak** Tattershall Bridge (01526 342413). A warm and friendly pub, serving bar and restaurant meals *lunchtimes and evenings every day,* with a vegetarian menu. Traditional bar games and country music at weekends. Children are welcome, and there is outside seating. A few yards walk from moorings with a shop nearby. B & B.

🍽 ✕ **Hornblowers** Dogdyke Road, Coningsby (01526 342124). A smart riverside pub with an 'aft of ship' bar and a fine garden, serving Courage and John Smith's real ales. Bar snacks, with vegetarian options, *lunchtimes and evenings,* plus an à la carte carvery *at weekends.* Children welcome.

🍽 ✕ **Packet Inn** Belle Isle, Dogdyke, Coningsby (01526 342294). A friendly riverside pub, serving real ale and restaurant and bar meals *08.00–23.00 daily,* with a vegetarian menu. Children are welcome, and there is a garden. Small caravan site. Showers are available, and *shops and PO are nearby.* (⚡ top-ups)

🍽 ✕ **The Crown Lodge** Chapel Hill (01526 342262). The old pub burnt down, and has been replaced by this friendly new establishment. Meals are served *12.00–24.00 (not Mon in winter).* Children welcome, and there is outside seating. Disco and karaoke at weekends. B & B.

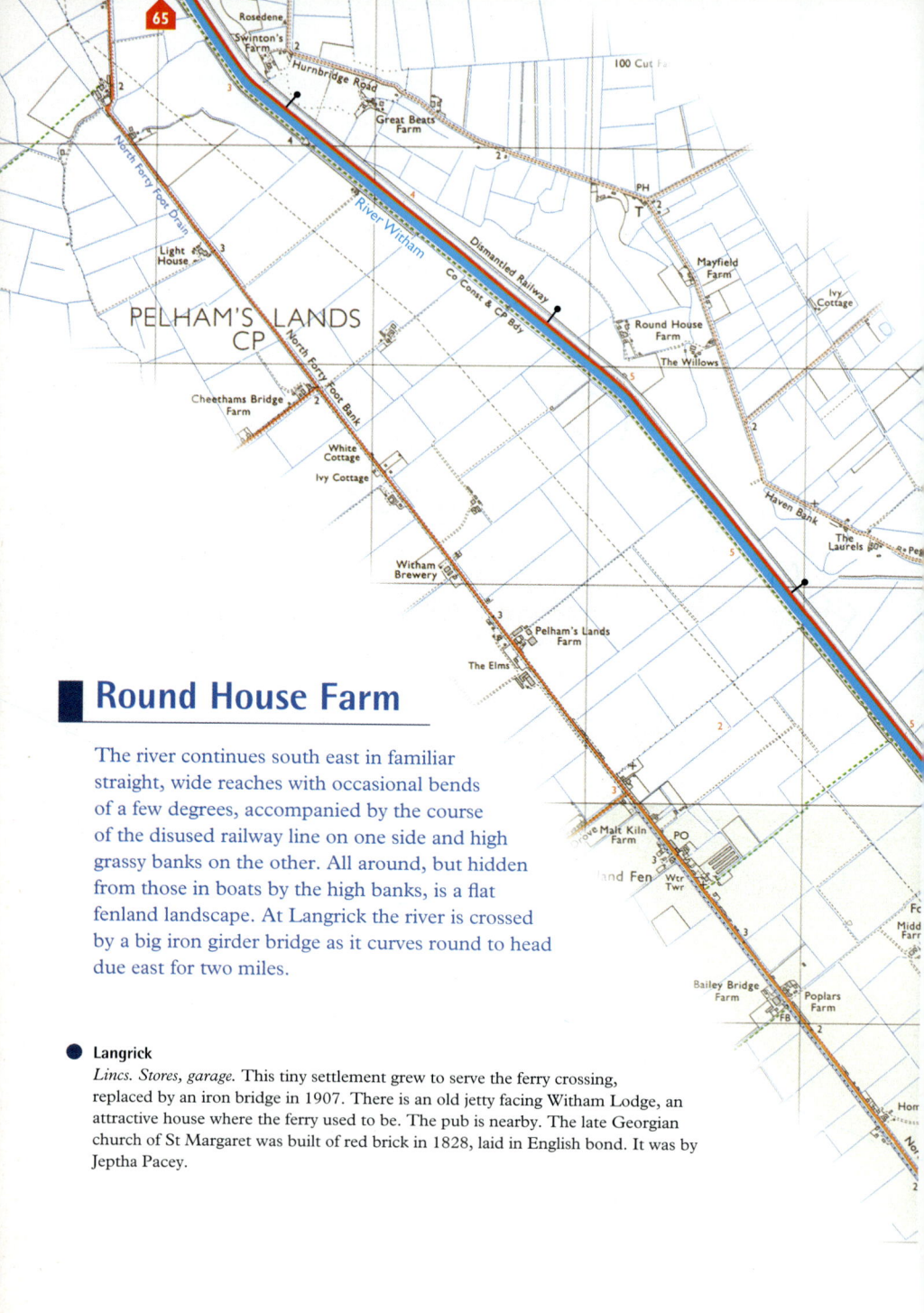

Round House Farm

The river continues south east in familiar straight, wide reaches with occasional bends of a few degrees, accompanied by the course of the disused railway line on one side and high grassy banks on the other. All around, but hidden from those in boats by the high banks, is a flat fenland landscape. At Langrick the river is crossed by a big iron girder bridge as it curves round to head due east for two miles.

● **Langrick**

Lincs. Stores, garage. This tiny settlement grew to serve the ferry crossing, replaced by an iron bridge in 1907. There is an old jetty facing Witham Lodge, an attractive house where the ferry used to be. The pub is nearby. The late Georgian church of St Margaret was built of red brick in 1828, laid in English bond. It was by Jeptha Pacey.

Pubs and Restaurants

🍺 **Ferry Boat Inn** Langrick (01205 280273). On the north side of the river. A plain yet handsome pub serving Home ales. Bar meals and snacks *lunchtime every day except Mon, Tue & Thur evenings*, with a vegetarian option. Children welcome. Garden and a large field out the back. H & M Johnstone's garage and shop is just over the bridge, with **P** & **D**.

✕ ♀ **Langrick Café** Main Road, Langrick (01205 280311). Serving food from *Mon–Fri 06.00–18.00 and Sat 06.00–noon*, including vegetarian menu. Fully licensed. Geordies Boat Sales operates in the grounds.

HE WHO LAUGHS LAST . . .

The line of a dismantled railway closely follows the north bank of the River Witham – it was opened on 17 October 1848 following an agreement between the proprietors of the navigation and the Great Northern Railway company, which leased the river for 999 years at £10,545 per annum. The competition between steam packet boats and railway trains was intense, with the railway ultimately providing *fourth-class* carriages at the fare of a halfpenny per mile, undercutting anything the boats could do, and finally putting them out of business in 1863. Railway trains also took freight from the river – 19,535 tons of coal passed through the Grand Sluice at Boston in 1847 but, after the railway opened, this had fallen to 3,780 tons in 1854. A large railway warehouse was built in 1897 alongside Brayford Pool in Lincoln, with a branch dock to provide shipment facilities. But swans now occupy what was the dock, and the railway is no more. The River Witham, made navigable by the Romans, flows quietly on.

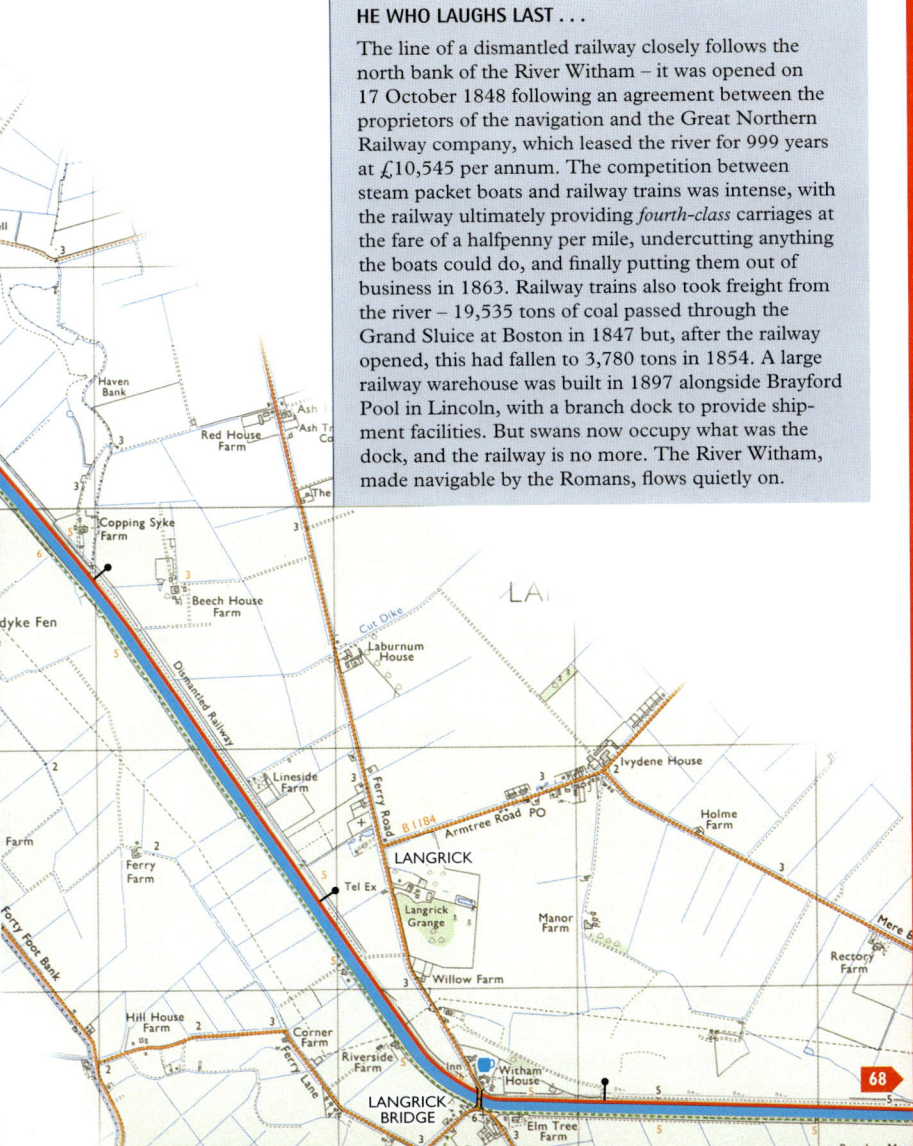

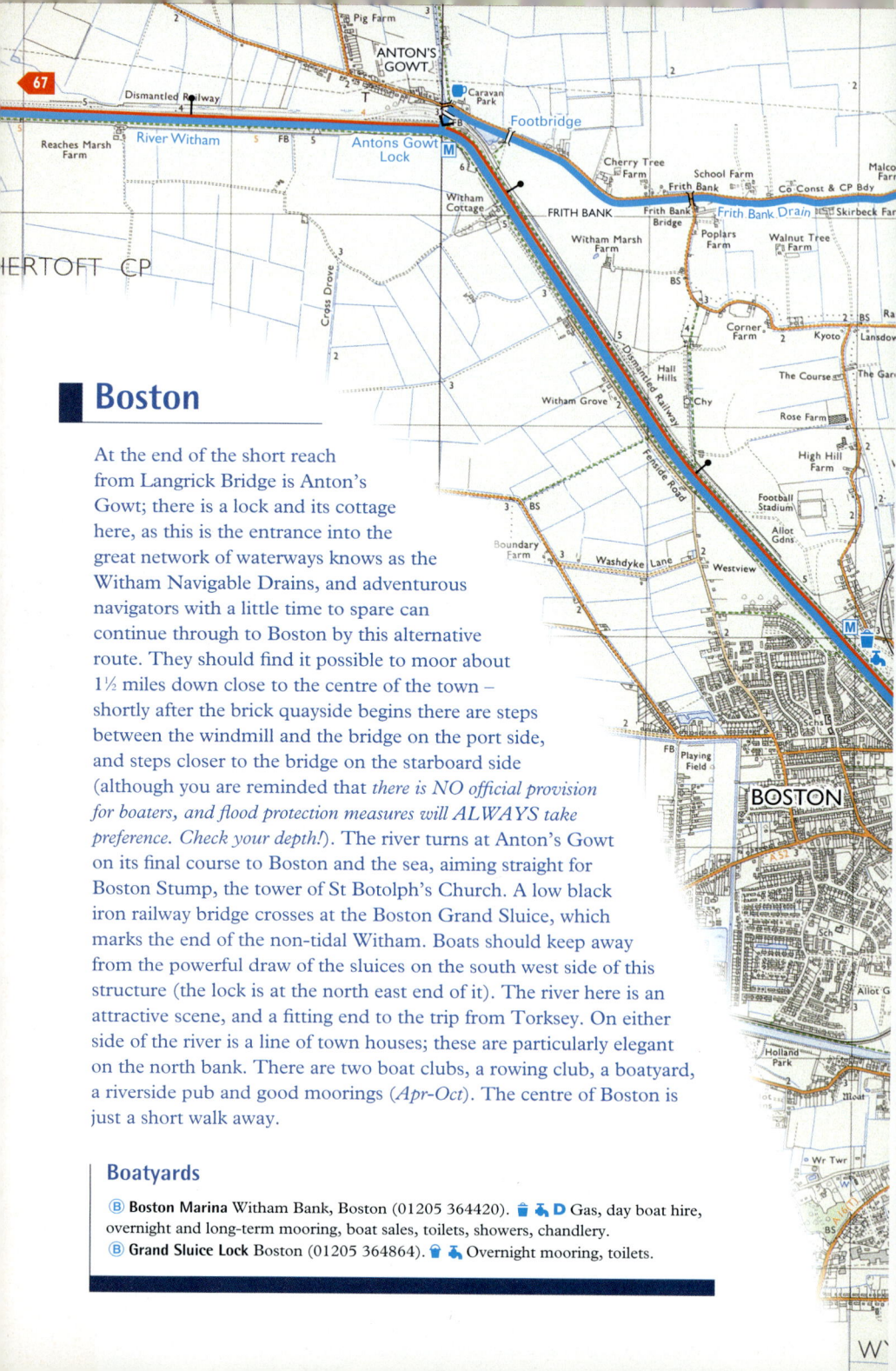

Boston

At the end of the short reach
from Langrick Bridge is Anton's
Gowt; there is a lock and its cottage
here, as this is the entrance into the
great network of waterways knows as the
Witham Navigable Drains, and adventurous
navigators with a little time to spare can
continue through to Boston by this alternative
route. They should find it possible to moor about
1½ miles down close to the centre of the town –
shortly after the brick quayside begins there are steps
between the windmill and the bridge on the port side,
and steps closer to the bridge on the starboard side
(although you are reminded that *there is NO official provision
for boaters, and flood protection measures will ALWAYS take
preference. Check your depth!*). The river turns at Anton's Gowt
on its final course to Boston and the sea, aiming straight for
Boston Stump, the tower of St Botolph's Church. A low black
iron railway bridge crosses at the Boston Grand Sluice, which
marks the end of the non-tidal Witham. Boats should keep away
from the powerful draw of the sluices on the south west side of this
structure (the lock is at the north east end of it). The river here is an
attractive scene, and a fitting end to the trip from Torksey. On either
side of the river is a line of town houses; these are particularly elegant
on the north bank. There are two boat clubs, a rowing club, a boatyard,
a riverside pub and good moorings (*Apr-Oct*). The centre of Boston is
just a short walk away.

Boatyards

Ⓑ **Boston Marina** Witham Bank, Boston (01205 364420). 🚽 ♿ **D** Gas, day boat hire,
overnight and long-term mooring, boat sales, toilets, showers, chandlery.
Ⓑ **Grand Sluice Lock** Boston (01205 364864). 🚽 ♿ Overnight mooring, toilets.

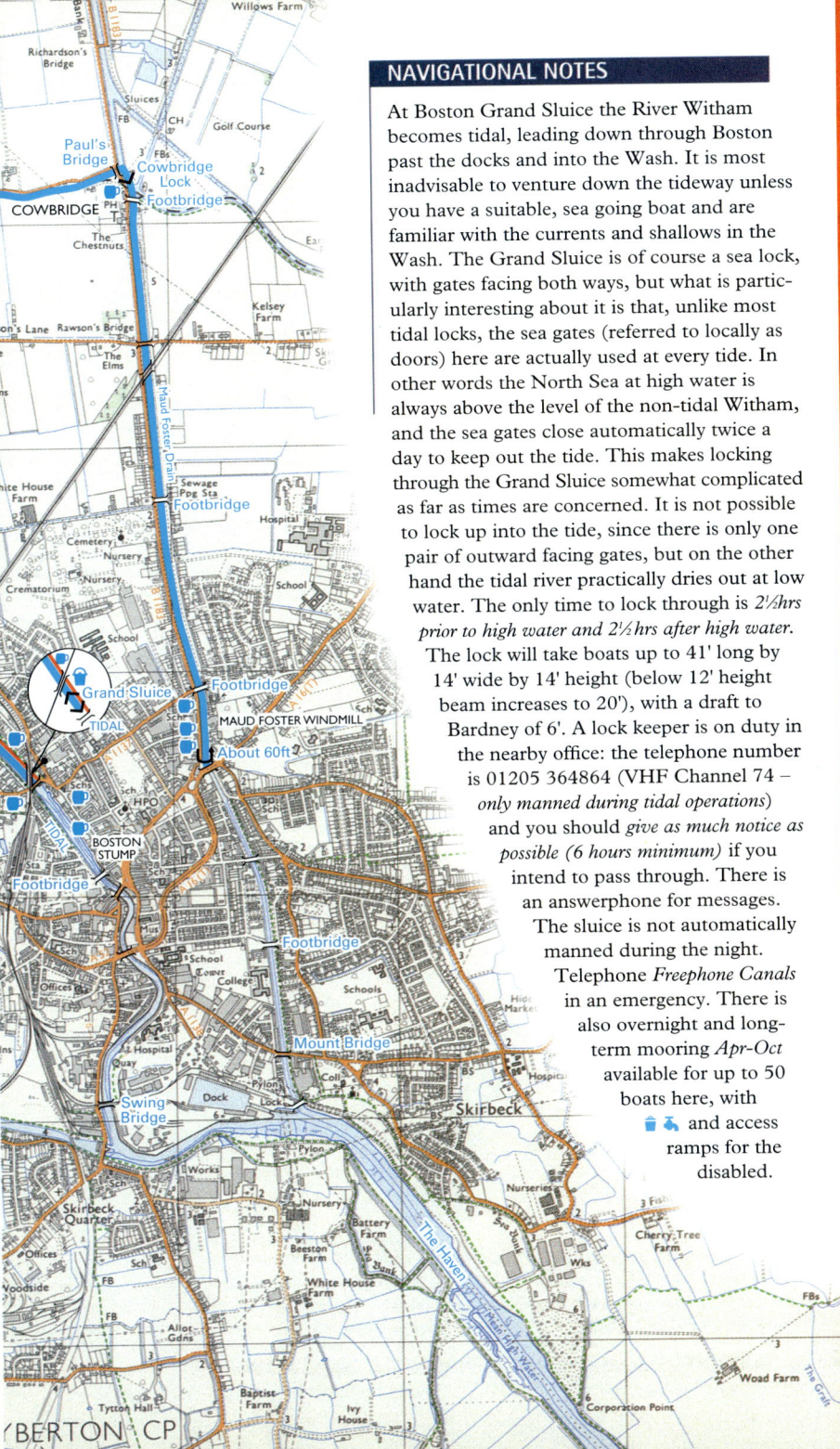

NAVIGATIONAL NOTES

At Boston Grand Sluice the River Witham becomes tidal, leading down through Boston past the docks and into the Wash. It is most inadvisable to venture down the tideway unless you have a suitable, sea going boat and are familiar with the currents and shallows in the Wash. The Grand Sluice is of course a sea lock, with gates facing both ways, but what is particularly interesting about it is that, unlike most tidal locks, the sea gates (referred to locally as doors) here are actually used at every tide. In other words the North Sea at high water is always above the level of the non-tidal Witham, and the sea gates close automatically twice a day to keep out the tide. This makes locking through the Grand Sluice somewhat complicated as far as times are concerned. It is not possible to lock up into the tide, since there is only one pair of outward facing gates, but on the other hand the tidal river practically dries out at low water. The only time to lock through is *2½hrs prior to high water and 2½hrs after high water*. The lock will take boats up to 41' long by 14' wide by 14' height (below 12' height beam increases to 20'), with a draft to Bardney of 6'. A lock keeper is on duty in the nearby office: the telephone number is 01205 364864 (VHF Channel 74 – *only manned during tidal operations*) and you should *give as much notice as possible (6 hours minimum)* if you intend to pass through. There is an answerphone for messages. The sluice is not automatically manned during the night. Telephone *Freephone Canals* in an emergency. There is also overnight and long-term mooring *Apr-Oct* available for up to 50 boats here, with and access ramps for the disabled.

Witham Navigable Drains

This remarkable network of waterways north of Boston exists to drain and irrigate a flat and highly vulnerable tract of fenland. The network is a vital part of the local economy and of the defence of the area against the encroachment of the North Sea. Castle Dyke Drain, Houghbridge Drain, Newham Drain, Frith Bank Drain, West Fen Drain, Medlam Drain, Stonebridge Drain, Maud Foster Drain, the Slea, (these last three are not managed for navigation purposes by the Witham Fourth Internal Drainage Board/WFIDB) are only navigable *early May–mid Sep.* Craft of 75' x 18' can pass through Anton's Gowt Lock, and the limiting size at Cowbridge is 70' x 10'. *Information regarding water levels* should be obtained by telephoning the WFIDB on 01205 310099 *before* you venture in. Access to Cowbridge Lock is by BW key or by calling 01205 310099 *during office hours,* or 01205 353758 *evenings & weekends.* However, it should always be remembered that navigation is NOT the top priority of the drainage authority, and sometimes a navigator is brought up sharply by a low bridge, often in a place where the channel is no wider than 30 feet for several miles. Anton's Gowt Lock is the only entrance to these waterways. The best (widest) course is to head east from this lock, along Frith Bank Drain for 2 miles, to the great junction of waterways at Cowbridge Lock. From here you can go north towards the Lincolnshire Wolds, or south for about 1¹/₂ miles to the outskirts of Boston along the Maud Foster Drain. BUT BE WARNED that levels on ALL the drains can rise or fall rapidly – moor cautiously, allowing plenty of slack in your warps. NOTE: THERE IS NO CONNECTION WITH THE TIDAL WITHAM VIA THE MAUD FOSTER DRAIN.

Boston

Lincs. MD Wed. All services. An immensely attractive town at the mouth of the Witham, Boston has been an important seaport for over 800 years – indeed in 1205 it was second only to London. There are many splendid buildings in the town, but of course the most conspicuous among them is the famous Boston Stump – the 272 foot tower of the parish church. There are two large market places, virtually contiguous. This area is the scene of much revelry in the spring, when the May Fair takes place. Under a charter of Elizabeth I dated 1573, the fair is held *3–10 May.*

St Botolph's Church beside the Witham. This enormous building, the largest parish church in England, is a magnificent example of the late Decorated architecture, and reflects the prosperity of Boston following the rise of its wool trade in the 13thC. The thriving guilds paid for the church, into which were built their respective chapels. Inside, the church is immensely spacious, the tall roof carried by slender quatrefoil columns. There are plenty of interesting things to look at here. The main south door is a remarkable piece of dovetailing, the pulpit is an elaborate Jacobean affair and the choir stalls are an excellent example of 14th-C carving. There are some good brasses and other monuments. The 272 foot tower may be ascended, at a small charge; with 365 steps up a claustrophobic narrow turret, this can be hard going, but one may walk right around a balcony near the top and of course the view over the fenland is unbeatable – on a clear day Lincoln, 32 miles away, is visible. The openness of the work at the top of the tower has led to speculation that it perhaps at one time carried a light for the benefit of shipping: speculation also suggests that it was intended to carry a tall tower – otherwise why call it the stump? Whatever plans there may have been, the church is much loved by the inhabitants of Boston, Massachusetts, who have largely financed its structural repairs this century.

Boston Guildhall Museum South Street (01205 365954). Near the river, south of the Market Place. An ancient and fascinating building constructed in 1450 for the Guild of St Mary, and now a museum illustrating Boston's history. It contains the cells that in 1607 held William Brewster and his friends after their unsuccessful attempt to leave the country. They were tried in the courtroom above. On the ground floor of this dark but historic building is the original kitchen. The roasting spit is self-propelled; the heat rising from the fire drives simple fans connected to a chain that operates the turning gear. This remarkably useful device is over 500 years old. There is also a Banqueting Hall, a Council Chamber and a Maritime Room to be visited. *Open all year, Mon–Sat 10.00–17.00; also Apr–Sep, Sun 13.30–17.00.* Modest charge (under 16 years old free), and *free every Thu.*

Fydell House next to the Guildhall (01205 351520). A superb town house built in 1726 by William Fydell, a successful wine merchant who was three times Mayor of Boston. The building was saved from demolition in 1935 by the pioneering Boston Preservation Trust, who have fully restored this and many other venerable buildings hereabouts. Fydell House is now part of the University of Nottingham (Pilgrim College). *Open daily 09.00–16.00, with limited access during holidays.*

Maud Foster Mill Willoughby Road, Boston (01205 352188). A beautifully preserved windmill, built in 1819. Organic stoneground flour is sold here. *Open all year Wed 10.00–17.00, Sat 11.00–17.00, Sun 13.00–17.00. Also Thu & Fri during August, and all B. Hol Mons, 11.00–17.00.* Charge. Tea shop.

Tourist Information Centre At the Black Friars Arts Centre, Spain Lane, Boston (01205 356656). Next to the Guildhall. This was once part of a 13th-C Dominican friary, and much of the old stone structure remains. The building has now been skilfully converted by the Boston Preservation Trust into Boston's only theatre. It backs onto Spain Court, a charming little square.

Pubs and Restaurants

Oak Tree Inn Frith Bank, Anton's Gowt (01205 360369). A well-situated pub with a pretty conservatory and garden. Serving Tetley's and Bateman's real ales. Bar and restaurant meals available *lunchtimes and evenings every day,* with a vegetarian menu. Children welcome. Working windmill nearby. Mooring.

Cowbridge House Inn Cowbridge (01205 362597). A 1930s style pub serving Home and guest real ales. Bar and restaurant meals are available *lunchtimes and evenings (not Mon),* with vegetarian menu. Children welcome. Garden. There are plenty of pubs in Boston, including:

Ropers Arms Horncastle Road (01205 355741). Opposite the pretty almshouses, this pub serves Bateman's real ale. Children welcome, and there is a patio. Fish & chips close by.

King William IV Horncastle Road (01205 361640). A plain local serving Bateman's real ale.

The Kings Arms Horncastle Road (01205 364296). A thriving brick-built pub opposite the windmill serving Bateman's real ale and bar meals *lunchtimes and evenings every day,* with vegetarian options. Children welcome. Outside seating. Occasional entertainment. B & B.

Coach and Horses Main Ridge (01205 362301). A sociable pub serving Bateman's real ales. Children welcome *during the day.* Traditional pub games. *Open evenings only Mon-Fri; usual hours at weekends.*

Witham Tavern Witham Bank East (01205 355570). Riverside, above the Grand Sluice. A sturdy, large brick-built pub overlooking the bridge and lock serving Courage and Bass real ales and bar meals *lunchtimes and evenings,* with vegetarian menu. Children's play area. Outside seating. Quiz nights *Mon & Tue.*

Carpenters Arms Witham Street (01205 362840). A lively and basic backstreet pub serving a variety of real ales including Bateman's, Boddingtons, Bass and Marston's. Children welcome. Outside seating. Live music *on Sunday.*

Goodbarnes Yard 8 Wormgate (01205 355717). Situated right by Boston Stump, this is a friendly, cosy pub with a pleasant riverside garden. Theakston, Courage and a guest real ale are served, along with food in large helpings *all day every day.* There are vegetarian choices. Children are welcome, although they should leave by *19.00 Thur-Sat,* when the pub can get *very* busy. If you have young children with you, be sure to visit Jakemans home-made sweet shop nearby.

Little Peacock Inn Wormgate (01205 365889). A nicely decorated local serving Bass, Courage, Mansfield, Marston's, Morland's, Theakston's, Wadworth's and Wells real ale and bar meals. Children welcome. Traditional pub games and live music *Fri & Sat.*

New Castle Inn Fydell Street, (01205 361144). A good local pub with one bar, serving Bateman's real ale. Children welcome. Garden. Regular quiz nights.

Maud Foster Mill

Kyme Eau

This remarkable navigation leaves the Fossdyke & Witham at Chapel Hill (see page 65), slipping through flood gates and beginning its journey across the flat fenlands, hemmed in by high banks and seeming at times to be impossibly narrow. Turning sharply south the nicely restored Bottom Lock is soon reached, opened in November 1986, standing alone amidst the fields. After passing Terry Booth Farm the navigation turns to the west and makes a pretty passage through South Kyme, where there is a pub, Kyme Tower and the remains of a priory. Once again the waterway enters open farmland, although those in boats will see only the high grassy banks. There is a brief flurry of interest at Ferry Bridge, where the navigation makes a sharp turn to head towards the present limit of navigation at Cobblers Lock. Those who fancy a challenge can then undertake to walk the remaining unrestored section into Sleaford (beware, the towpath is, in places, blocked), passing what appear to be the disproportionately large and, as yet, unrestored locks.

Kyme Eau Secretary: Steven Hayes, 10 Chelmer Close, North Hykham Lincs LN6 8TH (01522 689460). This 13-mile-long navigation leaves the Witham at Chapel Hill to reach Sleaford to the south west, through seven locks. Slea is taken from the old English sleow, meaning a slimy, muddy stream. Plans for a commercially viable waterway were mooted as early as 1343, and Gilbert d'Umfraville, one of the Lords of Kyme, received royal assent for charging tolls on a part of the river. It was not until 1773, however, that local businessmen initiated plans to make the river navigable. Their scheme was not accepted, and it was not until 1792 that a new plan by Creasey and Jessop was put forward and accepted. The Sleaford Navigation Company was formed, supported by local people and the City of Boston. William Jessop was appointed as engineer, and local funds were made available. The navigation opened in 1794 amidst great celebration, and the eagerly anticipated boom in

local prosperity duly followed. A builders, a coach-makers, a brick-works, an iron foundry, a mill and a brewery were all founded near Navigation Wharf in Sleaford. Navigation House, in Carre Street, still stands as a testimony to the waterway's early prosperity. However, as with all such local navigations, the coming of the railways brought about a rapid decline in prosperity. Tolls were lowered but to no avail, and navigation finally ceased around 1880. The opening in 1857 of the Boston, Sleaford and Midland Counties Railway had reduced the importance of the town of Sleaford, since it now became a mere stop on the line between Boston and Grantham. The Navigation Society was formed in 1976 and their restoration achievements have been considerable. Kyme Eau is now navigable through Kyme Eau Lower Lock (BW key needed) for over 4 miles to Cobblers Lock, where it is possible to wind. Maximum dimensions are 72' x 14' 6", with headroom of 6' 6". Progress can be slow on this

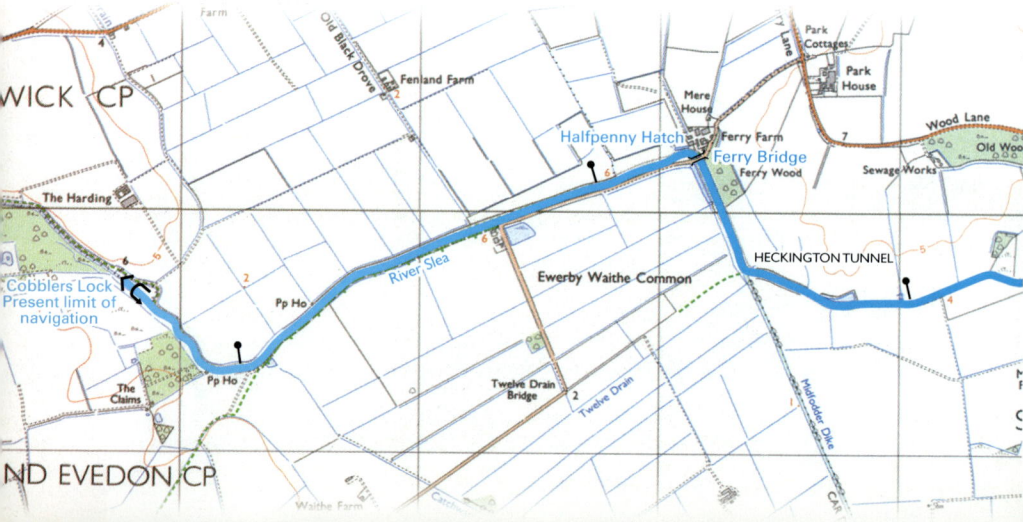

navigation. From *Oct–Mar* the gates at Kyme Eau Lower Lock are chained back for flood prevention reasons, and navigation is difficult in winter. Full restoration to Sleaford is planned.

● **South Kyme**
Lincs. PO box, tel. A quiet, remote and inauspicious fenland settlement, enlivened by the fine wooden sculpture of a kingfisher made by Simon Todd in 1990, and a handsome schoolhouse dated 1843. However, just to the west, and enclosed by the road and the navigation, are the timeless remains of a tower and priory, standing starkly amidst the fields. South Kyme Tower is a very impressive four-storey battlemented turret which dominates the surrounding flat landscape. It was built sometime between 1338 and 1381 by Sir Gilbert de Umfraville, and was probably at one time part of a larger house, dismantled around 1720. It now stands desolate and empty, with no floors above the second which, due to its pattern, was known as the Chequer Chamber. The nearby church was built in 1890 onto the surviving fragments of a grand priory of Augustinian Canons, founded in 1169. A fine Norman doorway survives, decorated with lions and other beasts, together with some fine Anglo Saxon carving dating from the 7th or 8thC, at the east end of the north wall. It depicts trumpet spirals and foliage, and is reminiscent of early manuscripts.

Pubs and Restaurants

🍺 **Hume Arms** South Kyme (01526 861004). An imposing public house, with a fishing lake in the grounds, serving Bateman's, Tetleys and a guest real ale – they have about 200 guests each year, usually from micros. Food is served *lunchtimes Wed–Sun, and evenings every day.* Children are welcome. B & B.

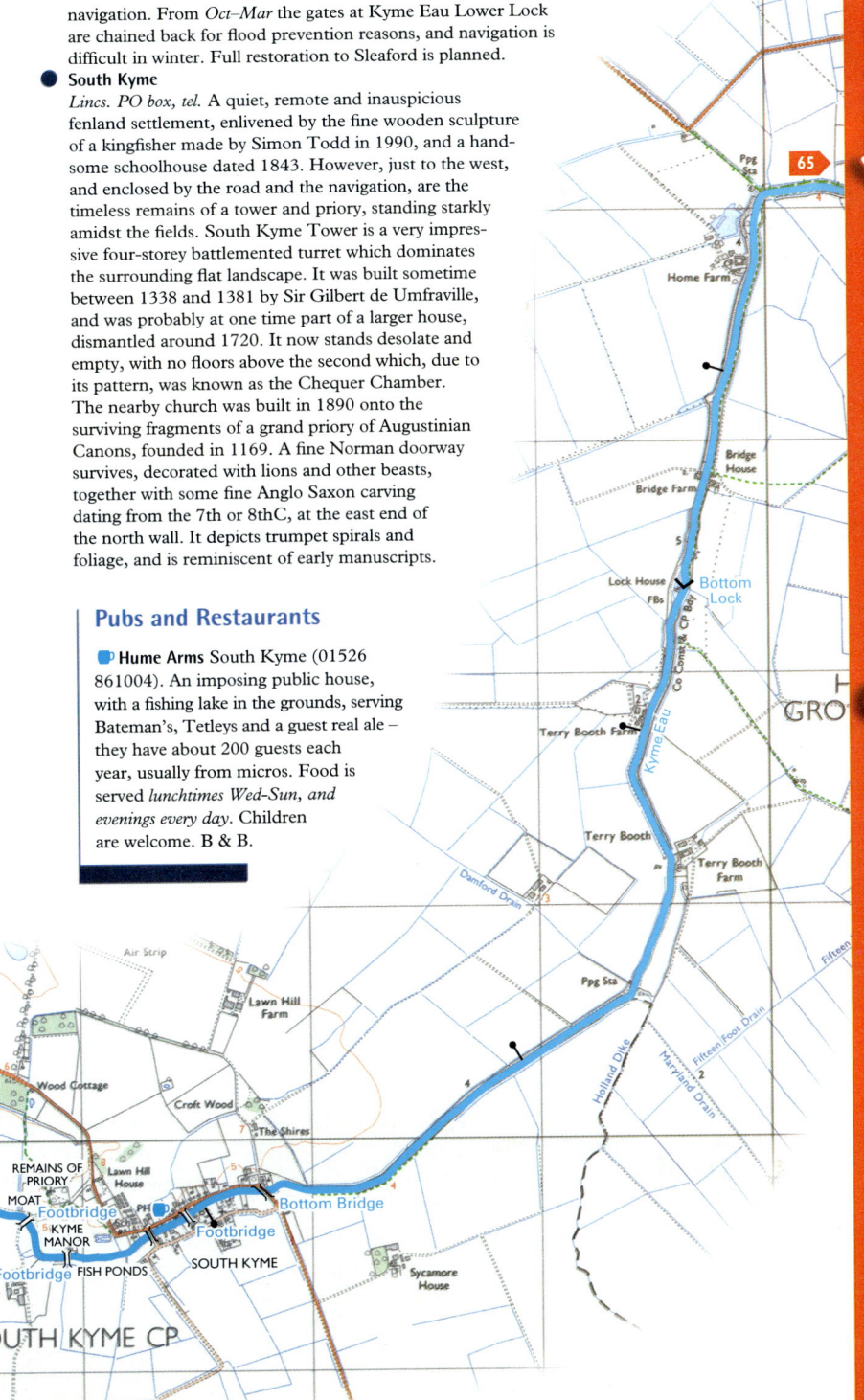

RIVER OUSE, RIVER URE AND RIPON CANAL

MAXIMUM DIMENSIONS

River Ouse

Naburn to York:
Length: 140'
Beam: 24'
Headroom: 25' 6"

York to Swale Nab:
Length: 57'
Beam: 15' 4"
Headroom: 16' 4"

River Ure
Length: 57'
Beam: 15'
Headroom: 10'

Ripon Canal
Length: 57'
Beam: 14' 3"
Headroom: 8' 6"

MILEAGE

RIPON to
Boroughbridge: 7$\frac{1}{2}$ miles
York: 28$\frac{1}{4}$ miles
Selby: 47$\frac{1}{4}$ miles
GOOLE: 63 miles

MANAGER
01904 728229

The River Ouse, flowing as it does through the flat lands of north east England, has long been navigable to York, and has provided a natural transport artery for that city. Indeed, at one time, coal was brought in from Newcastle: a 200-mile journey involving a trip by keel down the Tyne, then by ship to the Humber and then on by barge up the Ouse, rather than undertake an overland journey of 20 miles from the coalfields of the West Riding. In 1766 it was decided to extend navigation along the River Ure and then by a short canal as far as Ripon. Proposals for this scheme were submitted by John Smeeton. Royal assent was granted in 1767 and work began. Milby Lock and Cut were completed in 1769 and a cast-iron bridge, one of the first in the country, was built over the canalised section at Boroughbridge. This was only replaced in 1946. This northerly section of the inland waterways network was immediately prosperous, with Boroughbridge serving as the port for Knaresborough, one of Englands greatest linen manufacturing towns.

On the lower Ouse the Aire & Calder Navigation Company obtained an Act of Parliament in 1820 to extend to Goole, where a brand new port was to be created. When it opened in 1826, the population was 450: this increased to more than 20,000 over the following 100 years. The canal company built the grand and stately church of St John here in 1843–8.

The River Ouse escaped nationalisation in 1948, and today there is commercial traffic as far as Selby. Above York the river is quieter and more suited to the pleasure boater: beyond Boroughbridge the surroundings are particularly attractive with the added bonus of a short section of canal into Ripon. Restoration of this navigation was completed as recently as 1996. Cruising Notes for the River Ouse are available from British Waterways, Naburn Lock, Naburn, York YO1 4RU (01904 728229).

Ripon

The demure, yet pretty Ripon Canal terminates in a fine basin overlooked by a handsome warehouse. The navigation, having lain derelict for many years, now provides good moorings and excellent access to Ripon. Leaving the city on the most northerly artificial navigation in England still connected to the main network, the initial half-mile or so is closely accompanied by a main road. This is soon left behind, however, as the waterway swings to the south and descends Rhodesfield and Bell Furrows locks, passing to the west of Ripon Marina and the racecourse through quiet, open countryside. Ripon Boat Club's marina occupies a pretty spot near Littlethorpe, where the canal makes its approach to the River Ure, falling through Oxclose Lock. Entering the river, the character of the navigation is immediately less demure as it snakes towards Westwick Cut and Lock, set amidst flat farmland, with trees by the river. This unremarkable but pretty countryside makes Newby Hall and its attractively landscaped gardens stand out; its jetty beckons the passing boater, and its miniature railway makes quite a startling impression. At Cherry Island Wood there is another sharp turn as the handsome village of Roecliffe is approached.

Ripon

N. Yorks. PO, tel, stores, garage, bank, cinema. The horn you will hear blown at 9 o'clock each evening is that of the City Wakeman, dressed in traditional clothes and fulfilling the 1000 year custom of setting the watch. This traditionally signified that the town was under the Wakeman's care for the night. If there was then a robbery, he was obliged to make good the loss! Alas this is no longer the case today. His two storey 14th-C half-timbered house, standing in the square, was used as a museum but unfortunately the building is now unsafe for visitors and the museum and Tourist Information Centre have moved to new premises. The centre of Ripon remains elegant and quite well preserved, with narrow winding streets enclosed by buildings of many periods, mostly brick built. The fine open square is dominated by a tall obelisk erected in 1781, which commemorates William Aislabie of Studley Royal's 60 year membership of Parliament. On the south side of the square is the imposing Town Hall, built in 1801 by James Wyatt.
Ripon Cathedral The central tower of this imposing building stands over a Saxon crypt, believed to have been built by St Wilfred circa 670, and now used to display the cathedral's treasures. Wilfred's original church was destroyed in 950 by King Edred of Northumberland, and rebuilding did not begin again until about 1180. It was Archbishop of York Roger de Pont l'Évêque who began the reconstruction, with the superb west front being completed around 1230. Further substantial work was carried out by Christopher Scune, who built the Gothic nave around 1520. The building was restored in 1832, with the re-creation of the diocese and elevation to cathedral status. Look

out for the splendidly carved choir stalls 1489–94, the work of the Bromflets, a local family of wood carvers, and an interesting 1896 Arts & Crafts pulpit associated with William Morris.
Prison and Police Museum (01765 690799). Once in the market square in the old Wakeman's House, now in St Marygate, it houses items concerned with local punishment, including the stocks and pillory, public whipping and transportation. Open Apr–Jun and Sep–Oct, daily 13.00–17.00; Jul & Aug, Mon–Sat 11.00–17.00, Sun 13.00–17.00. Modest charge.
Ripon Workhouse Museum Allhallowgate, Ripon (01765 690799). Ripon's newest museum, established in the Men's Casual Wards of the Victorian workhouse, is dedicated to the lives and treatment of paupers who were the man-power in Ripon's workhouses. The cells, the ablutions, the day room and the workyard can all be seen. Open Apr–June and Sep–Oct, daily 13.00–17.00; Jul & Aug, Mon–Sat 11.00–17.00 and Sun 13.00–17.00. Modest charge.
Tourist Information Centre Seasonal at Minster Road, Ripon (01765 604625). Out of season contact Harrogate TIC (01423 537300) for a friendly and helpful service.
Fountains Abbey & Studley Royal Water Garden (01765 608888). Three miles south west of Ripon (bus service from the city). NT property. The glorious ruins of a Cistercian monastery set amidst 100 acres of beautiful grounds. Founded in 1132, this was one of the most complete sur-vivors of the dissolution. The superb water gar-den was designed by John Aislabie and his son William in the 1700s. Enjoy the Temple of Fame, the Octagon Tower and Serpentine Tunnel. Open Jan–Mar & Oct–Dec, daily 10.00–17.00; Apr–Sep, daily 10.00–19.00. Closed Fri Nov, Dec & Jan, & Xmas. Charge.

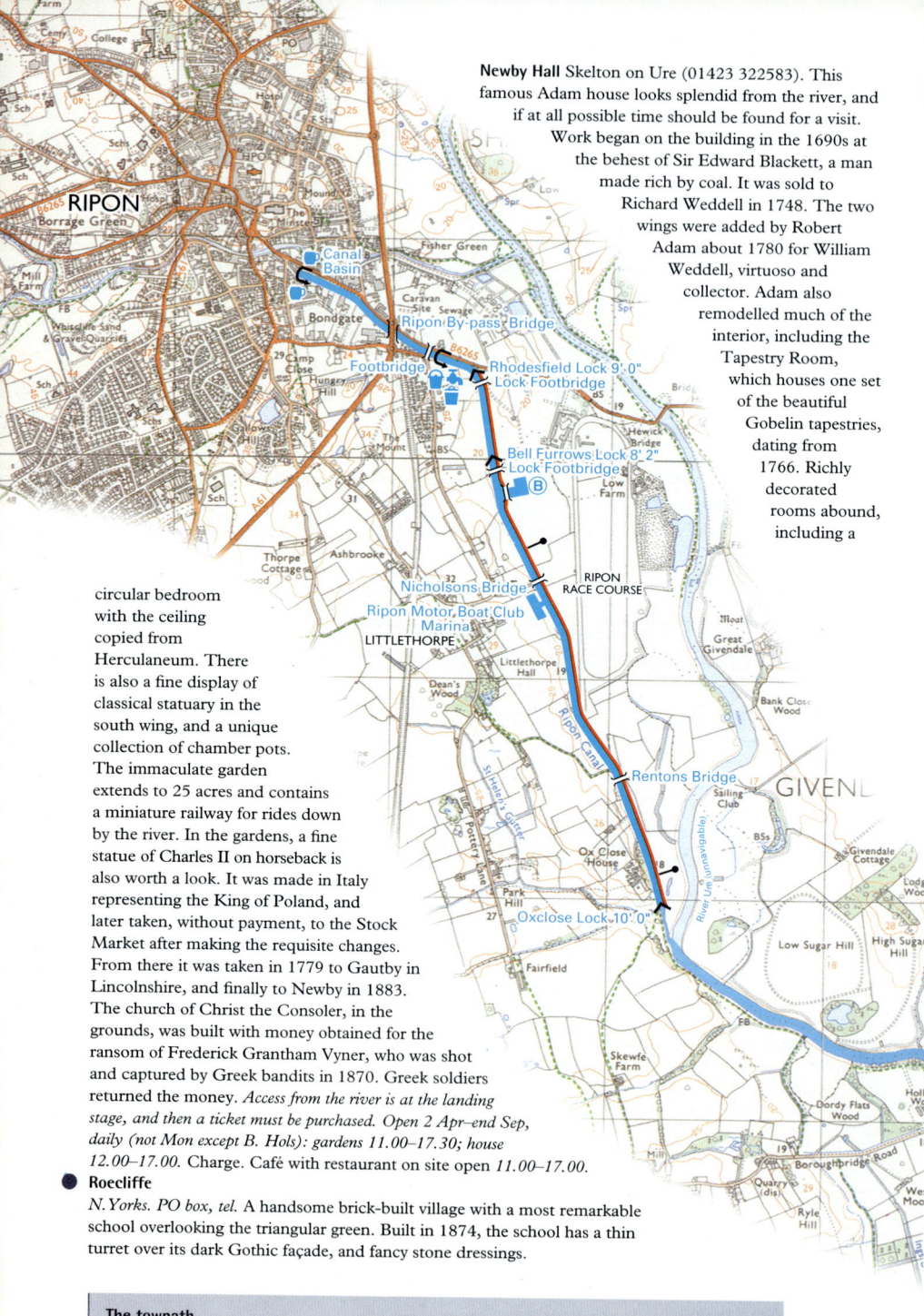

Newby Hall Skelton on Ure (01423 322583). This famous Adam house looks splendid from the river, and if at all possible time should be found for a visit. Work began on the building in the 1690s at the behest of Sir Edward Blackett, a man made rich by coal. It was sold to Richard Weddell in 1748. The two wings were added by Robert Adam about 1780 for William Weddell, virtuoso and collector. Adam also remodelled much of the interior, including the Tapestry Room, which houses one set of the beautiful Gobelin tapestries, dating from 1766. Richly decorated rooms abound, including a circular bedroom with the ceiling copied from Herculaneum. There is also a fine display of classical statuary in the south wing, and a unique collection of chamber pots. The immaculate garden extends to 25 acres and contains a miniature railway for rides down by the river. In the gardens, a fine statue of Charles II on horseback is also worth a look. It was made in Italy representing the King of Poland, and later taken, without payment, to the Stock Market after making the requisite changes. From there it was taken in 1779 to Gautby in Lincolnshire, and finally to Newby in 1883. The church of Christ the Consoler, in the grounds, was built with money obtained for the ransom of Frederick Grantham Vyner, who was shot and captured by Greek bandits in 1870. Greek soldiers returned the money. *Access from the river is at the landing stage, and then a ticket must be purchased. Open 2 Apr–end Sep, daily (not Mon except B. Hols): gardens 11.00–17.30; house 12.00–17.00. Charge. Café with restaurant on site open 11.00–17.00.*

● **Roecliffe**
N.Yorks. PO box, tel. A handsome brick-built village with a most remarkable school overlooking the triangular green. Built in 1874, the school has a thin turret over its dark Gothic façade, and fancy stone dressings.

The towpath
The towpath on the *canal* is excellent, however the river is only approachable in parts.

Pubs and Restaurants

🛈 **The Navigation** Canal Road, Ripon (01765 605676). Spacious and friendly pub just across the road from the pretty canal basin. John Smith's, Theakston's and guest real ales. Bar meals *lunchtimes only every day* with vegetarian selection. Children welcome *for meals only.* Outside seating at the front. Regular quiz nights on *Sun.* B & B.

🛈 **The Water Rat** Bondgate Green, Ripon (01765 602251). Just across the main road from the basin, this friendly pub serves Ward's real ale, along with bar meals *12.00–21.45 daily*, with a children's menu. Benches outside overlook the River Skell and Alma weir, and there is a picturesque view of the cathedral. Regular quiz evenings and live entertainment.

🛈 ✕ **Crown Inn** Roecliffe (01423 322578). A pretty end of terrace pub, with real fire for the winter and outdoor seating for summer. John Smith's, Tetley's and Theakston's real ales. Bar and restaurant meals *lunchtimes and evenings* with vegetarian menu. Also a function room. Children are welcome and there is some outside seating. Regular entertainment with speciality food nights and bands. Disabled access. Camping and caravan site to the rear. B & B.

WORKING ON SHIFTING SANDS

Our roads are now overcrowded – everyone who uses them knows this. In a region where there is much heavy industry, and good access to water transport, it makes sense to move bulk goods by barge.

Acaster's Water Transport who, amongst other activities, recently transported newsprint from Goole to the Yorkshire Evening Press in York (regrettably, this now goes by road), is a small family business which manages to survive in an uncertain world. Graham Acaster and his wife might work in Goole Docks on *Little Shifta* and *Little Shuva*, or on the Trent with their son Karl and his mate Vic Roberts, who shift bulk loads of gravel to Goole from Rampton. But the riverside quarry here is now nearing the end of its operational life, and Acaster's have adapted their boats *River Star*, *Twite* and *Poem 24* at Waddington's yard to create a 600-ton barge taking the name *River Star*, in the expectation of efficiently moving aggregates from a new quarry at Muddy Bank, near Cromwell Lock.

As this is written, there now seems to be some last-minute doubts about using water transport in this new venture, in spite of the government's protestations to the contrary. For the sake of the environment, let us hope this scheme goes ahead.

Boatyards

Ⓑ **Ripon Racecourse Marina (BW)** Boroughbridge Road, Ripon (01904 728229). Pump-out, toilets, showers, long-term mooring.

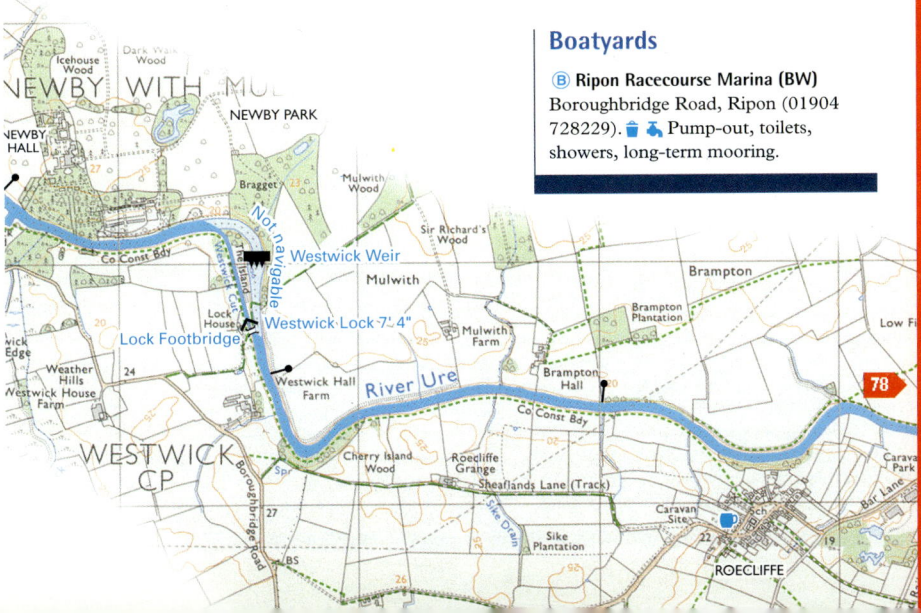

Boroughbridge

The navigation swings under Arrows Bridge and the busy A1 as it makes its approach to Boroughbridge, passing the marina and finally entering Milby Cut, leaving the weir stream to the south. The town lies beyond the weir stream, and imposes little, but there are good moorings, a sanitary station, and fuel and gas from Canal Garage, so a stop to explore is worthwhile. Beyond the town is open country as the river gently winds through pleasant farmland.

Pubs and Restaurants

Fox and Hounds Langthorpe (01423 322717). John Smith's and Theakston's real ale is served, and bar meals are available *lunchtimes and evenings (not Mon lunchtimes in winter)* with vegetarian menu. Children welcome. Outside seating. *Fri night* quiz, live entertainment on *Sat.*

The Grantham Arms Milby (01423 322261). John Smith's, Tetley's and Theakston's real ale, with bar meals *lunchtimes and evenings (not Sun evenings)*, with a vegetarian selection. Children are welcome, and there is outside seating. Regular entertainment. B & B.

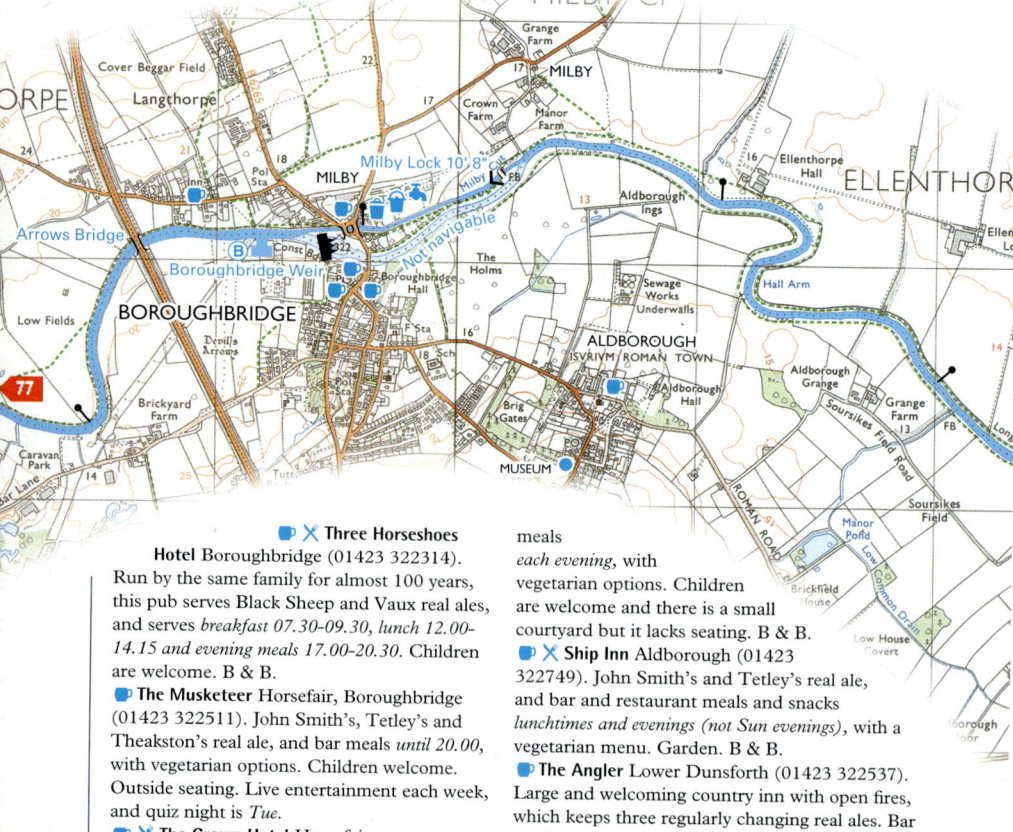

Three Horseshoes Hotel Boroughbridge (01423 322314). Run by the same family for almost 100 years, this pub serves Black Sheep and Vaux real ales, and serves *breakfast 07.30-09.30, lunch 12.00-14.15 and evening meals 17.00-20.30*. Children are welcome. B & B.

The Musketeer Horsefair, Boroughbridge (01423 322511). John Smith's, Tetley's and Theakston's real ale, and bar meals *until 20.00*, with vegetarian options. Children welcome. Outside seating. Live entertainment each week, and quiz night is *Tue.*

The Crown Hotel Horsefair, Boroughbridge (01423 322328). Black Sheep, Tetley's and Theakston's real ale, with bar meals *lunchtimes and evenings,* and restaurant meals *each evening,* with vegetarian options. Children are welcome and there is a small courtyard but it lacks seating. B & B.

Ship Inn Aldborough (01423 322749). John Smith's and Tetley's real ale, and bar and restaurant meals and snacks *lunchtimes and evenings (not Sun evenings)*, with a vegetarian menu. Garden. B & B.

The Angler Lower Dunsforth (01423 322537). Large and welcoming country inn with open fires, which keeps three regularly changing real ales. Bar meals served *lunchtimes and evenings every day*, restaurant meals served *lunchtimes and evenings during the summer, and evenings and weekends during the winter*. Children are welcome, and there is a garden. B & B.

Boatyards

B **Boroughbridge Marina (BW)** Off Roecliffe Lane (01904 728229). 🚽 🚿 ♿ (pump-out at BW facility 300yds away).

● **Boroughbridge**
N. Yorks. PO, tel, stores, garage. The Crown Hotel, just up the road from the bridge, used, when the town sat astride the Great North Road, to have stabling for 100 horses. The first mail coach passed through in 1789, but now the A1 thankfully bypasses the town. Boroughbridge was the 44th of some 400 settlements established by the Normans and their successors between 1066 and 1348 as part of a plan to unite their new kingdom, and served as the port for Knaresborough, 7 miles away. The present river bridge dates from between 1562 and 1784, having been continually repaired during that period. It replaced an earlier wooden structure, which in turn had replaced a ford downstream near Milby. The well, in the Market Place, is 250 feet deep.
Tourist Information Centre Seasonal at Fishergate, Boroughbridge (01423 323373).
Battle of Boroughbridge 1322 Rebel barons led by the Earl of Lancaster struggled with Edward II's supporters for control of the bridge over the River Ure. Eventually Lancaster was taken to his own castle at Pontefract, where he was executed.

Battle of Myton 1319 North of Swale Nab. Known as the white battle from the number of churchmen who were involved. While Edward II was holding Berwick-upon-Tweed under siege, an army of Scots infiltrated into the north of England in the hope of drawing Edward's attention away from the border town. They met a hastily assembled English force at Myton and defeated them. Heavy losses were incurred on the English side with some 3000 killed, including about 300 priests.
● **Aldborough**
N. Yorks. PO, tel, stores. Georgian village less than a mile from Boroughbridge. It was once the walled Roman town of *Isurium Brigantum*, and before that *Iseur*, built by the ancient Britons. It functioned for the Romans as the civitas, or civilian capital of the Brigantes, a tribe who occupied most of what is now Yorkshire and Lancashire. Once enclosed by mighty red sandstone walls, perhaps 20 feet high, the remains are modest but interesting.
Aldborough Roman Museum (01423 322768). Relics gathered from the Roman town. Museum and grounds *open early Apr–end Sep, daily 10.00–18.00 (closed for lunch 13.00–14.00).* Charge. During the winter season only the grounds are open and admission is free. Suitable for picnics.
● **Lower Dunsforth**
N. Yorks. The church of St Mary, 1860, at the eastern end of this small village, has a Norman door in the vestry.

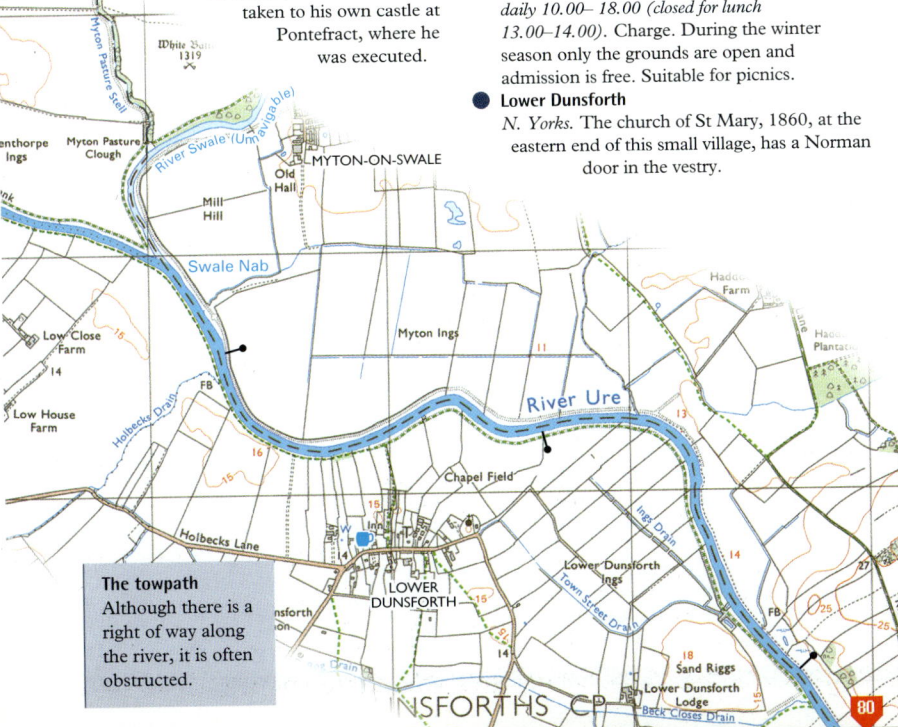

The towpath
Although there is a right of way along the river, it is often obstructed.

Linton Lock

The river continues to meander gently through quiet, unprepossessing, countryside with villages scattered alongside, but never actually on its banks. The rickety toll bridge at Aldwark provides the only river crossing on this stretch, emphasising its remote nature. Just before the river turns east at Cuddy Shaw Reach its name changes from Ure to Ouse, where the Ouse Gill Beck joins. To the north is Linton-on-Ouse RAF airfield, where training aeroplanes come and go noisily during the week, shattering the peace of an otherwise quiet area. The navigation falls through Linton Lock, leaving a fine large weir and salmon leap to the south. There are useful services, plus a shop and café, here. The river then turns sharply to the west of Newton-on-Ouse to pass the extensive and well-tended grounds of Beningbrough Park and Hall, rich with trees and beautifully landscaped. As the river widens to accept the River Nidd, the outstandingly attractive and interesting village of Nun Monkton, and its splendid church, is passed.

Pubs and Restaurants

🛑 **Bay Horse Inn** Aldwark (01347 838324). Black Sheep real ale and bar meals *lunchtimes and evenings* with vegetarian options. Children are welcome and there is a garden. Good moorings, signposted on the river. You will also find the PO here.

🛑 **College Arms** Linton-on-Ouse (01347 848312). Tetley's, Theakston's and John Smith's real ale. Bar meals available *evenings and Sun lunchtimes*, with vegetarian options on request. Children welcome. Regular quiz and disco nights.

🛑 **Dawnay Arms** Newton-on-Ouse (01347 848345). An 18th-C listed building, where you can enjoy Boddingtons, Flower's, Morland's and Theakston's real ale. Bar meals *lunchtimes and evenings*, with an extensive vegetarian menu. Children are welcome. Large riverside garden, and moorings. Quiz night *Tue.*

🛑 **Blacksmiths Arms** Cherrytree Avenue, Newton-on-Ouse (01347 848249). Opposite the church, and offering Camerons and Marston's real ale. Food is served *lunchtimes and evenings*. Garden.

- **Aldwark**
  N. Yorks. PO (at the Bay Horse Inn), tel. The pretty pebble and brick church was built to an original design in 1846–53 by E.B. Lamb.
- **Linton-on-Ouse**
  N. Yorks. PO, tel, stores. A village totally overwhelmed by the adjoining RAF airfield.
- **Newton-on-Ouse**
  N. Yorks. The church of All Saints was built in 1849 for Miss Dawnay by G.T. Andrews. The base of the tower dates from the 12thC: the top is finished with a fine recessed spire. **Beningbrough Hall** Newton-on-Ouse (01904 470666). A very fine Georgian House. The room settings are atmospheric with over 100 portraits and wood-carvings on loan from the National Portrait Gallery. Also on view is a glimpse of life 'downstairs', in the Victorian potting shed and laundry. Art exhibitions, children's play area. *Open Apr–Oct, Sat–Wed & G. Fri 11.00–17.00; also Jul & Aug, on Fri. Closed Nov–Mar.* Charge.

- **Nun Monkton**
  N. Yorks. PO box, tel. Following the Norman conquest the village, together with other surrounding estates, was given to the Norman knight Osbern de Arches. It was one of Osbern's descendants, William de Arches, who chose this site at the junction of the Rivers Nidd and Ouse to found a priory of Benedictine nuns dedicated to the Blessed Virgin Mary. Today only the nun's chapel survives as the church of St Mary. Built 1153–80 in Early English style, there is a late Norman porch and some very fine arcading above plain lower windows, access to which is gained via a staircase in the north west angle. Between the windows are 12 niches, which probably once contained effigies of the apostles. Set into the floor beneath the present altar is the pre-Reformation stone altar, with five crosses cut into it, thought to represent the five wounds of Christ. The church is quite properly considered to be one of the finest in Yorkshire, and will amply repay a visit. The village green has a splendid May pole, and a fine duck pond.

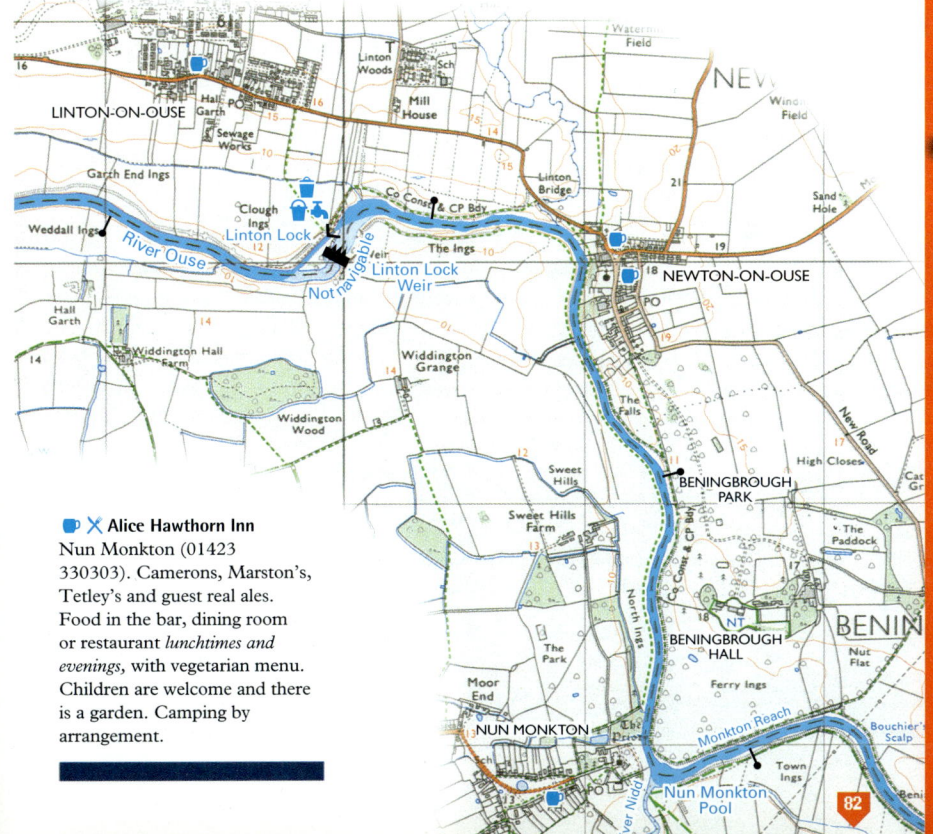

- **📱✗ Alice Hawthorn Inn**
  Nun Monkton (01423 330303). Camerons, Marston's, Tetley's and guest real ales. Food in the bar, dining room or restaurant *lunchtimes and evenings*, with vegetarian menu. Children are welcome and there is a garden. Camping by arrangement.

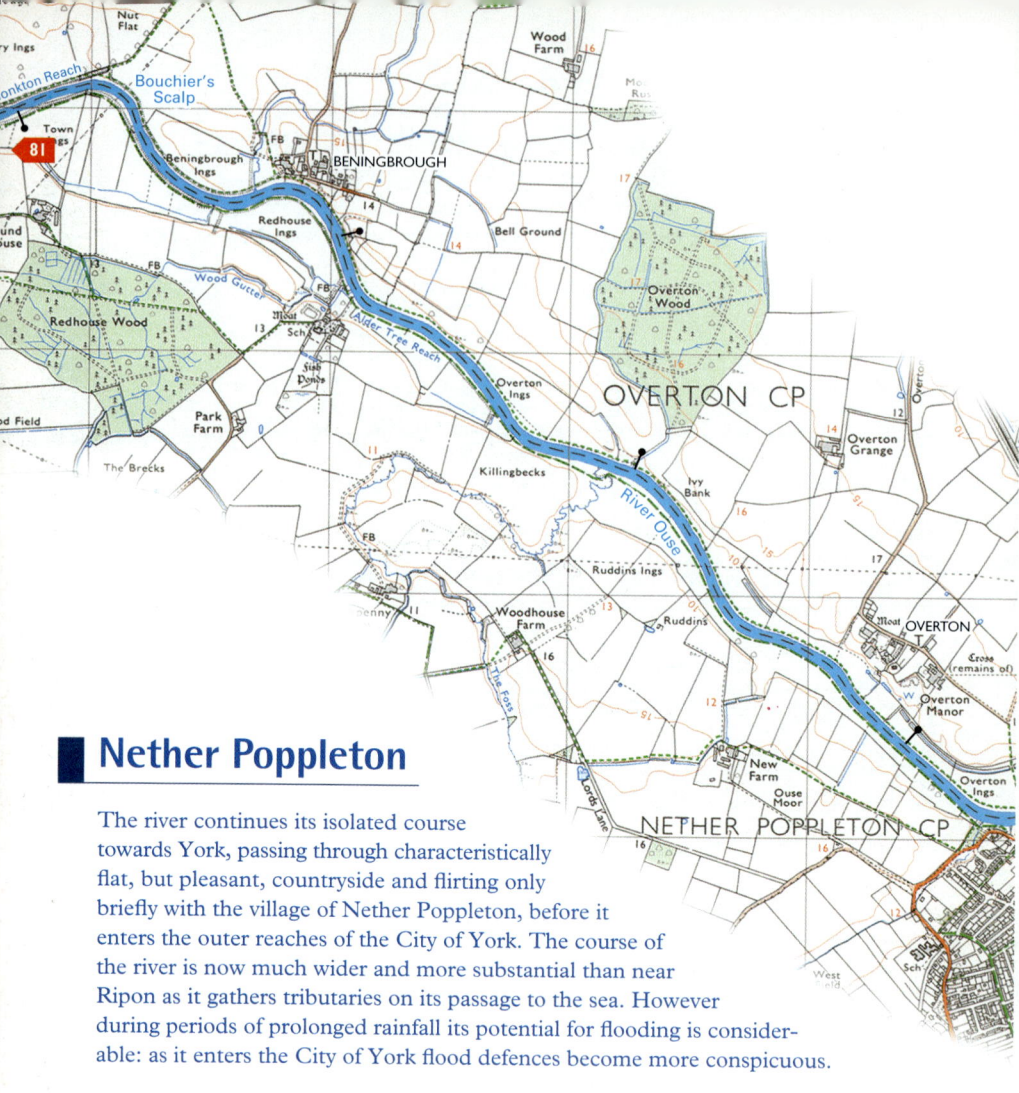

Nether Poppleton

The river continues its isolated course
towards York, passing through characteristically
flat, but pleasant, countryside and flirting only
briefly with the village of Nether Poppleton, before it
enters the outer reaches of the City of York. The course of
the river is now much wider and more substantial than near
Ripon as it gathers tributaries on its passage to the sea. However
during periods of prolonged rainfall its potential for flooding is considerable: as it enters the City of York flood defences become more conspicuous.

● **Beningbrough**
N. Yorks. PO box, tel. A remote farming settlement by the river.

● **Overton**
N. Yorks. A tiny settlement around Overton
Manor, which the abbots of St Mary, York once
used as their major country house. The moat can
still be traced, at the north end of the village, and
a farmhouse near the church re-used the stones.

● **Nether Poppleton**
N. Yorks. PO, tel, stores. A commuter village for
York, most attractive by the river. The small
church of St Everilda, at the far eastern end, is of
Norman origin, with relics of 14th- and 15th-C
glass in the east window. There are also some
fine monuments to the Huttons: Sir Thomas,

1620, is depicted kneeling; Ursula, her husband
and another woman, circa 1640, are smaller but
also kneel; Anne, 1651, is less formal, with more
movement in the figure.

● **Skelton**
N. Yorks. PO, tel. The church of St Giles is a
superb example of Early English work, built circa
1240, by the masons who had worked on York
Minster, for Walter de Gray, Archbishop of
York. Neatly constructed from magnesian
limestone, there is no tower – just a bellcote
separating the nave from the chancel. Toolmarks
left by the masons can be seen inside, together
with their marks. It was restored 1814–18 by
Henry Graham, who was nineteen when the work
started.

Pubs and Restaurants

🍺 **Lord Nelson** Main Street, Nether Poppleton (01904 794320). A handsome brick-built pub serving John Smith's and Magnet real ale. Bar meals available *lunchtimes* *& evenings*, with vegetarian options. Children are welcome and there is a garden with a bouncy castle and play area to amuse them. Caravan site to the rear of the pub.

The towpath
There is a right of way on the north bank from Beningbrough to Rawcliffe.

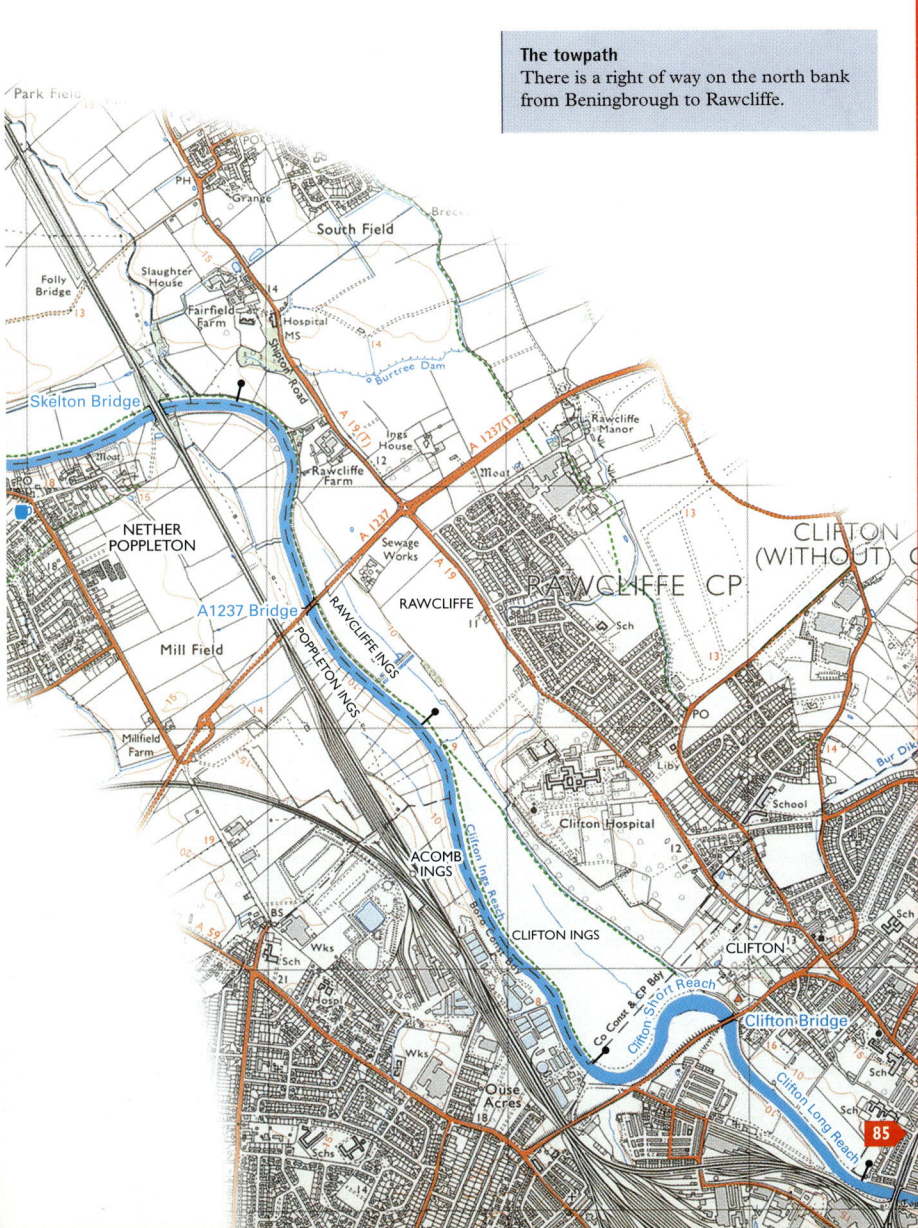

York

The River Ouse makes an intimate passage through York, and with all the major sights tightly enclosed within the city walls, none are more than a short walk away from the moorings. Trip boats ply back and forth, their commentaries adding to the general hub-bub of a working city and popular tourist venue. To the south of Skeldergate Bridge the River Foss joins from the east, and, whilst the entrance seems inviting and the first mile-and-a-half is navigable, there are no official moorings on the Foss, and the passage through the lock is very expensive. The riverside to the south of the city is extremely pleasant, with few factories to be seen. Look out, on the east bank, for the Roman Well, then swing round under the A64 and pass the extremely pleasant Bishopthorpe Palace and grounds. Enjoy what view there is to the west as you leave behind a very large sewage works on the east bank, then pass under Naburn Bridge to once again enter open countryside.

RIVER FOSS

York City Council, 9 St Leonard's Place, York YO1 2ET (01904 613161). The river is navigable for just over 1 1/2 miles from Blue Bridge, and the maximum craft size is 100' x 19'. Do not enter unless the flood lights are showing green. A licence is not required, but there is a substantial charge (plus a hefty deposit) for each passage through Castle Mills Lock. Keys are obtainable from the above address – telephone first for price and availability. There are no official moorings on the River Foss in York. One of the public river trips visits the river *each week*.

Boatyards

Ⓑ **Naburn Marina and Yacht Service** Naburn (01904 621021). 🚽 🚿 ⚓ P D Pump-out, gas, overnight and long-term mooring, winter storage, slipway, crane, boat and engine sales and repairs, public telephone, toilets, showers, chandlery. The re-created Viking boats are kept here.

● **York**

N. Yorks. All services. Everything you will wish to see is packed within the square mile or so contained by the limestone medieval city walls which, if you are feeling energetic, you can walk around. Or you can climb the 275 steps to the top of the Minster for a superb panorama of this fine walled city and its surroundings. You will see the river passing through its centre, crossed by three handsome bridges: the stone built Ouse Bridge, designed by Peter Atkinson; and the decorous cast-iron constructions of Lendal Bridge and Skeldergate Bridge. Just how much of this fine city you can enjoy will depend upon how long you plan to stay, but the Minster should be a high priority on everyone's list. Then perhaps wander south through the maze of 'snickleways', including the impossibly narrow and picturesque Shambles, to enjoy the Jorvik Centre and the museums to its south. York finds its origins in the Roman base of Eboracum, established during the first century AD. If you walk a short way along Museum Street from Lendal Bridge and turn into Museum Gardens, you can see the substantial remains of the Multangular Tower, the western corner of the original Roman fortress. Tidy Roman brickwork is surmounted by much less neat medieval stonework. When the Romans left, York became a Saxon settlement, and it was they who built a wooden church on the spot where the cathedral now stands. The Saxons were over-run by the Vikings in 867, and the damp soils surrounding the river thankfully preserved substantial remains of their stay here, which can now be seen in a spectacular presentation at the Jorvik Centre. Following the Norman conquest in 1066, William the Conqueror built two wooden towers to guard the Ouse. One of these was destroyed in 1190 and its replacement, built of stone, still stands close to the castle. The present cathedral was begun by Archbishop Walter de Gray during the early part of the 13thC, and was completed some 250 years later. After Charles I made York his northern headquarters in 1639, the Parliamentarians laid it siege in 1644 and, following the Battle of Marston Moor fought 6 miles to the west, Charles' garrison capitulated on the understanding that none of the city's fine

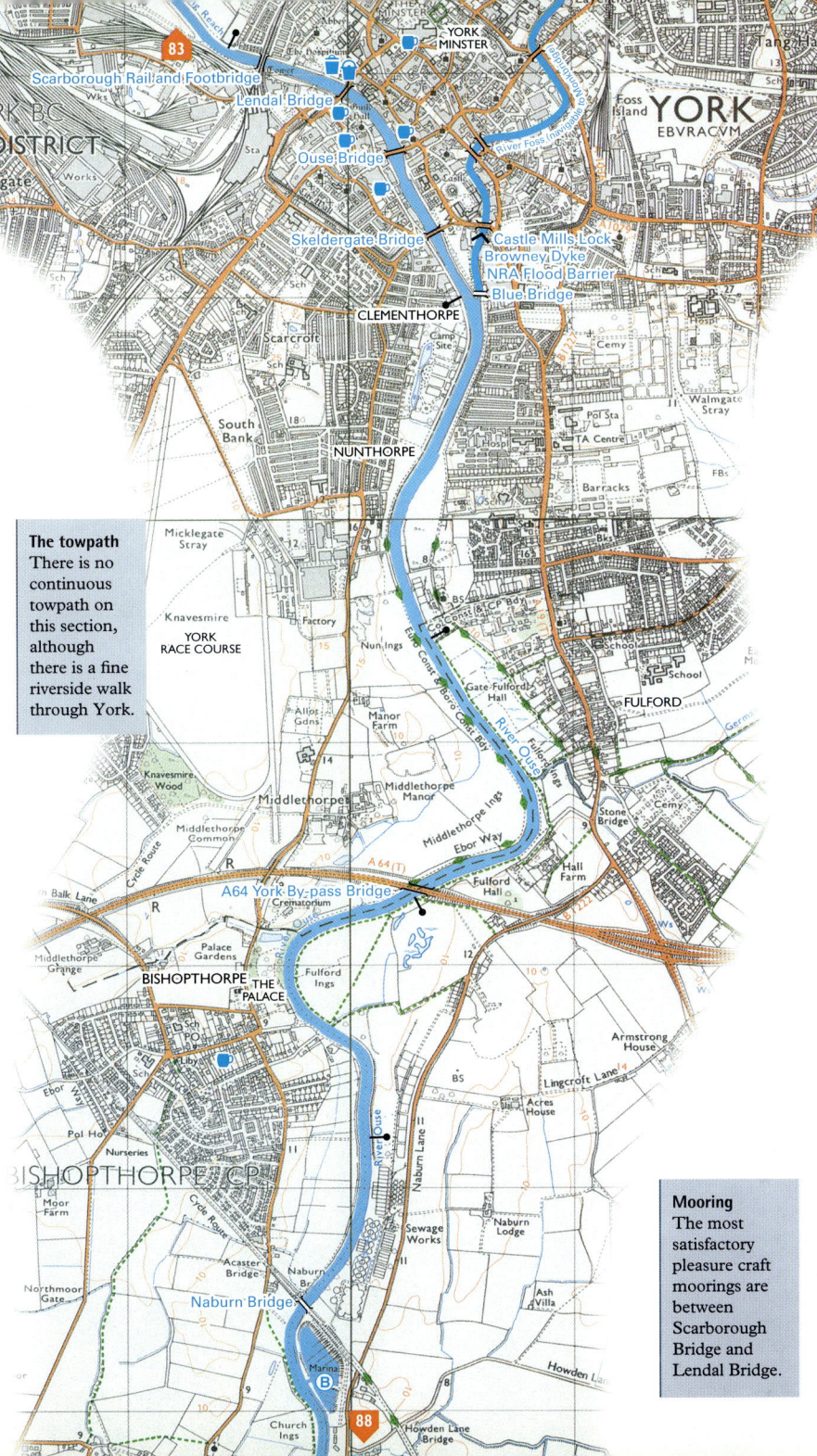

River Ouse, River Ure and Ripon Canal

York

83

Scarborough Rail and Footbridge

Lendal Bridge

Ouse Bridge

Skeldergate Bridge

Castle Mills Lock
Browney Dyke
NRA Flood Barrier
Blue Bridge

CLEMENTHORPE

Scarcroft

YORK
MINSTER

YORK
EBVRACVM

Foss Island

Walmgate
Stray

South
Bank

NUNTHORPE

FULFORD

The towpath
There is no
continuous
towpath on
this section,
although
there is a fine
riverside walk
through York.

Micklegate
Stray

Knavesmire

YORK
RACE COURSE

Nun Ings

Gate Fulford
Hall

River Ouse

Allot
Gdns

Knavesmire
Wood

Manor
Farm

Middlethorpe

Middlethorpe
Manor

Middlethorpe Ings

Stone
Bridge

Middlethorpe
Common

Ebor Way

Hall
Farm

Cycle Route

A 64 (T)

A64 York By-pass Bridge

Crematorium

Fulford
Hall

Palace
Gardens

BISHOPTHORPE
THE
PALACE

Fulford
Ings

Armstrong
House

Palace
Grange

Middlethorpe
Grange

BS

Lingcroft Lane

Acres
House

Nurseries

River Ouse

Naburn Lane

Cycle Route

Sewage
Works

Naburn
Lodge

Ash
Villa

BISHOPTHORPE CP

Moor
Farm

Acaster
Bridge

Naburn Bridge

Northmoor
Gate

Marina

Church
Ings

88

Howden Lane
Bridge

Mooring
The most
satisfactory
pleasure craft
moorings are
between
Scarborough
Bridge and
Lendal Bridge.

religious buildings be desecrated. York's 19th-C history is centred upon the birth of the railways and the prosperity this new means of transport brought to the city. George Hudson, three times mayor of York, successfully cashed in on this boom and although he fell from grace for a while due to some doubtful business deals, he was returned to favour this century, and his portrait now hangs in the fine 18th-C Mansion House. He also has a street named in his honour, off Micklegate (which was very fashionable in the 18th & 19thCs) on the west side. Shoppers can enjoy the vast array of shops in the streets by the Minster, and of course everyone will want to visit the Shambles, a narrow cobbled street which was once filled with butchers, but is now a good place for souvenirs. The university opened in 1963, reviving the city's reputation as a seat of learning. A lively student population keeps the city on its toes.

York Minster Deangate (01904 624426). Earliest records of a religious building near this site relate to a wooden church, recorded by the Venerable Bede as being built by the Saxons in 627 AD. The present Minster was begun by Archbishop Walter de Grey, and completed in 1472, after 250 years work. Built on a truly grand scale, it is 524 feet long and 249 feet wide (by volume, it is the largest cathedral in the country), topped by a central tower 234 feet tall, completed about 1730. This tower needed remedial work in 1967, when serious weaknesses were found. The work, however, revealed a rich hoard of Roman and Saxon treasures, many of which are now displayed in the Undercroft Museum, along with all other aspects of the Minster's history. There are over 100 stained-glass windows spanning a period of 800 years, making the interior surprisingly light and airy. The earliest glass is in the second window on the left from the west door of the nave, and dates from circa 1150. There is also a funeral procession of monkeys to look out for. Fine carvings around the capitals, the east window with Old and New Testament illustrations, and the stone choir screen, carved with England's rulers from William I to Henry VI are other delights. The Octagonal Chapter House, with no central pillar to support the roof, is also worth seeing. In 1984, following some controversial statements made by the Bishop of Durham, the roof of the south transept was struck by lightning, causing considerable damage and invoking comment about the wrath of God. This has now been repaired and incorporates designs submitted by *Blue Peter* viewers. Every hour a priest asks visitors to stop their sightseeing and pray. Excellent free tours can be taken, leaving from the information desk. *Open Nov–Mar 07.00–18.00; closing at 18.30 Apr, 19.30 May, 20.30 Jun–Aug, 20.00 Sep, 19.00 Oct.*

Merchant Tailors' Hall Fossgate (01904 624889). One of York's finest timbered buildings, with a fine undercroft and a beautifully panelled hall. *Open Apr–Oct, Tue only 10.00–16.00. Free.*

Treasurer's House Minster Yard (01904 624247). A Jacobean façade on a house of which much was built in the 12thC, on the site of a Roman building. It was at one time owned by Frank Green, an industrialist and obviously intensely practical man: he put nails into the floor to remind servants where the furniture should stand. Walled garden, tearoom and art gallery. *Open Apr–Oct, Sat–Thu 10.30–17.00. Charge.*

National Railway Museum Legman Road (01904 621261). This is reputedly the world's largest railway museum, housed in two vast hangars, and whilst there are of course many superb locomotives, the exhibits illustrate rail travel in its broadest sense. Here you will see photographs, paintings, ceramics, models, ticket displays and the re-creation of a section of the Channel Tunnel. Locomotives on display include the *Agenoria*, which hauled coals in Staffordshire from 1829, and the splendid *Mallard*, which reached a speed of 126mph in 1938, still the world record for a steam locomotive. A station has been re-created in the South Hall, and includes Queen Victoria's royal carriage, plus the carriage used by Queen Elizabeth II until 1977. Background recordings keep the railway atmosphere at a peak. Tours, demonstrations and rides. *Open daily 10.00–1800. Charge.*

York Model Railway Tea Room Square, York Station (01904 630169). A fascinating array of superb model railways. *Open Mar–Oct 09.30–18.00; Nov–Feb 10.30–17.00. Closed Xmas. Charge.*

The York Dungeon 12 Clifford Street (01904 632599). Branding, boiling, roasting and beheading of people are just a few of the attractions of this startling place, which is definitely *not recommended for the squeamish*. The story of Guy Fawkes is also vividly re-told including, of course, his torture and execution. *Open Apr–Sep, daily 10.00–17.30; closing 16.30 Oct–Mar. Closed Xmas Day. Charge.*

Jorvik Viking Centre Coppergate (01904 643211). The superbly re-created Viking town of Jorvik, discovered whilst excavating the Coppergate Shopping Centre and now superbly displayed. Sit in a time-car to journey back in time through 1000 years of English history, culminating at the Viking port discovered on this site. Journey along a Viking street surrounded by the smell of wood smoke and pigs, listening to the sounds of herring being unloaded, together with an informative commentary. *Open Apr–Oct, daily 09.00–17.30; Nov–Mar, Mon–Fri & Sun 09.00–15.30, Sat 09.00–16.30. Charge.*

Archaeological Research Centre St Saviourgate (01904 654324). A hands-on archaeology centre established in a church building, giving afficionados of all ages the chance to play at the real thing. *Open Mon–Fri 10.00–15.30, Sat 13.00–15.30. Closed Sun, G. Fri, and three weeks around Xmas. Charge.*

Fairfax House Castlegate (01904 655543). Built in 1762, this superb town house houses the Terry collection of furniture and clocks. Special 18th-C Christmas exhibition each year. *Open Mon–Thu & Sat 11.00–16.30, Sun 13.30–16.30; also Fri in Aug; closed early Jan–mid Feb.* Charge.

Cliffords Tower Tower Street (01904 646940). There is a good view of the city from the top of this tower, which once stood in Jewbury, where the city's Jews lived. In 1190 they were attacked by townsfolk complaining about loan repayments, and took refuge in the tower. There they committed mass suicide rather than convert to Christianity. *Open all year, daily 10.00–18.00 (closes 16.00 Nov–Mar). Closed Xmas & N. Year.* Charge.

Bar Convent Museum Blossom Street (01904 643238). The country's oldest convent, founded in 1686. The dome of the chapel was remarkably hidden under a pitched roof. *Open Mon–Fri 10.00, last admission 16.00. Closed Jan–Feb.* Charge.

York Castle Museum The Eye of York (01904 653611). A fascinating array of objects and displays kept in two 18th-C prisons, one of which includes the cell where Dick Turpin spent his last night. Reconstructions of a Victorian pub, Kirkgate, a Fancy Repository and a toyshop are packed full of fascinating artifacts. Many visitors will remember similar 1950s front rooms, complete with a television. Shop and coffee bar, which has a Wurlitzer juke box. *Open Apr–Oct, daily 09.30–17.30; Nov–Mar, daily 09.30–16.30. Closed Xmas & N. Year.* Charge.

Theatre Royal St Leonard's Place (01904 623568). Shakespeare, ballet, opera and large popular productions. Café and restaurant.

Tourist Information Centre Exhibition Square, York (01904 621756).

BOAT TRIPS

White Rose Line The Boatyard, Lendal Bridge (01904 628324). Comfortable city and country sightseeing cruise boats leave from Lendal Bridge and King's Staith, for a *1 hour* river trip with commentary running from *mid Feb–late Nov.* Charge. All boats have a licensed bar and most serve tea and coffee and other refreshments.

Castle Line 18 Swinegate (07836 799799). Leaving from the jetty by the Bonding Warehouse, Skeldergate Bridge, they run river trips and longer dining cruises to the Ship Inn, both with a commentary. Their two boats are the historic *Empress*, built in 1933 at Wroxham, and the *Duchess.* Run *all year round.* Charge.

York Marine Services Ferry Lane, Bishopthorpe (01904 704442). A riverbus service from Bishopthorpe to York (*Easter–end Oct*), plus lunch and dinner cruises (*all year – telephone to book*). Charge. Also self-drive motorboat hire and a fleet of weekly holiday cruisers for hire.

Pubs and Restaurants

There are many fine pubs in York, including;

🔵 **The Maltings** Tanners Moat, just past Lendal Bridge (01904 655387). An atmospheric small pub, voted Cask ale pub of Great Britain in 1998, which runs its own beer festivals each year (telephone for details). Black Sheep and at least six guest real ales along with four real draught ciders are kept. Bar meals are available *Mon–Fri 12.00–14.00, Sat & Sun 12.00–16.00,* with vegetarian options. Jazz on *Mon* night and folk on *Tue.*

🔵 **The First Hussar** North Street (01904 656097). A friendly free house decorated with military memorabilia, and dedicated to the promotion of real ale. Bar meals *lunchtimes.* Children are welcome. No-smoking family room and garden. Quiz night is *Tue*, with folk & blues *Wed.*

🔵 **York Arms** 26 High Petergate, by the Minster (01904 624508). Samuel Smith real ales. Bar meals *lunchtimes (and some evenings)*, with vegetarian options. Children are welcome if you are eating.

🔵 **Yates Wine Lodge** Church Lane, Low Ousegate, Church Lane (01904 613569). Bar meals available *all day 10.00–17.00,* with vegetarian menu. Children are welcome. Some outside seating in the courtyard, and there is regular live entertainment.

🔵 **Kings Arms** Kings Staith (01904 659435). The last surviving remnant of the Water Lanes, this is also York's famous flooding pub, with water levels over the last 100 years recorded. Stone floors, brick walls, exposed beams and open fires. Bar meals *lunchtimes*, with vegetarian options. Children are welcome, and there is outside seating. Moorings. During the summer, an evening ghost walk starts from here at *20.00.*

🔵 **The Bluebell** 53 Fossgate (01904 654904). Over 200 years old, this pub is reputed to have the smallest and oldest interior in York. Vaux, Wards and guest real ales are served, and sandwiches are available *12.00–16.00.*

🔵 **Cock & Bottle** Skeldergate (01904 654165). Reputedly York's most haunted pub, serving Courage, Greene King, Marston's and John Smith's real ales. Bar meals are served at *lunchtimes*, and children are welcome. Disco *Thur* and live music on *Sun.*

The towpath
There is a right of way on the west bank, as far as Acaster Selby.

Naburn Locks

Having left the excitement of York, the river resumes its quiet passage through unassuming countryside, passing Naburn and Acaster Malbis on its way to Naburn Locks. Here the elegant British Waterways buildings, swing bridges and crane create a fine riverside scene, marking the start of the tidal river and a gradual change in surroundings. Now the intimacy of the upper river is slowly replaced by bare banks and more open countryside around the tidal waters. Bell Hall, just half a mile south of the lock, was built in 1680, and is a fine example of its period. Moreby Park, also on the east bank, provides almost a mile of pleasing parkland and relief from the generally flat countryside. Acaster Selby, a small farming settlement, lies inconspicuously behind a bend as the river continues its languorous route south.

NAVIGATIONAL NOTES

A detailed chart of the tidal Ouse is available from: Pat Careless, 1 Chelmsford Avenue, Aston, Sheffield S26 2AU (0114 287 5129).

● **Naburn**
N. Yorks. Tel. A charming and compact brick-built village nestling on a bend in the river. The church of St Matthew, built in 1854, stands separately to the south, with the famous locks a mile further on. The large Banqueting House, by the lock, was built 1823–4 as a meeting place for members of the Ouse Navigation Company.

● **Acaster Malbis**
N. Yorks. PO box, tel. A pretty but non-descript village, with caravan parks at each end. A half-mile to the north is the large 14th-C church of the Holy Trinity, with its fine weather-boarded Victorian bell turret and spire. Look for the pretty stained glass in the east window, circa 1320, and the effigy of John Malbis, from about the same time, in the south chapel. The pulpit is an elaborate 17th-C piece.

● **Acaster Selby**
N. Yorks. A small farming settlement around what is left of Acaster Hall, built circa 1670.

Boatyards

ⓑ **Waterline Leisure** The Airfield, Acaster Malbis (01904 702049/mobile 07885 255711). Riverside yard just upstream of Naburn Locks. Ⓓ Overnight mooring, winter storage, slipway, 10 ton crane, boat and engine sales and repairs, boatbuilding, telephone. Engineer available for emergencies on 01904 700070, mobile 07711 041285.

Pubs and Restaurants

🍺 **Blacksmiths Arms** Naburn (01904 623464). A very comfortable and friendly pub, which for over 300 years was a blacksmith's shop. The bar has a fine collection of plates and teapots, and you can enjoy a pint here, or retreat into a cosy alcove. Mansfield and guest real ales, and good bar meals *lunchtimes and evenings (not Sun evenings)* with vegetarian options. Children are welcome. There are two large gardens. Regular quiz nights.

🍺✕ **The Ship Inn** Acaster Malbis (01904 705609). A large, stylish, 17th-C coaching house, once used by Oliver Cromwell's men, and now a popular venue for visitors by road and river. Taylor and Tetley's real ales and bar meals *lunchtimes and evenings,* with vegetarian menu. Children are welcome and there is a garden. Quiz on *Mon* night. B & B. River trips leave from here.

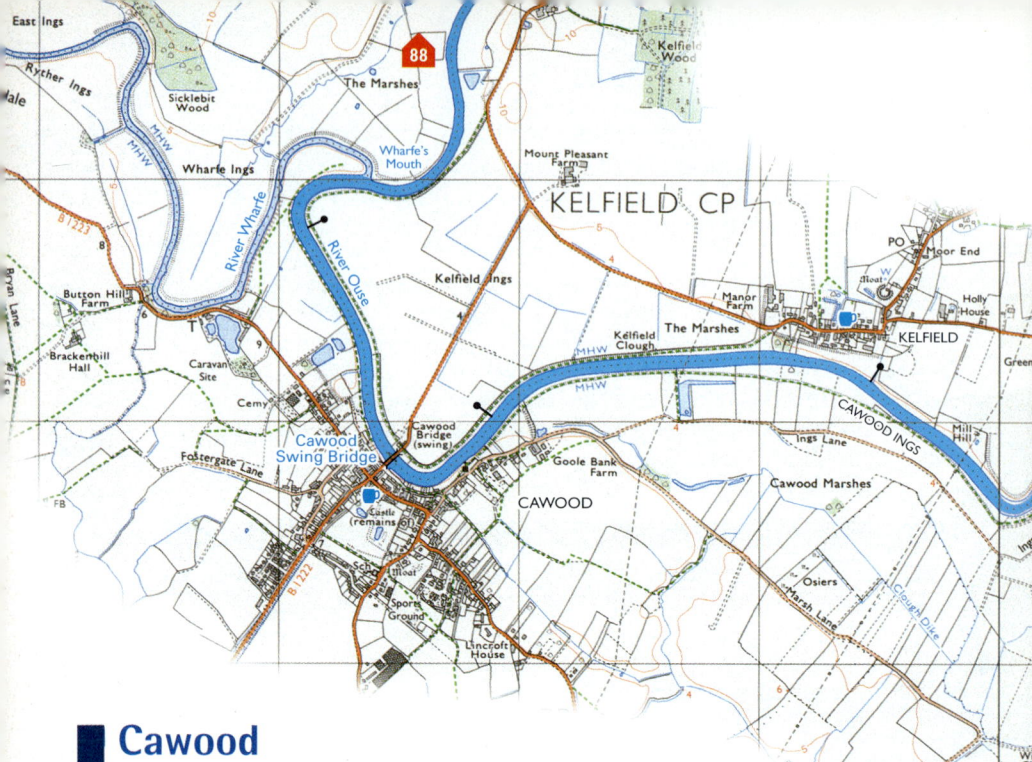

Cawood

The Ouse now starts to gather momentum as the River Wharfe, coming down from Tadcaster, joins from the west (see below). Sweeping eccentrically past Cawood, the Ouse passes under the only river crossing on this section. Enclosed by flood banks and surrounded by rich farmland, the river now pursues an isolated course, with towns and villages showing a healthy respect by keeping their distance.

● **Cawood**
N. Yorks. PO, tel, stores. A pretty red brick and tile village, with narrow streets, nestling on the south bank and joined to the north by the swing bridge. A castle owned by the Archbishops of York once stood here, dating from 930 AD. Cardinal Wolsey visited, and was arrested here in 1530 for high treason. His fate is recalled in the nursery rhyme Humpty Dumpty. All that now remains is a white stone gate house, dating from the first half of the 15thC. It has been renovated by the Landmark Trust and is available for lets (01628 825925). The church of All

Saints stands to the east of the village, and has a fine Perpendicular tower containing a monument to George Mountain, Archbishop of York, who died 1623.

● **Kelfield**
N. Yorks. PO, tel. Seeming to totally ignore the river, this village contains a chapel dated 1852, beautifully converted into a house.

● **Riccall**
N. Yorks. PO, tel, fish & chips. The church of St Mary has a Norman doorway, dating from 1160, and Norman arcading from the 13thC. The south door is 12th-C.

NAVIGATIONAL NOTES

River Wharfe
Although in theory navigable for just over 9 miles to Tadcaster Weir, this is not advisable without local knowledge. The lower reaches are not particularly attractive and shallows around Ulleskelf, known locally as huts, are one of the problems you may encounter.

Pubs and Restaurants

🍺 **The Greyhound** Riccall (01757 248224). John Smith's real ale is served, and there is a family room and a play area in the garden.

🍺 **Jolly Sailor** Market Place, Cawood (01757 268758). Adjacent to Cawood Castle, this sociable pub serves Rudgate's, Tetley's, Theakston's, Tomlinson's, John Smith's and guest real ales. Bar meals are available *lunchtimes and evenings*, with vegetarian options. Children are welcome, and there is a patio garden.

🍺 **The Grey Horse** Main Street, Kelfield (01757 248339). Black Sheep, John Smith's and Tetley's real ale and bar meals every *evening and Sun lunch*, with vegetarian options. Children welcome, and there is a garden.

🍺 **Hare & Hounds** Silver Street, Riccall (01757 248255). John Smith's real ale and bar meals *lunchtimes and evenings (not Mon, or Sun & Tue evenings)*, with vegetarian options. Children are welcome. Garden. Quiz night is *Sun*.

🍺 **Bay Horse** York Road, Barlby (01757 703878). John Smith's real ale, and snacks at *any time*. Children welcome *during the day*. Large garden. Quiz nights on *Tue & Thur*, and live music *one Sat each month*.

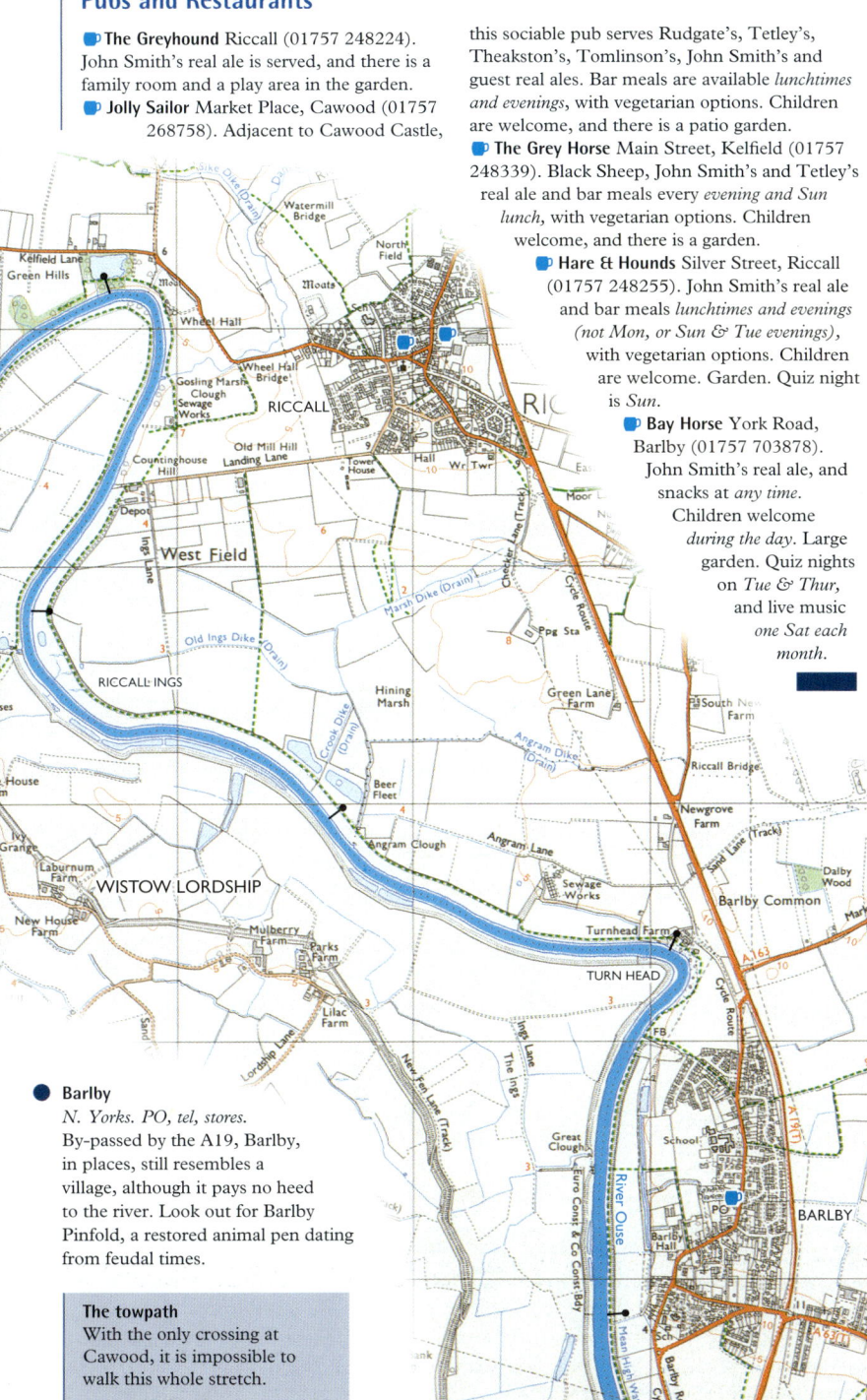

🔴 **Barlby**
N. Yorks. PO, tel, stores.
By-passed by the A19, Barlby, in places, still resembles a village, although it pays no heed to the river. Look out for Barlby Pinfold, a restored animal pen dating from feudal times.

The towpath
With the only crossing at Cawood, it is impossible to walk this whole stretch.

91

The towpath
Continuous on this section, on the north bank.

SELBY

Road Swing Bridge
Railway Swing Bridge
Selby Lock
Selby Swing Bridge
Bawtry Road Bridge

101
Brayton Railway Bridge

BARLOW CP

Barlow

Selby

Turning sharply at Selby and passing under two bridges, the size of the navigation becomes very apparent as coasters can be seen loading and unloading at the wharf. The Selby Canal, with its links to the Aire & Calder Navigation and then on to the rest of the waterways network, adds to the interest of what is very much a working port. Now the tidal effect is much stronger as the river sweeps relentlessly on towards the Humber. The River Derwent joins from the north east at Barmby, further adding to the flow.

NAVIGATIONAL NOTES

The Ouse is now a working river, with large craft and a strong tidal effect. Navigation should not be attempted without the requisite experience and a suitable craft. Visitor moorings are available in Selby Basin. A transit licence is available for craft on River Registration to use the canals between Selby and Keadby on the Trent (missing Trent Falls).

● **Selby**
N. Yorks. All services. Away from the River Ouse, this is a handsome market town, dominated by its sparkling Abbey. The present road bridge was built in 1970, and became toll-free in 1991: it replaced an earlier structure which had stood since 1791.
Selby Abbey (01757 703123). Founded for the Benedictines, as a result of Benedicts vision of seeing three swans landing on a river coming to fruition here. The east window shows the family tree of the Kings of Israel and dates from the 14thC. Below the south east window is the grave slab of Laurence Selby, abbot from 1486–1504. Notice that the three swans seen by Benedict are featured in a shield by his shoulder. *Open Apr–Sep 09.00–17.00,*

Oct–Mar 09.00-16.00, although if there is a ceremony taking place some of the abbey will be cordoned off to visitors.
Selby Park A very pleasant 5 acres of trees and plants, with a children's play area, picnic tables, mini-golf and bowls. *Open Mon–Fri 10.00–21.00, Sat & Sun 10.00–17.00.*
Selby Market Over 150 stalls, food and entertainment in front of the Abbey. *Every Mon 08.00–15.30.*
Abbey Leisure Centre Scott Road, Selby (01757 213758). Open *Mon–Fri 07.00–23.00, Sat 07.00–19.30, Sun 08.00–21.00.* Charge.
Tourist Information Centre Park Street, Selby (01757 703263).
● **Hemingbrough**
N. Yorks. PO, tel. The very tall slender spire of the church of St Mary can be seen for miles across the flat Yorkshire countryside, standing fully 189 feet high.
Drax Power Station (01757 618381). This is Europe's largest coal-fired power station, producing 10 per cent of England's electricity. Opened in 1973 it dominates the area for miles around. Guided tours for groups only, by prior arrangement.
● **Barmby on the Marsh**
N. Yorks. PO box, tel. Village with some Georgian houses hemmed in by the Rivers Ouse and Derwent.

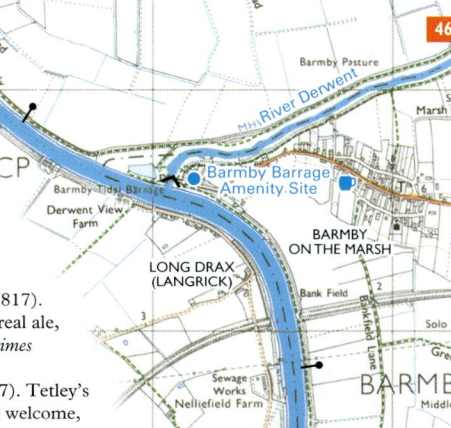

Pubs and Restaurants

● **The Three Swans** Church Hill, Selby (01757 702951). A basic boozer serving John Smith's real ale. Children are welcome, and there is a disco *Fri & Sat evenings.*
● ✕ **The Londesborough Arms Hotel** Market Place, Selby (01757 707355). Bar and restaurant meals are available, with vegetarian options and a children's menu, *lunchtimes and evenings.* B & B.
● **The Rose & Crown** New Street, Selby (01757 703388). Children welcome.
● **Albion Vaults** The Crescent, Selby (01757 213817). A cosy traditional corner house serving Old Mill real ale, brewed in nearby Snaith. Food is available *lunchtimes daily*, and children are welcome. Garden.
● **Fox & Pheasant** Hemingbrough (01757 638327). Tetley's and John Smith's real ale are served. Children are welcome, and there is a garden.
● **The Crown** Hemingbrough (01757 638434). A changing range of real ales, along with food *lunchtimes and evenings (not Mon)*. Children are welcome, and there is a garden.

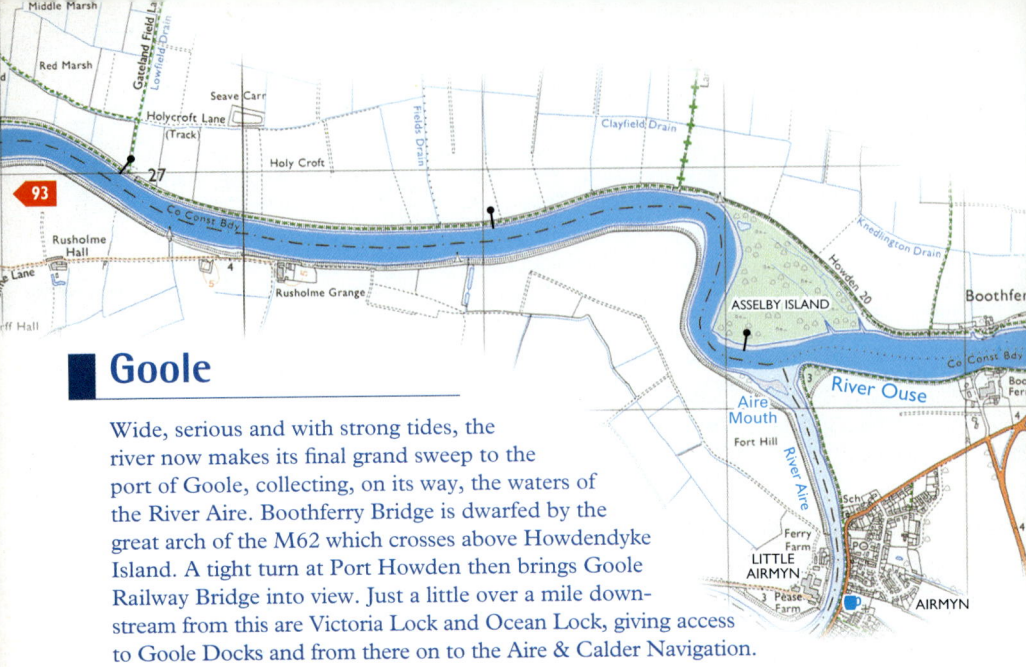

Goole

Wide, serious and with strong tides, the river now makes its final grand sweep to the port of Goole, collecting, on its way, the waters of the River Aire. Boothferry Bridge is dwarfed by the great arch of the M62 which crosses above Howdendyke Island. A tight turn at Port Howden then brings Goole Railway Bridge into view. Just a little over a mile downstream from this are Victoria Lock and Ocean Lock, giving access to Goole Docks and from there on to the Aire & Calder Navigation.

NAVIGATIONAL NOTES

1 The Ouse is now a working river, with large craft and a strong tidal effect. Navigation should not be attempted without the requisite experience and a suitable craft. Cruising notes are available free of charge from Selby Locks (01757 703182) and Naburn Locks (01904 728500), or BW Naburn Office (01904 728229). The lock keeper at Goole will willingly offer advice and information on navigating the tideway. For his part the boater must inform Associated British Ports (ABP) that he is on the river and make his position known (see note 2). ABP maintain a continuous watch on channel 14.

2 At the west end of South Dock, Goole, the navigation is under the jurisdiction of ABP. They may be contacted on VHF radio channels 14 and 19 – call *Goole Docks* – or by telephoning 01405 760924.

3 To the west of this point ocean-going shipping is manoeuvring and contact must be made with Ocean Lock Control before entering the docks.

4 Overnight mooring will incur a substantial charge and temporary mooring, whilst awaiting a lock or bridge swing, is only permitted if the crew are in attendance. Mooring on any pier whilst on the tideway (unless awaiting a lock) will also incur a charge.

5 Lock operating times are $2\frac{1}{2}$ *hours before high tide and 1 hour after* for which no charge is made. Outside these times special pens are always available on payment of a fee, which is in turn dependent on the time of day or night.

6 A detailed chart of the tidal Ouse is available from: Pat Careless, 1 Chelmsford Avenue, Aston, Sheffield S26 2AU (0114 287 5129).

7 It is about 5 miles from Swinefleet to Trent Falls. See notes on pages 156-7.

● **Airmyn**
E. Riding. PO, stores, tel. A small village of brick-built cottages with a sturdy clock-tower, facing the raised banks of the River Aire.

● **Goole.**
E. Riding. MD Wed & Fri. All services. When the Aire and Calder Navigation applied for an Act to build a canal from Knottingley to Goole in 1819, Goole was no more than a few cottages scattered around the marshes on the banks of the Ouse. Work commenced on cutting the canal in 1822 and by 1828 foreign trade had begun with Hamburg and the local people entertained themselves by going down to the docks in the evening to await the arrival of foreign vessels on the spring tides. It is said of Goole that it was 'born under Victoria and died with her'. The docks are still very much the focal point, handling cargoes from Europe and Scandinavia.

Waterways Museum & Adventure Centre Dutch Riverside, Goole (01405 768730). Museum displays, boat tours of Goole docks. Café. *Open Mon-Fri 10.30–15.30 and Sat & Sun Easter 12.00-17.00.* Charge.

Boatyards

Ⓑ Goole Boathouse The Timber Pond, Dutch Riverside, Goole (01405 763985). Gas, overnight & long-term mooring, winter storage, slipway, telephone chandlery, toilets, showers, limited groceries. Charts of the Ouse are sold here.

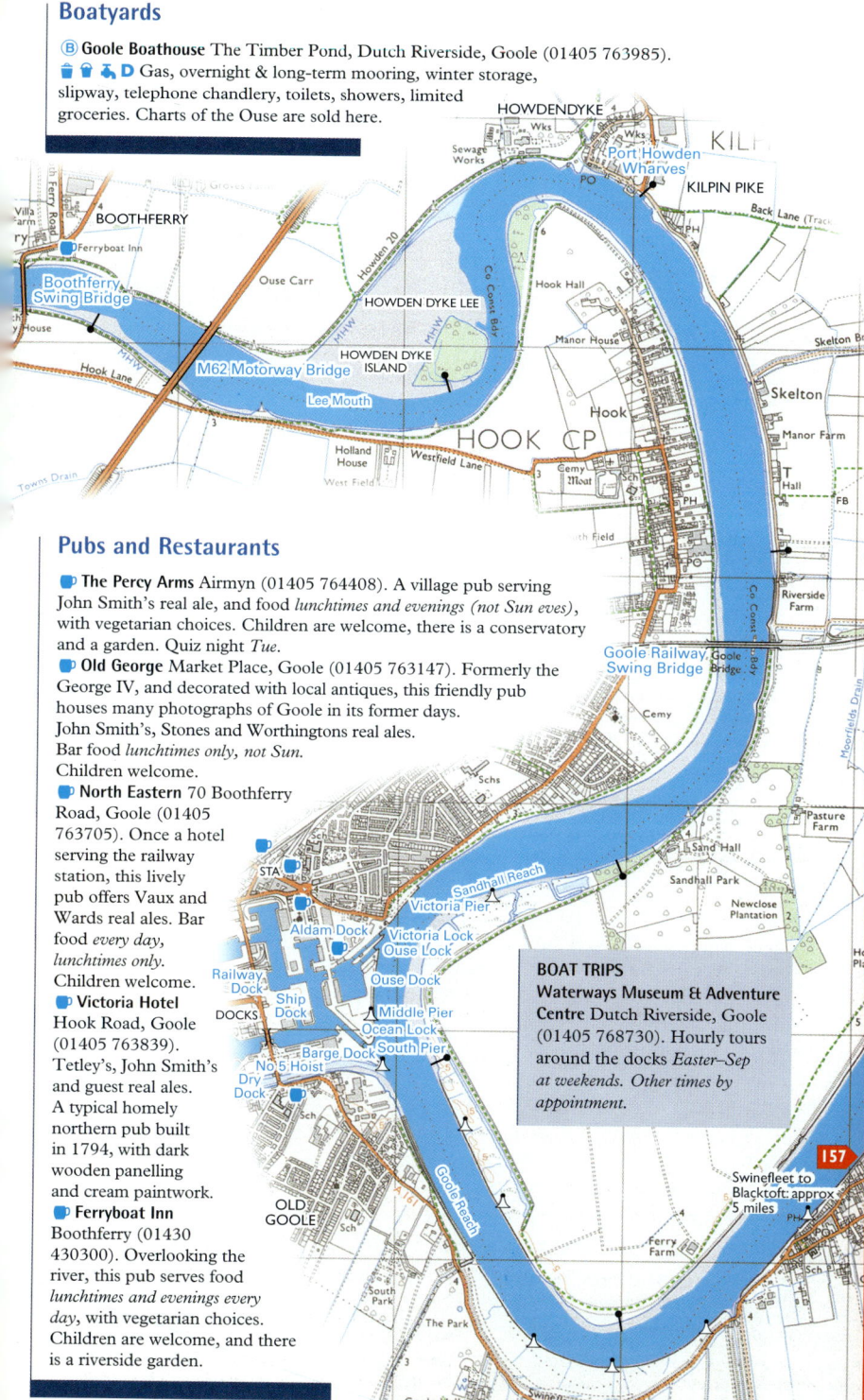

Pubs and Restaurants

The Percy Arms Airmyn (01405 764408). A village pub serving John Smith's real ale, and food *lunchtimes and evenings (not Sun eves)*, with vegetarian choices. Children are welcome, there is a conservatory and a garden. Quiz night *Tue*.

Old George Market Place, Goole (01405 763147). Formerly the George IV, and decorated with local antiques, this friendly pub houses many photographs of Goole in its former days. John Smith's, Stones and Worthingtons real ales. Bar food *lunchtimes only, not Sun*. Children welcome.

North Eastern 70 Boothferry Road, Goole (01405 763705). Once a hotel serving the railway station, this lively pub offers Vaux and Wards real ales. Bar food *every day, lunchtimes only*. Children welcome.

Victoria Hotel Hook Road, Goole (01405 763839). Tetley's, John Smith's and guest real ales. A typical homely northern pub built in 1794, with dark wooden panelling and cream paintwork.

Ferryboat Inn Boothferry (01430 430300). Overlooking the river, this pub serves food *lunchtimes and evenings every day*, with vegetarian choices. Children are welcome, and there is a riverside garden.

BOAT TRIPS
Waterways Museum & Adventure Centre Dutch Riverside, Goole (01405 768730). Hourly tours around the docks *Easter–Sep at weekends. Other times by appointment.*

Swineleet to Blacktoft: approx 5 miles

SELBY CANAL

MAXIMUM DIMENSIONS

Bank Dole Junction, Knottingley, to junction with the River Ouse, Selby
Length: 78' 5"
Beam: 16' 6"
Draught: 4'
Headroom: 8'

MANAGER
01904 728229

MILEAGE
Bank Dole Junction, Knottingley to
Haddlesey Flood Lock: 6^1/2 miles
Selby, junction with the River Ouse: 11^3/4 miles

Locks: 4

Bank Dole and West Haddlesey Locks give access to river sections of the navigation. River level gauge boards indicate conditions as follows:

GREEN BAND – Normal river levels safe for navigation.

AMBER BAND – River levels are above normal. If you wish to navigate the river section you are advised to proceed on to and through the next lock.

RED BAND – Flood conditions unsafe for navigation. Lock closed.

In 1774 the Aire and Calder Navigation Company obtained an Act to construct a navigation from the River Aire at Haddlesey to the Ouse at Selby. This was not, however, the first attempt to improve communication by navigable waterways in the area. During the 17thC local industry had transported goods by packhorse along the Hambleton Causeway to Selby Dock from where they were shipped to their destination. When the Aire was eventually made navigable to small vessels, Selby's trade declined. For some 70 years the traders battled with the difficulties that navigating the Aire presented until, in 1770, there were rumours that there was to be a new canal created, covering some 23^1/2 miles and linking Leeds directly to Selby. The proprietors of the Aire and Calder Company soon realised the gravity of this threat. In making a connection with a tidal waterway at each end of its navigation, the Leeds and Liverpool Canal Company could very soon put the Aire and Calder Canal Company out of business. The latter employed the services of John Smeaton and William Jessop in the hope of eliminating the tideway on the river. Instead an Act was finally secured in 1774 which took the shortest and cheapest option. That was a direct route from the Aire's lowest lock at Haddlesey to Selby, a mere 5^1/2 miles. The navigation opened on 29 April 1778. It was built to Jessop's design and cost £20,000. As a result Selby flourished. The town was in the enviable position of being at the junction of two great waterways and at a point where river, canal and road met. The manufacturers of the West Riding were able to send goods directly to Hull and London as well as being within more easy access of York and Leeds. By 1821 one third of the people living in Selby were making their living from the waterways. The town was busy with ship and boat building, rope and sail making, flax dressing and linen manufacture. Industries in Leeds, Castleford and Knottingley improved, to all of which Selby had direct access. The building of a customs house at Selby enabled traffic to go straight out into the North Sea without having to stop at Hull to complete the necessary paperwork. The 8 acres of land around the lock were thriving with a counting house, rigging house, tarring house and sailmaker's shop. A small cut was made parallel with the Ouse where smaller vessels could be kept for transhipment of goods from larger vessels on the river. (This land is now mostly filled in and is the site of Rigid Paper Products.) A sailing packet left Selby every Monday for Hull returning Thursday if weather conditions permitted. The fare

Steam driven narrow boat on the Selby Canal

was two shillings return with food available on board at a cost of sixpence for men and fourpence for ladies. As trade increased so did the amount of traffic and the size of loads carried on the navigation. The one shortcoming of the quick and cheap construction of the canal, namely the shallow draught of only 3' 6", proved to be its downfall. The Aire and Calder Canal Company was under fire from merchants and traders, all dissatisfied by the lack of capacity that the navigation offered for larger vessels. The rise in the production of coal from the Selby coalfield highlighted a serious deficit in the capacity of larger vessels and soon the Company was under pressure to provide an alternative course. By 1826 the new and deeper canal from Knottingley to Goole was in operation and trade on the Selby Canal, although not entirely abandoned, suffered greatly as a consequence.

Today the canal is used primarily for leisure and recreational purposes. The recent acquisition of the River Ouse by British Waterways has resulted in the Selby Canal being promoted as a through-route to the city of York. Since 1988 boating numbers have doubled with over 2000 boats now passing through Selby Lock each year. The towpath now forms part of the Selby Horse Shoe Walk. A recent Canal Corridor Study has recognised the potential of the canal in creating a linear urban park. At present the industries which line its banks are turning their backs on the water but an imaginative scheme set to reverse this trend promises to inject some life and create a valuable recreational resource along the banks of the canal. It is hoped that before too long Selby's canal will once again be recognised for the important role it once played in the life of the town.

Beal

The navigation from Knottingley provides a welcome escape from the intensive industry of the area. However, the concentration required to navigate safely on the commercial waterways cannot be abandoned as the Aire adopts a fairly tortuous course as it meanders across more open countryside towards Haddlesey. Care needs to be taken on the countless

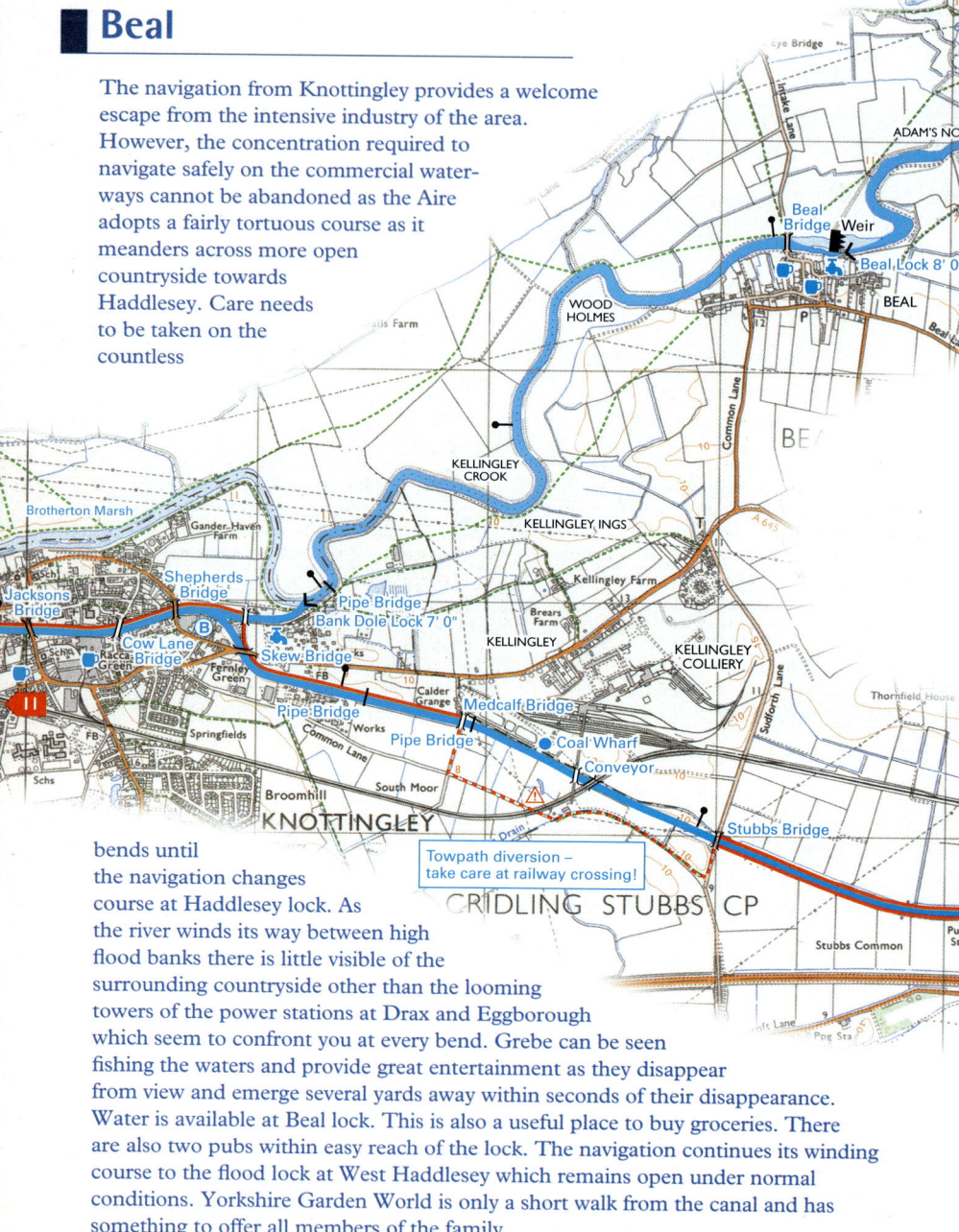

bends until the navigation changes course at Haddlesey lock. As the river winds its way between high flood banks there is little visible of the surrounding countryside other than the looming towers of the power stations at Drax and Eggborough which seem to confront you at every bend. Grebe can be seen fishing the waters and provide great entertainment as they disappear from view and emerge several yards away within seconds of their disappearance. Water is available at Beal lock. This is also a useful place to buy groceries. There are also two pubs within easy reach of the lock. The navigation continues its winding course to the flood lock at West Haddlesey which remains open under normal conditions. Yorkshire Garden World is only a short walk from the canal and has something to offer all members of the family.

NAVIGATIONAL NOTES

Bank Dole Lock is unmanned. Temporary mooring is available on the river alongside all locks although the landing stages should be approached with care. Care is needed in locking up as the paddles are quite fierce. Caution should also be taken on entering the lock at West Haddlesey as the wind can easily catch the boat, forcing it against the approach wall.

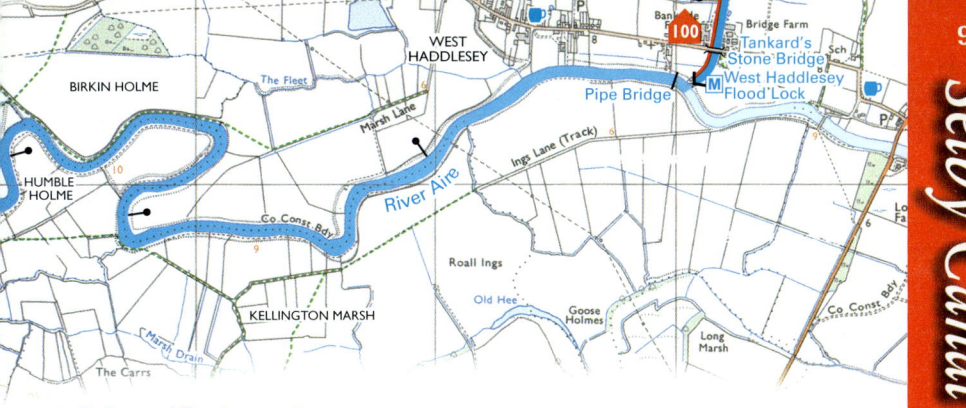

Pubs and Restaurants

🍺 **Kings Head** Beal (01977 673487). Tetley's, John Smith's and a guest real ale are served in the old tap room, unchanged for 50 years. Food, including vegetarian, is available *Tue–Sat evenings only, Sun lunchtimes and evenings*. Quiz nights *Sun and Wed*. Children welcome. Outside patio.

🍺✗ **Hungry Fox** Beal (01977 607180). Bar and restaurant serving well-kept John Smith's and Theakston real ales. Generous portions of home-made food with special rates for pensioners and children are available *lunchtimes and evenings*. Booking advised *at weekends*.

Quiz *Tue*. Children welcome. Outside patio. Facilities for disabled.

🍺 **George and Dragon Inn** West Haddlesey (01757 228198). One mile to the west of the lock. Tetley's and Ruddles real ales are served from the bar where you can enjoy a real fire and home-cooked food *Thu–Sat evenings only*. Children welcome. There is an outside patio and facilities for disabled people.

🍺 **The Jug** Chapel Haddlesey (01757 270307). A regular choice of five real ales including Marston's. Food, including vegetarian, is available *lunchtimes and evenings*. Children welcome. Riverside beer garden. Pub games, regular folk evenings and disabled access.

For pubs in Knottingley, see page 15.

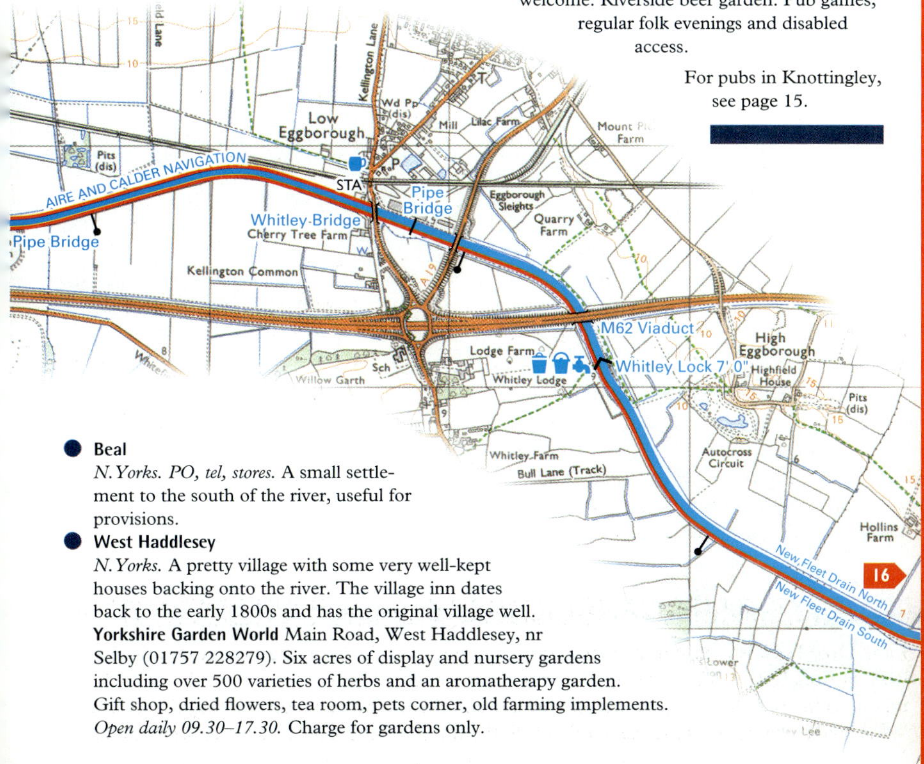

⬤ **Beal**
N. Yorks. PO, tel, stores. A small settlement to the south of the river, useful for provisions.

⬤ **West Haddlesey**
N. Yorks. A pretty village with some very well-kept houses backing onto the river. The village inn dates back to the early 1800s and has the original village well.
Yorkshire Garden World Main Road, West Haddlesey, nr Selby (01757 228279). Six acres of display and nursery gardens including over 500 varieties of herbs and an aromatherapy garden. Gift shop, dried flowers, tea room, pets corner, old farming implements. *Open daily 09.30–17.30*. Charge for gardens only.

Selby

Leaving West Haddlesey and the River Aire behind, the navigation now enters the Selby Canal whose course provides a welcome contrast. The rich vegetation on both banks changes with the seasons but is never without interest. The towpath, which follows the north bank, is popular with the local people and the banks are well-populated with fishermen, particularly during competition time when the short stretch to Selby may attract as many as 1000 competitors! Several old milestones can be seen along the bank marking the distance from the River Ouse. Just to the north of Burton Bridge is Burton Hall, built on the site of a medieval manor and beyond it the wooded hill of Brayton Barff which provides excellent views over the Vale of York to Selby. Barff is an ancient British name for barrow or burial place. There is a pub at Burn Bridge and also mooring providing access to Brayton to the north, where there are further pubs, two stores, a post office and a butcher. The graceful 15th-C spire of St Wilfrid's Church at Brayton can be seen across the fields. Passing under Brayton Railway Bridge, which carried the old east coast line, the canal enters the short industrial corridor into Selby basin. The railway, which once headed directly north from Selby, had to be diverted to the west to avoid subsidence due to the newly opened deep mines to the north east of the town. Selby Swing Bridge is boater-operated with a BW key. There are showers and pump-out facilities in the basin, operated by a card (for which there is a charge) available from the lock keeper.

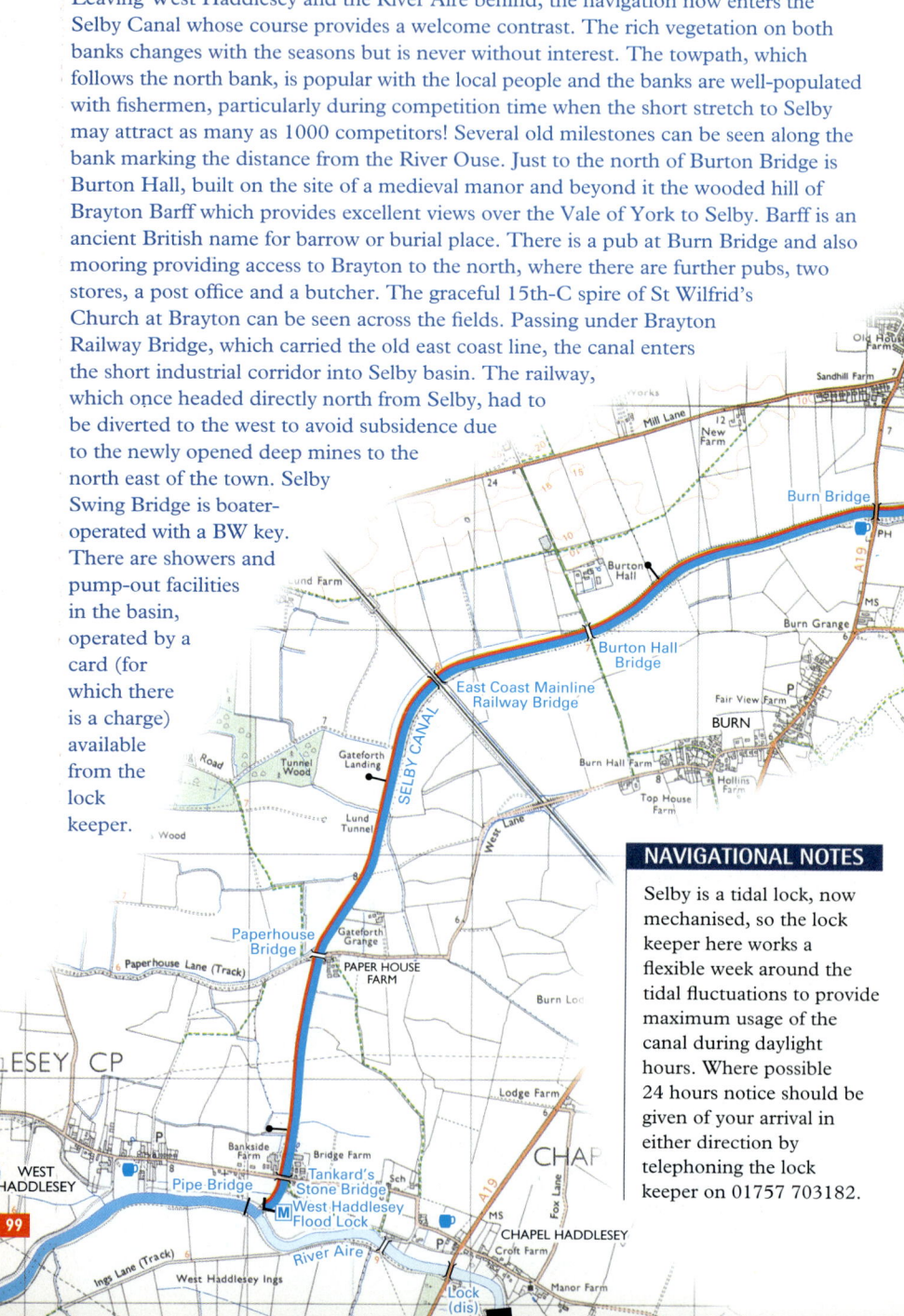

NAVIGATIONAL NOTES

Selby is a tidal lock, now mechanised, so the lock keeper here works a flexible week around the tidal fluctuations to provide maximum usage of the canal during daylight hours. Where possible 24 hours notice should be given of your arrival in either direction by telephoning the lock keeper on 01757 703182.

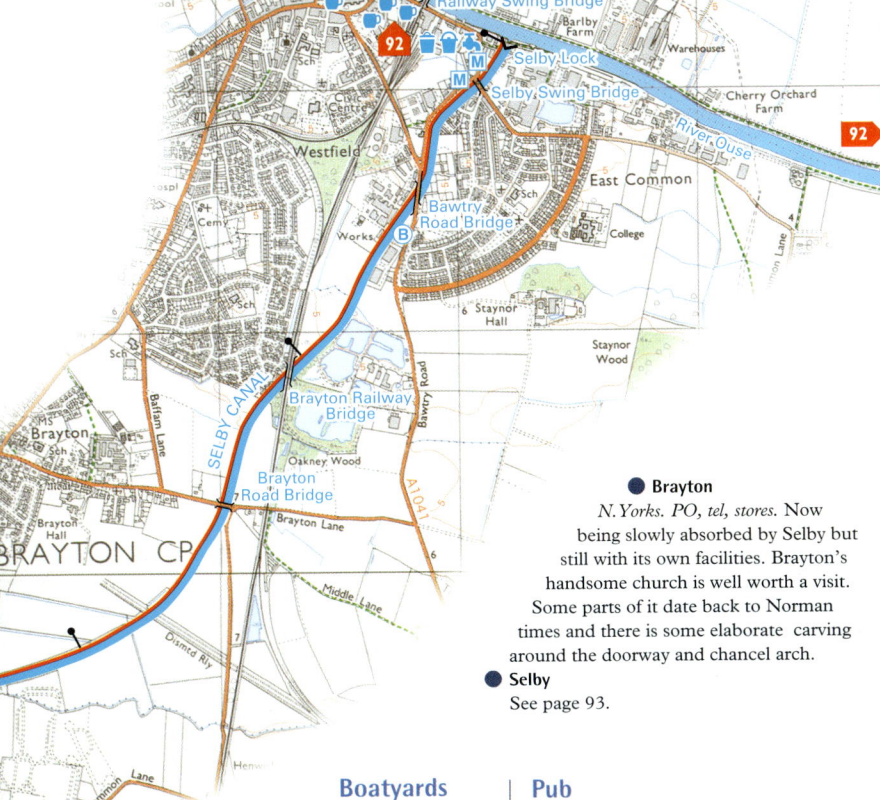

● **Brayton**
N.Yorks. PO, tel, stores. Now being slowly absorbed by Selby but still with its own facilities. Brayton's handsome church is well worth a visit. Some parts of it date back to Norman times and there is some elaborate carving around the doorway and chancel arch.

● **Selby**
See page 93.

Boatyards

Ⓑ **Selby Boat Centre**
Bawtry Road, Selby (01757 212211). **D E** Pump-out, gas, gas installations, narrow boat hire, day craft hire, overnight moorings, long-term moorings, winter storage, slipway, engine repairs, (including outboards), crane, boat and engine sales, boat repairs and fitting-out, DIY facilities, solid fuel, chandlery, books, maps and gifts. *24 hour* emergency call-out.

Pub

🛶 **The Anchor Burn** (01757 270255). Canalside pub serving John Smith's real ale and food *lunchtimes and evenings.* Children will enjoy the extensive collection of animals including chipmunks and lop-eared rabbits as well as some beautifully kept aquariums. Outside seating. Quiz *Thur.* Live music *Sat.*

There are many pubs in Selby. See page 93 for details.

BURSTING AT THE SEAMS

It is difficult to conceive whilst cruising quietly around the waterways of Yorkshire that underground lies the biggest coal mining complex in Europe. Only the effects of subsidence remind us of the extensive activity below. The six mines that comprise the Selby coalfield extract some 11 million tons of coal, providing work for 4000 people. Shafts sunk in the 1960s and 1970s at a cost of £1 billion extend eastwards towards the North Sea at a depth of 700 feet, some seams measuring two or three miles in length. In spite of being the most modern and productive complex in Europe, this high tech operation still chooses to employ the cleanest and most environmentally-friendly mode of transport at one of its collieries – the canal. In 1996 Kellingly Colliery celebrated the transportation of the 35-millionth ton of coal by barge to Ferrybridge power station. In fact coal from five of the six pits goes no further than a 15 mile radius to feed the many power stations in the area which in turn supply power to the national grid.

Victoria Quay, Sheffield

SOUTH YORKSHIRE NAVIGATIONS

MAXIMUM DIMENSIONS

Sheffied to Rotherham
Length: 61' 6"
Beam: 15' 3"
Headroom: 10'
Rotherham to Sykehouse
Length: 230'
Beam: 20'
Headroom: 10' over 16' width

Bramwith to Keadby
Length: 61' 7"
Beam: 17'
Headroom: 11' over 16' width

New Junction Canal
Length: 200'
Beam: 20'
Headroom: 11' 5"

MANAGER
01302 340610

MILEAGE
SHEFFIELD Basin to
Rotherham: 6 miles, 15 locks
Swinton Junction: 12 miles, 18 locks
Doncaster Lock: 21½ miles, 23 locks
Bramwith Junction: 28 miles, 24 locks
Thorne: 33 miles: 26 locks
Crowle Wharf: 39½ miles, 26 locks
KEADBY, Junction with River Trent: 43 miles, 27 locks

Four separate waterway developments combine to make up the South Yorkshire Navigations. Prior to their improvement, trade with the industrial heartland of South Yorkshire was by horse and cart to Bawtry and then by the natural line of the River Idle into the Trent and so into the Humber estuary. The River Don was largely given over to powering water wheels along its upper length, whilst its lower reaches split into two channels west of Thorne and drained into the Trent. In 1627 Cornelius Vermuyden was employed to drain Hatfield Chase and the Isle of Axholme. His scheme involved blocking one of the River Don's outlets into the Trent, thereby forcing all its waters into the tidal River Aire. This was unsuccessful, and resulted in flooding and made what had been an already difficult river navigation into a hazardous one. A new channel, the Dutch River, was cut east from the River Don into the Ouse. This improved drainage, but not navigation.

Upstream, the river between Doncaster and Mexborough had, by 1729, been considerably improved, with complete navigation to Tinsley, four miles from Sheffield, a reality by 1751. All goods to and from Sheffield for shipment by water travelled by road between a river wharf at Tinsley and the city. It was not until 1815 that an Act of Parliament was obtained to build a canal into the city centre. The Sheffield Canal was opened on 22 February 1819. For the first time the city was linked directly to the sea, via the Trent and Humber.

The Trent link had in fact been made 17 years earlier, with the construction of the Stainforth & Keadby Canal, which bypassed the tidal reaches of the old Dutch River. The navigation declined until 1888, when the Sheffield & South Yorkshire Navigation Company was formed, and improvements made. The Straddle Warehouse built over Sheffield Basin dates from this period, as did the negotiations with the Aire & Calder Navigation to link Sheffield directly to the port of Goole and the more northerly coalfields. These negotiations resulted in the opening of the New Junction Canal on 2 January 1905, the last canal to be constructed in the country. In 1983 the navigation was upgraded to the 700-tonne Eurobarge standard. Unfortunately, with no established traffic, the annual tonnage of goods carried is now just a fraction of the record one million tonnes achieved in 1951. The navigation's future now seems to be firmly in the area of leisure and recreation, along with some freight traffic.

Sheffield

The restored Sheffield Basin is dominated by the impressive Straddle Warehouse, built on columns over the water in 1895 by the South Yorkshire Navigation Company. Immediately behind this stands the Grain Warehouse, beyond which is the original Terminal Warehouse of 1819, standing an imposing seven storeys high. Leaving the basin, the canal initially curves away beneath a railway bridge. Bridge 6, Bacon Lane, built in 1819, was also known as Needle's Eye, due to the problems its narrow width posed. The sharp eyed will be able to spot evidence of boats having been forced through with a crowbar. It is now renowned as the place where the *Full Monty* was filmed. Staniforth Road Bridge provides useful access to pubs, cafés, restaurants and shops on Attercliffe Road. At Darnall Road Aqueduct the landscape is dominated by stadiums built to accommodate the Universiade, or World Student Games, in 1991. Access to the Don Valley Stadium, shops, pubs and cafés can be made by leaving the towpath at the aqueduct. At Greenland Road Bridge the towpath crosses to the north side of the canal. The water here was once polluted, but this has now been eliminated and wildlife has recovered well. Fishermen can be seen along the banks, as can clumps of Michaelmas daisies, toadflax and valerian. Ahead the canal enters the top lock of the Tinsley flight which descends under the shadow of the massive steel viaduct carrying the M1 across the valley. A total of 11 locks, with tranquil wide pounds and open views, lower the navigation from its summit level, with the bright-green domed roofs of the Meadowhall Shopping Centre dominating the outlook to the west. The canal joins the River Don at Halfpenny Bridge, and bends sharply right after passing the head of a large weir. Three locks, almost equally spaced, continue the descent towards Rotherham. The chamber of Rotherham Lock is quite tiny – retaining the original keel length of 61' 6" – and looks very pleasant in front of the new court house, where barristers and defendants alike can be seen crossing the canal to the car park. There then follows a very tight right turn before the waterway seems to burrow underground and snake through the heart of the town.

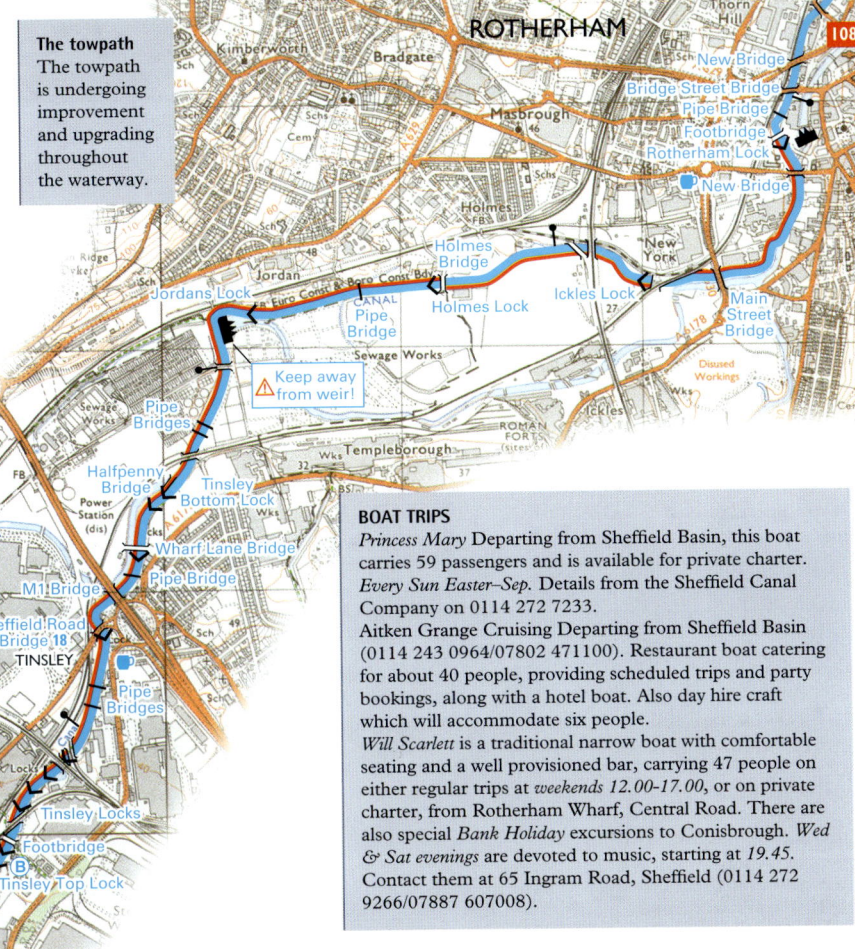

The towpath
The towpath is undergoing improvement and upgrading throughout the waterway.

BOAT TRIPS

Princess Mary Departing from Sheffield Basin, this boat carries 59 passengers and is available for private charter. *Every Sun Easter–Sep.* Details from the Sheffield Canal Company on 0114 272 7233.

Aitken Grange Cruising Departing from Sheffield Basin (0114 243 0964/07802 471100). Restaurant boat catering for about 40 people, providing scheduled trips and party bookings, along with a hotel boat. Also day hire craft which will accommodate six people.

Will Scarlett is a traditional narrow boat with comfortable seating and a well provisioned bar, carrying 47 people on either regular trips at *weekends 12.00–17.00,* or on private charter, from Rotherham Wharf, Central Road. There are also special *Bank Holiday* excursions to Conisbrough. *Wed & Sat evenings* are devoted to music, starting at *19.45.* Contact them at 65 Ingram Road, Sheffield (0114 272 9266/07887 607008).

NAVIGATIONAL NOTES

1 Although it is possible to moor at several points along this stretch of waterway, it is advisable to use Sheffield Basin or Tinsley Marina for an overnight stop.
2 Passage through the Tinsley Flight requires assistance from one of the lock keepers. Telephone 07710 175488 during the day, or 0114 244 1981 in the evening, *and ensure that you give 24 hours notice.*
3 From Tinsley to Doncaster Town Lock the boater is entering a river navigation with a series of artificial cuts. Many of the locks are accompanied by large weirs, so keep a sharp lookout for signs which direct you safely into the locks.
4 Once the river level rises 2 feet above normal (gauging sticks are fixed at the top of all locks) pleasure craft may well experience difficulty due to the current, floating debris and the pull at weirs. Seek advice from BW staff before proceeding.
5 All locks require a standard BW key for operation. Obey the traffic light signals.
6 All weirs are protected by weir booms.
7 Much of the towpath is currently being upgraded, making long lengths suitable for walking and cycling.

Sheffield

S. Yorks. MD Tue, Fri, Sat. All services. Sheffield is England's fourth largest city and owes its world-famous reputation to the manufacture of steel, cutlery and silverware. The unique landscape into which Sheffield was built, steep hills sliced by deep cut valleys, contributed to its importance during the Industrial Revolution. Five rivers facilitated the operation of water wheels, and hills rich in iron ore made Sheffield a natural pioneer of the steel industry. Today the city bustles with life, and new shopping complexes merge with the existing Georgian and Victorian architecture to give a lively mix. Overhead the two-car units of the Supertram shuttle back and forth, and the station close to the canal basin makes access to this excellent means of transport quite easy. Tudor Square brings together the internationally famous Crucible Theatre with the Lyceum Theatre, now restored to its former Victorian splendour (from Park Square, by the Canal Basin, walk along Commercial Street, then turn left into Arundel Gate to find them). Also nearby are the award-winning Ruskin Gallery and Graves Art Gallery. Just across Exchange Street an open market is useful for supplies.

Town Hall Pinstone Street (0114 273 4793). Built in 1897 and designed by Mountford, the Town Hall has a clock tower, 210 feet high, crowned with a statue of Vulcan, Roman God of Fire. There is a sculptured frieze outside depicting the industries of Sheffield. Public tours for pre-booked parties only.

Cutlers' Hall Church Street (0114 272 8456). Built in 1832, the Cutlers' Hall houses the Cutlers' Company collection of silver. Tours for parties. Telephone for details.

City Museum Weston Park, Western Bank (0114 276 8588). The museum contains the largest collection of Sheffield Plate in the world and has a unique section devoted to cutlery. Also Bronze Age antiquities, local geology and wildlife gallery. *Open Tue–Sat 10.00–17.00 and Sun 11.00–17.00.* Free. Touch sessions for visually impaired people available.

Cathedral of St Peter & St Paul Opposite the Cutlers' Hall in Church Street. A largely 15th-C church with 12th-C foundations and an interesting extension incorporating a new glass and steel porch, elevated to cathedral status in 1914. Five years later it was decided to enlarge the building, whilst retaining much of the original, to designs by Sir Charles Nicholson. Visitors will enjoy the stained glass windows depicting local history and the Chaucer window in the Chapter House. *Open daily.* Guided tours can be arranged, contact the Head Verger on 0114 275 3434.

Sheffield Industrial Museum Kelham Island off Alma Street (0114 272 2106). The museum takes the visitor through Sheffield's industrial past with a chance to see craftsmen at work in the Little Mesters workshops. Occasionally the River Don Engine (a 12,000 bhp engineering wonder) is in steam. *Open Mon–Thu 10.00–16.00, Sun 11.00–17.00.* Charge. Café on site.

Abbeydale Industrial Hamlet Abbeydale Road South (0114 236 7731). Four miles south west of the city centre. A superb example of industrial archaeology which displays a restored community, built around a water-powered scythe and steel works. *Telephone for opening hours.* Charge. Café. Bus from the High Street (continuation of Commercial Street, off Park Square).

The National Centre for Popular Music Paternoster Row (0114 296 6060 – bookings 0114 296 2626). From Billie Holiday to Björk, from Glenn Miller to glam rock, from the Specials to the Spice Girls, this is a unique pop-music experience. Play a guitar, record a song, enjoy Soundscapes. *Open daily 10.00–18.00 (closed Xmas).* Charge.

Bishop's House Meersbrook Park, Norton Lees Lane (0114 255 7701). A timber-framed Yeoman's house of 15thC origins with 16th- and 17th-C additions. Other displays include Sheffield in Tudor and Stuart times and changing local history exhibitions. *Open Wed–Sat 10.00–16.30, Sun 11.00–16.30.* Charge. Bus 434/439 from the Transport Interchange, opposite the BR station in Pond Street, south of Park Square.

South Yorkshire Steam Railway Barrow Road, Meadowbank (0114 242 4405). Industrial steam locomotives can be seen here. They are aiming to re-open the 3½ mile stretch of track between Meadowhall and Chapletown. *Open all year, Sat and Sun 10.30–17.00.* Charge. Bus from the Transport Interchange, opposite the BR station in Pond Street, south of Park Square.

Tourist Information Centre Peace Gardens, Sheffield (0114 273 4671/2). An invaluable source of information.

Boatyards

ⓑ **Sheffield Canal Co** Victoria Boatyard, Sussex Street (0114 272 7233). Just outside Sheffield Basin. 🛶 🚽 ♿ D E Gas, pump-out, overnight and long-term mooring, winter storage, slipway, wet and dry dock, chandlery, boat and engine sales and repairs, boat refurbishing, showers, toilets, books and maps, gifts.

ⓑ **Trafalgar Canal Boat Company** Trafalgar Works, Effingham Road (0114 275 1389). Boat building and fabrication.

ⓑ **Tinsley Marina (BW)** Tinsley Top Lock (01302 340610). 🛶 🚽 ♿ Overnight and long-term mooring, toilets, showers.

Rotherham

S. Yorks. MD Mon, Sat. All services. An attractive town set amidst the industrial heartland of South Yorkshire where the buildings, although dating from a variety of periods, integrate well to form a coherent town centre. A part of the medieval town plan remains while the old town hall, in its new guise of arcade, presents a fine renovation. In ancient times Rotherham was an important seat of learning, the College of Jesus being founded in 1482 by Archbishop Thomas and surviving until the dissolution. The pinnacled tower of All Saints church dates from 1409, and the remainder was almost entirely constructed during the same century. Its position, whilst maintaining an intimate contact with the town, is nevertheless imposing. Standing on the remaining four arches of the bridge which spans the River Don, the Chapel of Our Lady was built in 1483 and again fell victim to the dissolution, after which it variously became an almshouse, a prison and a tobacconist's. It was finally restored and re-consecrated in 1924 and forms an attractive feature in the lower part of the town. The key is available from the vicar of All Saints, nearby.

Rotherham's modern growth dates from 1746 when Samuel Walker, a former schoolmaster, established its first ironworks. Coal mining developed, as well as the production of brass, steel, rope and glass, yet it is probably for the production of quality steels, in the form of fine-edge tools, that the town is best known.
Clifton Park Museum Rotherham (01709 382121). A collection containing gemstones and examples of Rockingham and other local pottery can be seen here. Loan exhibitions of paintings. Roman remains from Templeborough are displayed in the park, *Open Mon–Thu & Sat 10.00–17.00, Sun 13.30–17.00. Closed Fri.* Free.
Meadowhall Shopping Centre Tinsley. Immense indoor shopping mall accessible from above Lock 9 on the Tinsley flight.
Elsecar Heritage Centre (01226 740203). Access by train from Sheffield. Follow the signs from Elsecar Station. These Victorian engineering workshops dating from the early 1800s have been transformed into an exciting centre. *Open daily 10.00-17.00. Closed Xmas & New Year.* Charge.
Tourist Information Centre Central Library, Walker Place, Rotherham (01709 835904).

ART GALLERIES IN SHEFFIELD

Graves Third floor, Central Library Building, Surrey Street (0114 273 5158). A fine collection of English watercolours, drawings and prints, European paintings and Old Masters (16thC to present). *Open Mon–Sat 10.00–17.00.* Free. Coffee bar.
Mappin Weston Park (0114 272 6281). Victorian paintings including pre-Raphaelites. English 18th- and 19th-C paintings including Constable and Turner. Occasional concerts, performances and artists workshops. *Open Tue–Sat 10.00–17.00, Sun 11.00–17.00.* Free. Gift shop and coffee bar on site. Disabled facilities. Bus from the High Street, west of Park Square.
Ruskin Norfolk Street (0114 273 5299). A fine collection of minerals, plaster casts and architectural details, paintings, watercolours, illuminated manuscripts and books collected by John Ruskin for the people of Sheffield. Craft gallery. *Open Mon–Sat 10.00–17.00.* Free. South west of Park Square.

Pubs and Restaurants

There are many pubs and restaurants in Sheffield. The following are simply a selection of those nearest to the navigation.
Sheaf Quay Victoria Quays, Wharf Road (0114 273 7370). A large and sociable pub in what was once a cutlery factory. Courage and John Smith's real ale are served, and a wide choice of food, including a children's menu and vegetarian dishes, is available *lunchtimes and evenings every day.* Children are welcome, and there is a patio.
The Norfolk Arms Dixon Lane, Sheffield (0114 249 3108). A friendly little local serving Stones real ale. Sing-along on *Sat & Sun evenings* with the organist.
Alexandra Exchange Street, Sheffield (0114 253 6581). 500yds west of the basin. A large

yet friendly traditional pub serving Stones real ale. Bar meals *lunchtimes only,* plus a vegetarian menu.
The Plumpers Plumpers Road, Tinsley (0114 244 1457). A modern pub serving Stones real ale, along with regular entertainment. Tinsley Transcafé next door, for good solid food.
Moulders Rest 110-2 Masbrough Street (01709 560095). Near to Millmoor football ground. A large, popular and comfortable corner pub, with its own football team, serving John Smith's and guest real ales. Food, including vegetarian dishes, *lunchtimes Mon-Fri and evenings Mon-Thu.* Children welcome. Outside seating. Regular entertainment with quiz and traditional games nights. B & B.

Swinton

The exit from Rotherham is marked by a very large expanse of water before Rawmarsh Road Bridge, beyond which the Rotherham Cut eventually rejoins the River Don. When Eastwood Locks were combined on the upper site the river was re-aligned along the old canal bed. The new lock, opened on 1 June 1983, by the then Chairman of BWB (now BW) was called Sir Frank Price Lock in his honour (it is now Eastwood Lock), completed the modernisation to the 700-tonne barge standard of the South Yorkshire Navigations. It is worth noting, however, that from Sheffield the navigation has remained virtually unchanged since its original construction, a lasting tribute to its designers. Now, unfortunately, about 20 of Waddingtons barges lie disused here. At Aldwarke Lock a short channel bypasses the weir and a new concrete flyover has taken over from Wash Lane bridge. Built in 1834, this listed structure bears the marks of much abuse from both barges and road traffic alike. The navigation now follows the course of the River Don, twisting and turning between high and often tree-lined banks, passing gaunt modern factory complexes, largely engaged in specialist steel manufacture. All discharges from these works are now carefully monitored for purity and to this end brightly coloured booms surround each outfall, containing their emissions for regular testing by the Environment Agency.

Pottery Road Bridge

Dearne & Dove Canal (disused)

SWINTON BRIDGE

110

Footbridge

Swinton Lock

Swinton Junction

SWINTON

Burton Ings Bridge

Kilnhurst Cut

Kilnhurst

Wentworth Road

Hooton Road Bridge

Weir

Pipe Bridge

Pipe Bridge

Disused Workings

Tip (dis)

Mine

Kilnhurst Hall Farm

Kilnhurst Flood Lock

Thrybergh Bridge

Weir

Thrybergh Park (CH)

THRYBERGH PARK (Golf Course)

Don Bridge

THRYBERGH

River Don

Quarry (dis)

Works

Aldwarke

Parkgate Works Bridge

Whinney Hill

Opencast Workings

Toll

Industrial Estate

Eastwood Lock

Wash Lane Bridge

Aldwarke Lock

Dalton

A630

27

Footbridge

Rotherham Cut

Trading Estate

Rawmarsh Road Bridge

105

Greasbrough Road Bridge

St.

Eastwood

ROTHERHAM

Within recent memory the Don was fast becoming one of the most polluted rivers in Europe, but stringent control measures have reversed this trend and fishing on this stretch of water is now quite popular. Overlooked to the east by Thrybergh Park, it is not at all unpleasant. Kilnhurst Cut is entered at Kilnhurst Flood Lock, where the towpath crosses the river – without the benefit of a bridge, barge horses were obliged to use flat-decked chain ferries. At Hooton Road Bridge there is a reasonable mooring, a grocer and post office, together with two pubs. To the east Hooton Common, criss-crossed with hedges and trees, rises to a more distant skyline. Once a tar works and a colliery lined the left bank, the former receiving the bulk of its deliveries by barge from local town gas works, before natural gas made these plants redundant. At Swinton Junction, the remains of the Dearne & Dove Canal climbs the locks off the mainline towards Barnsley. Waddington's boats throng the junction in a jumble of boilers, pipes and cranes, using the first pounds of the closed canal as a dock. The lock on the main line here was re-named Waddington Lock in recognition of the contribution that E.V. Waddington's barges once made to the life of the navigation. Let us hope they will soon contribute again.

Boatyards

Ⓑ **Tulley Marine Services** Rotherham (01709 836743). Gas, overnight and long-term mooring, winter storage, slipway, boat and engine sales and repairs, boat building, telephone, toilets, chandlery, DIY facilities.

Ⓑ **Waddingtons of Swinton** (01709 582232). In existence for 200 years, this proud and famous water freight company now finds operating conditions onerous, but still maintains its fleet of 90 craft in excellent condition, waiting for the return of waterways traffic. . .

● **Eastwood**
S. Yorks. PO, tel, stores. A suburb of Rotherham, with an excellent variety of corner shops dotted throughout the streets.

● **Kilnhurst**
S. Yorks. PO, tel, stores. A non-descript village merging into the conurbation linking Mexborough with Rotherham. Once the site of an ironworks and, more recently, a colliery, now closed down. It was also known for the production of earthenware pottery.

● **Swinton Junction**
Here the Dearne & Dove Canal left the mainline and provided a route to Barnsley and thence via the Barnsley Canal to Wakefield. Together they made up the southern loop for the so-called Yorkshire Ring. Both waterways have long since fallen into disrepair but ambitious plans have been mooted to re-open them. Once a busy waterway junction and boat building centre, it still forms an interesting canal settlement, worthy of exploration.

Pubs and Restaurants

🛥 **Crinoline Bridge** The Rawmarsh Road, Rotherham (01709 370748). Comfortable pub serving Wards real ale and food *lunchtimes Mon–Fri*, with vegetarian menu. Outside seating.

🛥 **Ship Inn** East end of Hooton Road Bridge, Kilnhurst (01709 584322). Cosy stone-built pub over the railway, serving John Smith's and Stones real ale and bar food *lunchtimes and evenings every day*, with vegetarian options. Garden. Children are welcome.

🛥 **Commercial** Victoria Street, West end of Hooton Road Bridge, Kilnhurst (01709 587905). A sturdy corner house serving Stones and Tetleys real ale. PO next door.

Conisbrough

The fruits of EU land reclamation grants have been in evidence between Sheffield and here, in the form of both landscaping and tree planting, as the concept of waterways as linear parks comes nearer to reality. The Earth Centre provides a focus for such ecological inspiration on the north bank at Conisbrough, overlooked by the well-restored keep of the Castle.

● **Mexborough**
S. Yorks. MD Mon, Fri, Sat. All services. The tiny church of St John the Baptist has a 13th-C tower arch. Gardens and a fine reconstructed archway face the canal.

● **Conisbrough**
S. Yorks. All services. A relatively attractive town. **Conisbrough Castle** (01709 863329). A Norman castle – circa 1185 – with a circular keep capped by a conical wooden roof, superbly sited 90 feet above the River Don. Excellent visitor centre. *Open Apr–Sep, Mon–Fri 10.00–17.00 and Sat & Sun 10.00–18.00. Oct–Mar, daily 10.00–16.00. Evening tours also available. Closed Xmas eve, Xmas day & New Years Day.* Shop, tea room. Charge.
The Earth Centre Denaby Main, Conisbrough

(01709 512000). Offers fun with an underlying message of sustainable development and regeneration. Visit the Planet Earth Gallery, the Wilderness Play Area, the Water and Nature Works, 21st Century Terraced Gardens, Water Conservation Garden, Forest Gardens, Bog Gardens and Action for the Future Gallery. It is still developing. *Open daily 10.00–18.00.* Organic café. Charge.

● **Sprotbrough**
S. Yorks. PO, tel, stores. A useful source of provisions, even on *Sundays.* Sir Walter Scott is reputed to have written part of *Ivanhoe* here. The church of St Mary dates from the 13thC, and is well worth a visit. In the chancel floor are brasses to William Fitzwilliam, 1474, who left £40 towards the building of the church tower.

Boatyards

Ⓑ **Yorkshire Rose Marina** Unit 9, Leach Lane, Mexborough (01709 571555). 🛠 **D** Pump-out, gas, narrow boat hire, overnight and long-term mooring, boatbuilding, boat sales, boat and engine repairs, telephone, chandlery. 🛠 🚮 🚻 and moorings *nearby.*

Ⓑ **Waddingtons of Swinton** (01709 582232). In existence for 200 years, this proud and famous water freight company now finds operating conditions very onerous, but still maintains its fleet of 90 craft in excellent condition, waiting for the return of waterways traffic. . .

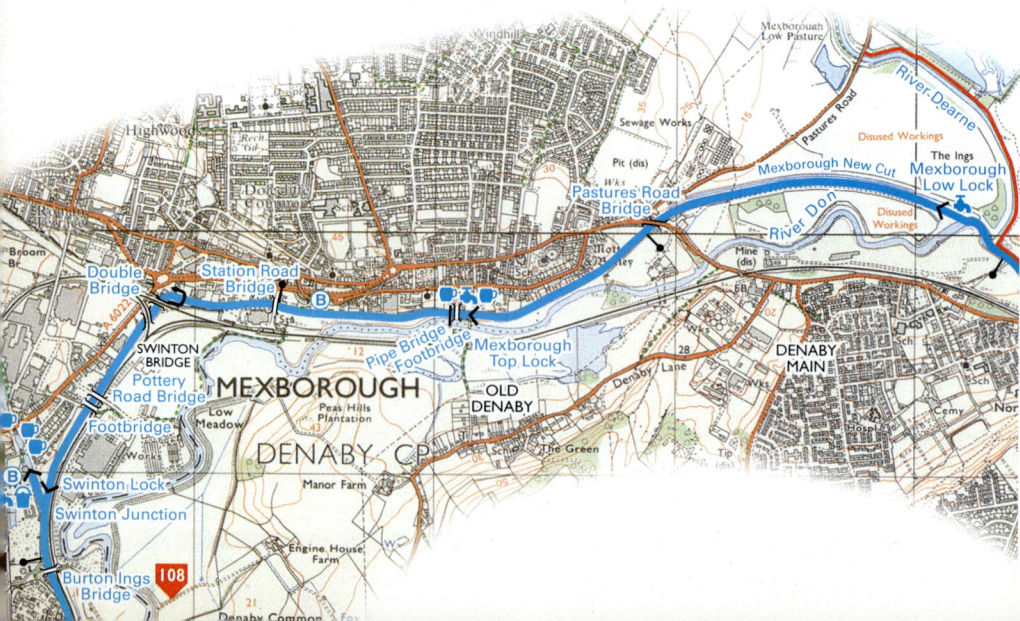

Pubs and Restaurants

Ferryboat Church Street, Mexborough (01709 586382). Close to the canal, north of Mexborough Top Lock. Spacious 400-year-old pub serving John Smith's and Stones real ale. Outside seating area and children's play area. Children welcome, live music *at weekends* and *B. Hol* barbeques.

George & Dragon Church Street, Mexborough (01709 584375). Near to the Ferryboat. Serves Vaux, Wards and guest real ales. China ornaments and wooden cats decorate a very comfortable wood panelled pub, and the service is friendly. Garden and children's play area.

Cadeby Inn Cadeby (01709 864009). Fine village pub, with open fires, in a converted farmhouse. Serves John Smith's, Tetley's, Samuel Smith and guest real ales and bar food *lunchtimes and evenings daily*, with vegetarian choices. Children welcome. Garden.

Boat Inn Sprotbrough (01302 857188). Off Boat Lane. On the north bank above the lock. Former coaching house where Sir Walter Scott wrote *Ivanhoe*. Since 1652 this building has regularly alternated between farmhouse and pub. After lying derelict for 20 years, it was renovated to the present high standard and now serves John Smith's, Courage and Magnet real ales. Bar meals available *lunchtimes and evenings every day,* with a restaurant open *Wed–Sat evenings,* and vegetarian choices. Courtyard. In summer Morris dancers occasionally entertain here.

Ivanhoe Malton Road, Sprotbrough (01302 853130). ¹/₂ mile from the river at the top of the village. Lively, comfortable pub overlooking the cricket pitch. Samuel Smith real ale, together with bar meals *lunchtimes and evenings and Sun all day until 17.00,* with a vegetarian menu. Children welcome. Garden.

BOAT TRIPS

Alan Oliver (Cruises) (01302 856513). Waterbus service from above Sprotbrough Lock on *Sun and B. Hols* aboard ex-Clyde ferry *Wyre Lady*.

Doncaster

The waterway now enters a pleasant tree-lined valley, only briefly intruded upon by the noise of motorway traffic crossing overhead on the slender Don viaduct. Passing beneath two iron-girdered railway bridges the waterway sweeps around wide bends towards Doncaster. Just before Doncaster Town Lock the navigation finally parts company with the River Don, although the river is never far away for many miles to come. Ahead lies a jumble of transport systems as road crosses railway, which in turn crosses the canal, all just beyond Doncaster Town Lock. Then the navigation is in Doncaster, widening out opposite the church and beside the disused coal staithe. Factories sprawl around the outside sweep of a wide bend, while all the time the River Don hugs the left-hand bank, obscured by flood embankments. There is little of interest between the centre of Doncaster and Long Sandall Lock, with its tower-shaped Control Cabin looking down on manicured lawns and neat flower beds. Dickens visited Long Sandall in 1857 and described it as being thronged with 'horse-mad, betting-mad, drunken-mad, vice-mad crowds'. Some say it is quieter now. There are moorings by Doncaster Waterways Office.

Pubs and Restaurants

There are plenty of pubs and restaurants in Doncaster, but none beside the navigation.

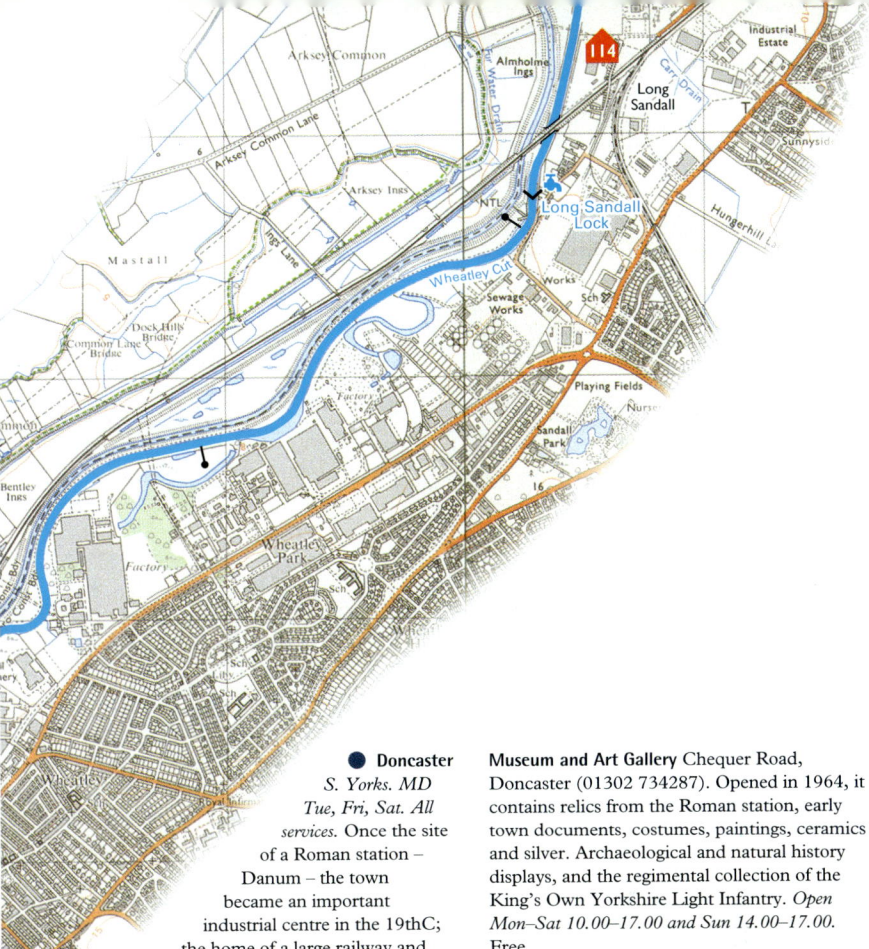

● **Doncaster**

S. Yorks. MD
Tue, Fri, Sat. All
services. Once the site
of a Roman station –
Danum – the town
became an important
industrial centre in the 19thC;
the home of a large railway and
carriage works and ringed by a girdle
of mining villages. Exploited for almost a
century, the pits of the South Yorkshire
Coalfield yielded open-cast coal to the
west, whilst to the east of a dividing ridge of
magnesium limestone, deep mines were sunk. In
the early part of the 19thC, when the town was
largely an agricultural community straddling the
Great North Road, its High Street was regarded as
the finest along the route between London and
Edinburgh. Alas, most of the buildings of the last
fifty years pay little regard to the original character.
One consistent link with the past is, however,
provided by the annual St Leger horse race, first
run in 1776, and pre-dating the Derby by two years.
Parish Church of St George Built to a design by
Gilbert Scott in 1858 on an almost Cathedral scale
(the crossing tower is fully 170 feet tall), it replaced
a medieval church burnt down in 1853. A very fine
example of Victorian Neo-Gothic.
Mansion House High Street, Doncaster (01302
734011). An impressive civic building designed
by James Paine and finished in 1748. *Open by*
appointment only.

Museum and Art Gallery Chequer Road,
Doncaster (01302 734287). Opened in 1964, it
contains relics from the Roman station, early
town documents, costumes, paintings, ceramics
and silver. Archaeological and natural history
displays, and the regimental collection of the
King's Own Yorkshire Light Infantry. *Open*
Mon–Sat 10.00–17.00 and Sun 14.00–17.00.
Free.
Cusworth Hall Museum Cusworth Park,
Doncaster (01302 782342). The Georgian
house (rebuilt and then altered by James Paine
in the 1750s) set in landscaped parkland,
contains a museum which illustrates South
Yorkshire's history, industries, agriculture and
social life. *Open Mon–Fri 10.00–17.00, Sat*
11.00–17.00 and Sun 13.00–17.00. Closes 16.00
in winter. Free.
Brodsworth Hall (01302 722598). About 5 miles
north west of Doncaster, off the A635, and
worth the effort. A rare example of a Victorian
country house which has survived, largely
unaltered, with much of its original furnishings
and decorations intact. It was built during the
1860s, and retains a faded grandeur which
speaks of an opulent past. The gardens are
delightful. *Open Apr-Oct, Tue-Sun 13.00-18.00.*
Gardens only Nov-Mar, Sat & Sun 11.00-16.00
(house closed in winter). Charge. Tea room and
shop. (Telephone 01709 515151 for details of
buses from Doncaster.)
Tourist Information Centre Central Library,
Waterdale, Doncaster (01302 734309).

Stainforth

At Sandall Grove there is a tiny, though delightful, hotch potch of a church, nestling beside a farmyard, beyond which Barnby Dun comes into view. Then the waterway splits – straight ahead lies the Aire & Calder Navigation;

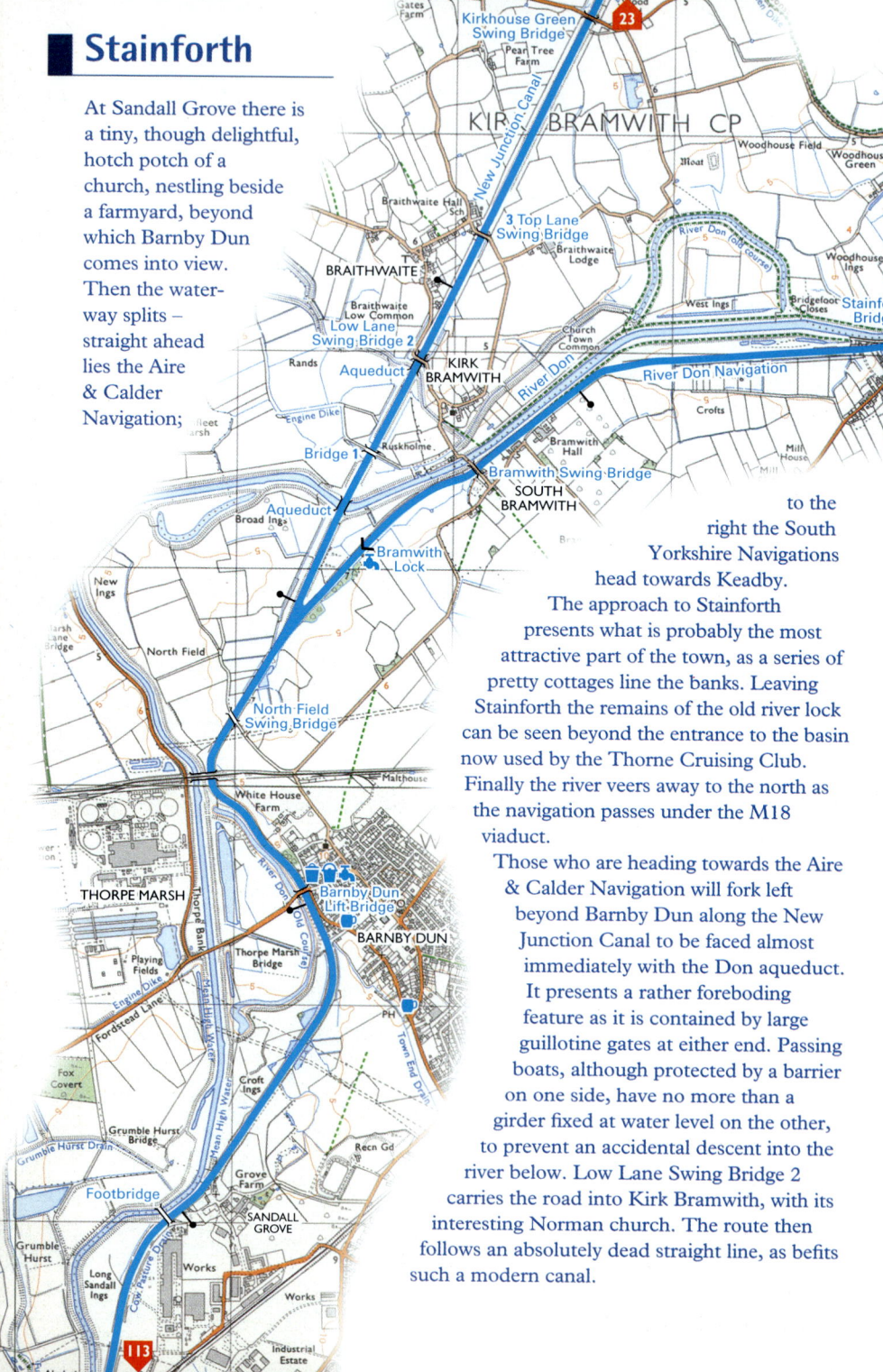

to the right the South Yorkshire Navigations head towards Keadby. The approach to Stainforth presents what is probably the most attractive part of the town, as a series of pretty cottages line the banks. Leaving Stainforth the remains of the old river lock can be seen beyond the entrance to the basin now used by the Thorne Cruising Club. Finally the river veers away to the north as the navigation passes under the M18 viaduct.

Those who are heading towards the Aire & Calder Navigation will fork left beyond Barnby Dun along the New Junction Canal to be faced almost immediately with the Don aqueduct. It presents a rather foreboding feature as it is contained by large guillotine gates at either end. Passing boats, although protected by a barrier on one side, have no more than a girder fixed at water level on the other, to prevent an accidental descent into the river below. Low Lane Swing Bridge 2 carries the road into Kirk Bramwith, with its interesting Norman church. The route then follows an absolutely dead straight line, as befits such a modern canal.

● **Barnby Dun**
S. Yorks. PO, tel, stores, garage. An attractive
village laid out along one side of the canal on
slightly rising ground. Once a picturesque
mix of old cottages, more recent infilling
threatens to overpower the original village
and turn it into a Doncaster suburb. It is
reported that the once boggy marshland
around the village yielded a surprising find:
the vertebrae of a whale. While the shop
beside the lift bridge keeps irregular hours, a
walk further along the street that almost
parallels the canal will be rewarded by a
butcher, an excellent farm shop selling fresh
local produce, two pubs and a restaurant. The
church of St Peter and St Paul is a virtually
intact example of 14th-C work, with some
remarkable gargoyles. It is well worth a visit.

● **Stainforth**
*S. Yorks. All services. Open air market Fri
evening.* An unprepossessing town strung out
along the main road south of the canal.

NAVIGATIONAL NOTES

All locks and moveable bridges can be boater-operated using a BW sanitary station
key. There are lengthsmen who will assist passage if working in the area.

Pubs and Restaurants

● **White Hart** Top Road, Barnby Dun
(01302 882959). John Smith's and
guest real ales are dispensed in this cosy
and welcoming local pub. The bar and
seating area are liberally decorated with
antiques, particularly china, while the
portions of food are generous in the
extreme, and an extensive menu is
offered *lunchtimes and evenings*, with
vegetarian options. Children welcome.
Outside seating.
● **Star** High Street, Barnby Dun
(01302 882571). East of the canal, this
is a typical brewery-owned pub, serving
bar food *lunchtimes Mon–Sat.*

NEW JUNCTION CANAL
This waterway, completed in 1905, provides
a link between the South Yorkshire
Navigations and the Aire & Calder
Navigation. It is 5 1/2 miles long and
completely straight all the way, the
monotony being broken only by a series
of swing and lift bridges. There are
aqueducts at each end of the long corridor
formed by the navigation, the one in the
south carrying the canal over the River
Don. Both aqueducts are equipped with tall
guillotine gates, which serve either to isolate
the canal in times of flood, or to facilitate
repairs. Moorings are available to the north
of Kirkhouse Green Bridge, and to the
north of Sykehouse Bridge (see page 23).

Thorne

Stanilands Marina, immediately beyond the railway bridge, provides both safe moorings and a range of services, Thorne town centre being only 1/4 mile away. Beyond Thorne bridge there are further moorings, available to visitors, at the marina. Leaving Thorne the landscape again opens up and a rich, fertile plain borders the navigation. Boaters will no doubt enjoy operating Wykewell Lift Bridge, which together with the road barriers and flashing red lights, is controlled by pressing the appropriate buttons in the grey box. At Moor's swing bridge a line of farms can be seen to the north of the canal. Here there is still evidence of the old strip system of farming, where each dwelling is backed by a long narrow strip of land. These units of land would vary in size according to the type of soil and the lie of the land. The one-acre strip (220yds long by 22yds wide) was a rarity in most parts of the country, farms generally possessing strips much smaller than this. Much of the land along the length of the navigation from Stainforth to Keadby

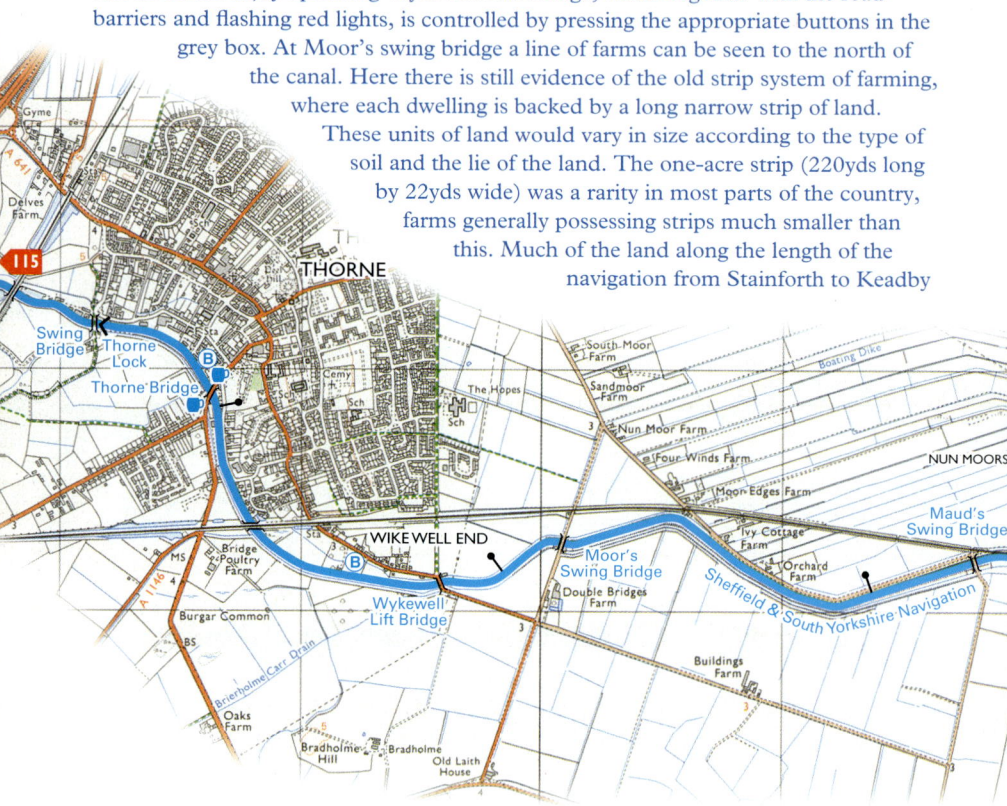

● **Thorne**
S. Yorks. MD Tue, Fri, Sat. All services. A small brick-built market town with an attractive pedestrian precinct around Finkle Street. Thorne's early industries were rope making, sacking and weaving with a canal traffic of coal, pig iron and stone. The town was in fact dependent on the river and the canal for its water supply, the only boreholes supplying Darley's brewery and the workhouse. Regettably the brewery ceased to function as such in 1986, although the memory of brewing in the town is kept alive in Thorne Best Bitter, now brewed in Sheffield. St Nicholas' church displays a variety of 13th-C work, including the south doorway and an unbuttressed west tower.

Pubs and Restaurants

There are many pubs in Thorne. The following are right by the navigation:

● ✕ **Canal Tavern** South Parade, Thorne (01405 813688). North of Thorne Bridge. A lively canalside pub with a beer garden serving Boddingtons, John Smith's, Tetley's, and guest real ales. Bar and restaurant meals available *lunchtimes and evenings every day.* Children welcome in the restaurant. Canalside garden and mooring for patrons. Disco *Fri & Sat,* country and western *Sun,* and quiz nights *Tue, Thur & Sun,* plus pool, darts and TV.

● **Rising Sun** Hatfield Road, Thorne (01405 812688). South of Thorne Bridge. A busy pub with a real fire and a garden.

was prone to seasonal flooding and consequently benefited greatly from the drainage schemes established during the 17thC. Herons, which abound in this area, display considerable patience while standing poised, ready to strike with lightning reflex at frogs, fish and water voles. In spite of their great size, take-off seems effortless and once airborne the head is drawn back and the legs trailed behind in a slow but majestic flight. Grebe too can be seen along the more overgrown sections of the waterway, where their floating nests are anchored to the reeds. Only a hundred years ago these birds had been all but exterminated in England due to fashionable Victorian ladies wishing to display not just the odd feather, but occasionally the entire plumage, in their hats. It is comforting to note that there is now a healthy population of more than 4000 adult birds in the country. At Maud's Bridge, again boater-operated, instructions for its operation are to be found on the white box. Now the railway adds some excitement by joining the canal and running along the north bank to Medge Hall and Crook o'Moor Swing Bridge, where it moves briefly away only to rejoin the line of the navigation at Godnow Bridge. Both these bridges are manned at present although boater-operation of the latter is possible at weekends.

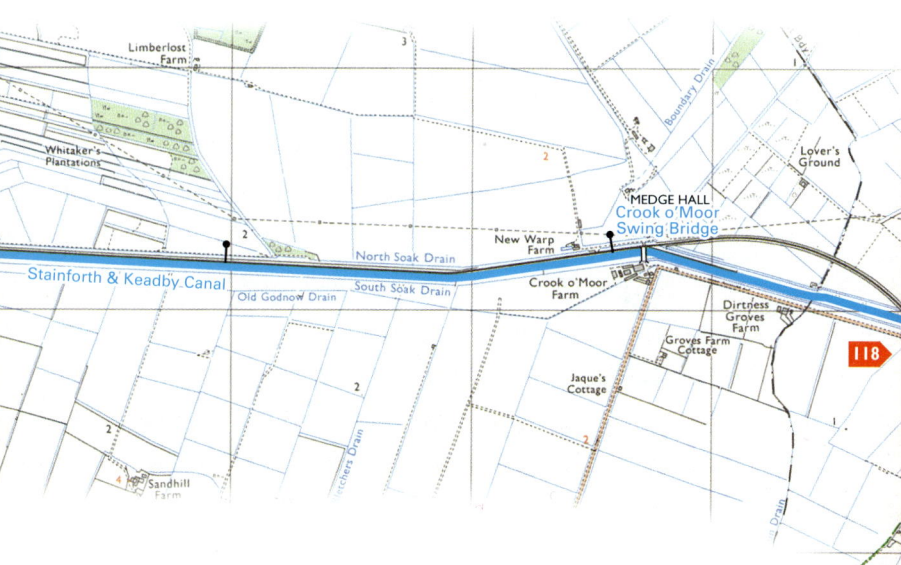

Boatyards

ⓑ ✕ 🍷 **Stanilands Marina** Lock Lane, Thorne (01405 813150). 🚿 🛁 🔧 D Gas, overnight and long-term mooring, slipway, crane, boat building, boat and engine sales, boat repairs, toilets, showers, chandlery. Clubhouse bar with restaurant serving meals *lunchtimes Sat & Sun.*

ⓑ **Thorne Boat Services** South Parade, Thorne (01405 814197). (🚿 🛁 🔧 next door)

D Pump-out gas, engine sales and repairs, chandlery, breakdown service.

ⓑ 🍷 **Blue Water Marina** South End, Thorne (01405 813165). 🚿 🛁 🔧 D Pump-out, gas, overnight and long-term mooring, slipway, crane, boat and engine sales and repairs, toilets, showers, chandlery. Club house open *Fri, Sat, Sun and B. Hols in season.* Visitors welcome.

Keadby

The village of Crowle can be reached from either Godnow Swing Bridge or Crowle Bridge. It is a mile to the north, and is worth the walk since it has a selection of shops and pubs, and an interesting church. In 1747 the body of a woman was found nearby in the peat moor, buried upright at a depth of six feet. From her sandals it appeared that she had been there for several centuries, but was remarkably well preserved. Just beyond Crowle Station there is evidence of the site of the old Axholme Joint railway bridge, demolished in 1972. The bridge must have proved an impressive landmark, consisting of four brick archways and a circular brick abutment upon which the railway pivoted through 90 degrees, thus allowing the passage of the tall sailed keels. Ahead lies the long straight to Keadby. It is not without excitement, however, as immediately beyond Vazon Swing Bridge there is a remarkable railway bridge, skewed across the canal only a couple of feet above the water. Built in 1915 the bridge is supposedly one of only three of its kind in Europe. In order to allow the passage of boats, winches slide the bridge deck sideways, so clearing the navigation and by a further series of wire cables and pulleys, winch the deck back into place. The entire operation is controlled from the nearby signal box. Once beyond the bridge the canal passes the rebuilt Keadby Power Station, which dominates the north bank.

Ahead is Keadby
Swing Bridge and Lock, allowing entry
into the tidal Trent. There is a pub and a post office nearby and a boatyard offering basic services. Moorings are available immediately before the swing bridge.

NAVIGATIONAL NOTES

1 Commercial river traffic operates on VHF channel 6 upsteam of Keadby Bridge on the River Trent. It is useful for VHF users to monitor this channel to establish the where-abouts of large craft on the river.
2 See notes 4 & 5 on page 152.

Boatyards

Ⓑ **Keadby Marine** Canalside, Keadby (01724 782302). 🚿 🚽 ♿ **D** Gas, overnight and long-term mooring, winter storage, boat and engine sales and repairs, telephone, toilets, showers.

● **Crowle**
Humberside. All services. A straggling village one mile north of the canal. There are some attractive Georgian houses in the vicinity of the church. The Market Square retains some of its character and is dominated by the elaborate Victorian façade of the old ballroom, now used for discos. The church of St Oswald is a handsome structure containing much Norman work, and some fine incised door-ways. During the restoration of the tower in 1840 an Anglo-Saxon cross shaft, probably inspired by the Vikings and some 7 feet in length, was found over a doorway. It is believed to date from the 11thC and now stands at the back of the church.

● **Ealand**
Humberside. PO, tel, stores. A small settlement next to the canal.

There are some pretty cottages in the village, and a station.

● **Keadby**
Humberside. PO, tel, stores. A dull settlement which has declined since the Stainforth & Keadby Canal ceased to carry commercial traffic. The only real activity is provided by craft entering the tidal Trent, and the commercial vessels unloading at the river wharf.

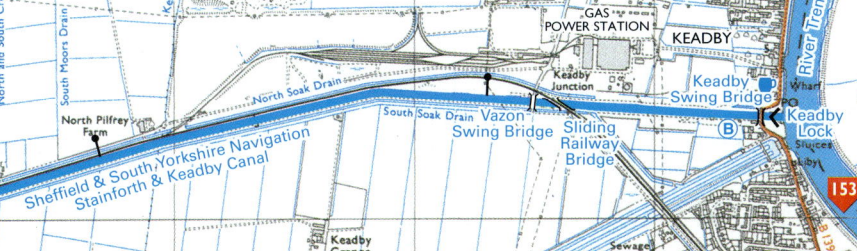

Pubs and Restaurants

🍺 **New Trent Inn** Crowle Wharf, Ealand (01724 710315). A friendly pub selling Mansfield real ale. Bar meals *lunchtimes and evenings Tue-Sat, and Sun lunchtimes*. Children welcome, and there is a garden.
🍺 **The Old South Yorkshire** The Trentside, Keadby (01724 783518). Basic and lively pub serving Webster's real ale and food *lunchtimes and evenings*. Children welcome, garden, and moorings nearby.

RIVER TRENT

MAXIMUM DIMENSIONS

Shardlow to Meadow Lane Lock,
Nottingham
Length: 81'
Beam: 14' 6"
Headroom: 8'
Meadow Lane Lock to Gainsborough
Length: 165'
Beam: 18' 6"
Headroom: 13'

MANAGER

0115 946 1017 *Derwent Mouth to Beeston,*
and the Nottingham Canal

01636 704481 *Trent Bridge northwards*

MILEAGE

DERWENT MOUTH to
Cranfleet Lock: 2³/₄ miles
Beeston Lock: 7 miles
Meadow Lane Lock, Nottingham: 12 miles
Gunthorpe Bridge: 22 miles
Fiskerton: 29³/₄ miles
Newark Castle: 35¹/₂ miles
Cromwell Lock: 40¹/₂ miles
Dunham Bridge: 53 miles
TORKSEY Junction: 57 miles
Littleborough: 60¹/₂ miles
GAINSBOROUGH Bridge: 67 miles
WEST STOCKWITH: 71³/₄ miles
KEADBY Junction: 84¹/₄ miles
TRENT FALLS: 93³/₄ miles

Locks: 12

The River Trent is a historic highway running for about 100 miles from the Midlands to the Humber ports and the North Sea and has long been of prime economic and social importance to the areas through which it flows. It is thought that as long ago as the Bronze Age the Trent was part of the trade route from the Continent to the metal-working industry in Ireland. The Romans recognised the value of the river as a route to the centre of England from the sea. In about AD 120, in the time of Emperor Hadrian, they built the Foss Dyke canal to link the Trent valley with Lindum Colonia (now Lincoln), the River Witham and the Wash. The Trent later acted as an easy route for the Danish invaders, who penetrated as far as Nottingham. In about AD 924 Edward the Elder expelled the Danes from Nottingham and built the first bridge there. The second bridge at Nottingham was built in 1156 (some 20 years earlier than Old London Bridge) and lasted 714 years. Its remains can still be seen. The third bridge was built in 1871 and forms the basic structure of today's Trent Bridge. The first Act of Parliament to improve the Trent as a navigation was passed in 1699. In 1783 an Act authorised the construction of a towpath, thus allowing for the first time the passage of sail-less barges. Ten years later the Trent Navigation Company's engineer drew up a comprehensive scheme to build locks and weirs, to increase the depth in certain reaches and build a number of training walls to narrow and thus deepen the channel. In 1906, the Royal Commission on Inland Waterways adopted it as the official future plan, authorising locks at Stoke Bardolph, Gunthorpe, Hazleford and Cromwell. The works were completed in 1926. Trade soon increased fourfold.

At its peak in the 19thC and early 20thC, the Trent formed the main artery of trade for the East Midlands, connecting with the South Yorkshire Navigations, the Chesterfield Canal, the Fossdyke, the Grantham Canal, the Erewash Canal, the River Soar Navigation and the Trent & Mersey Canal. Although it remains connected today to all but the Grantham Canal, the large trade between these waterways had dwindled away with railway competition and in particular as a result of railway ownership of most of those connecting waterways. Today most of the commercial carrying is from gravel pits at Besthorpe, Girton and Rampton to Hull, Goole and Whitwood.

The Trent remains a useful through route for pleasure craft, easy to navigate and with many interesting connections. British Waterways has improved facilities for pleasure craft with landing stages at locks, moorings and easier lock operating systems.

Thrumpton

Downstream from Derwent Mouth (see books 3 and 4), the navigation goes through Sawley Cut, avoiding the weir to the north, by the M1 bridge. Near the head of the Cut is a flood lock, which under most conditions is open. Beyond this lock and the main road bridge is a wide stretch of waterway, where both banks are crowded with moored boats. Just at the tail of Sawley Locks (a pair – one manual, one mechanised with a keeper – 0115 973 5234) is a large railway bridge over the river; this line carries oil and coal trains to Castle Donington and Willington Power Stations. To the east the cooling towers of the huge Ratcliffe Power Station are clearly visible, but they are discreetly tucked away behind Red Hill and their intrusion into the landscape is thus minimised. Trent Lock marks the junction of the Erewash Canal with the River Trent, while at the wooded Red Hill is the mouth of the River Soar. It is important not to get lost here, for there is a large weir just downstream of the railway bridges. Boats aiming for Nottingham should bear left at the big sailing club house, entering Cranfleet Cut. A pair of protective flood gates will be passed, then another railway bridge (the line disappearing into the decorative tunnel through Red Hill), another long line of moored motor cruisers (many belonging to the Nottingham Yacht Club) and an attractive white accommodation bridge. At the end of the Cut is Cranfleet Lock; from here one may enjoy a view of the woods hiding Thrumpton Park. The old lockhouse at Cranfleet is now the headquarters of the Nottingham Yacht Club. Steep wooded slopes rise behind Thrumpton, while the towers of the power station still overlook the whole scene. Below Thrumpton, the river winds through flat land, passing the village of Barton in Fabis.

Pubs and Restaurants

◖ ✕ **Chandlery Restaurant** Sawley Marina (0115 973 4278). Part of the marina complex this new pub serves food *all day, every day,* specialising in large portions of predictable Italian fare at low prices.

◖ **Plank & Leggit** Tamworth Road, Sawley (0115 972 1515). A new pub 200 yds south of Sawley Cut, behind the marina, serving Courage, Mansfield, Marston's, Theakston and guest real ales. A wide ranging, inexpensive menu, majoring on healthy eating, is available *all day* as are inexpensive children's and special menus (wide vegetarian choice). Indoor and outdoor children's play areas, outside seating and summer barbeques. Dogs welcome on outdoor patio area.

◖ ✕ **Harrington Arms** Sawley (0115 973 2614). North of the flood lock. Hardys & Hansons real ales and inexpensive bar and restaurant meals served *lunchtimes and evenings* in this cosy, 400-year-old coaching inn. Traditional *Sunday lunch;* children and vegetarians catered for. Outside seating. B & B.

◖ **Nag's Head** Sawley (0115 973 2983). North of the Flood Lock. Marston's real ale and *lunchtime* sandwiches. Children welcome, outside seating.

◖ ✕ **White Lion** Sawley (0115 973 3961). North of the flood lock. Marston's real ale and food available *lunchtimes and evenings.* Children and vegetarians catered for. Outside seating. Traditional pub games.

◖ **Navigation Inn** Trent Lock (0115 973 2984). Large, popular, family pub with a garden and play area. Home, Marston's and guest real ales. Wide range of reasonably priced food available *lunchtimes and evenings, 7 days a week.* Vegetarians catered for. Moorings.

◖ **Steamboat Inn** Trent Lock, on the Erewash Canal (0115 946 3955). Built by the canal company in 1791, when it was called the Erewash Navigation Inn, it is now a busy and popular venue. The bars have been handsomely restored and decorated with suitably nautical objects. Theakston, Marston's, Morland and guest real ales. Bar meals available *lunchtimes and evenings (not Sun evenings).* Garden, animal farm and children's playground. Quiz *Mon.* Attached to the pub is Trattoria il Nautica.

● **Sawley**
Notts. PO, tel, stores, garage. The tall church spire attracts one across the river to Sawley, and in this respect the promise is fulfilled, for the medieval church is beautiful and is approached by a formal avenue of lime trees leading to the 600-year-old doorway. Otherwise Sawley is an uninteresting main road village on the outskirts of Long Eaton.

● **Sawley Cut**
In addition to a large marina and a well-patronised BW mooring site, the Derby Motor Boat Club have a base on the Sawley Cut. All kinds of boats are represented here: canal boats, river boats and even sea-going vessels. It is certainly no place to be passing through on a summer Sunday late-afternoon, for there will be scores of craft queuing up to pass through the locks after spending the weekend downstream. There are windlasses for sale at Sawley Lock, as well as the more conventional facilities.

● **Trent Lock**
A busy and unusual boating centre at the southern terminus of the Erewash Canal (see book 3).

a dead end. Motorists only go there if they have good reason to. Hence Thrumpton is a quiet and unspoilt farming village, with new development only up at the far end. Although the impressive Hall is hidden away at the west end of the village, its large uncompromising gateway serves to remind the villagers what they are there for. The tiny church, with its narrow nave and a tower, was built in the 13thC but restored in 1872 by the well-known architect G.E. Street, at the expense of Lady Byron. The single street winds past it down to the river – there used to be a ferry here.

Thrumpton Hall Basically a James I mansion built around a much older manor house. The Hall is famous for its oak staircase, which dates from the time of Charles II. The ground floor rooms are well-used, and elegantly decorated; the grounds are delightful,

There are two boatyards and two pubs here, together with the Waterway Office (0115 946 1017), who can also be contacted during office hours on Marine VHF – call sign Trent Base.

● **Thrumpton**
Notts. PO, tel. This little village beside the Trent is, like so many other places on the river,

encompassing a backwater off the River Trent. The house is private.

● **Barton in Fabis**
Notts. Tel. A small and isolated village, composed mainly of modern housing and set well back from the river. The 14th-C church seems unbalanced in several respects; it has a great variety of styles. The building has, however, considerable charm; it is light, and attractively irregular. It contains several monuments to the Sacheverell family.

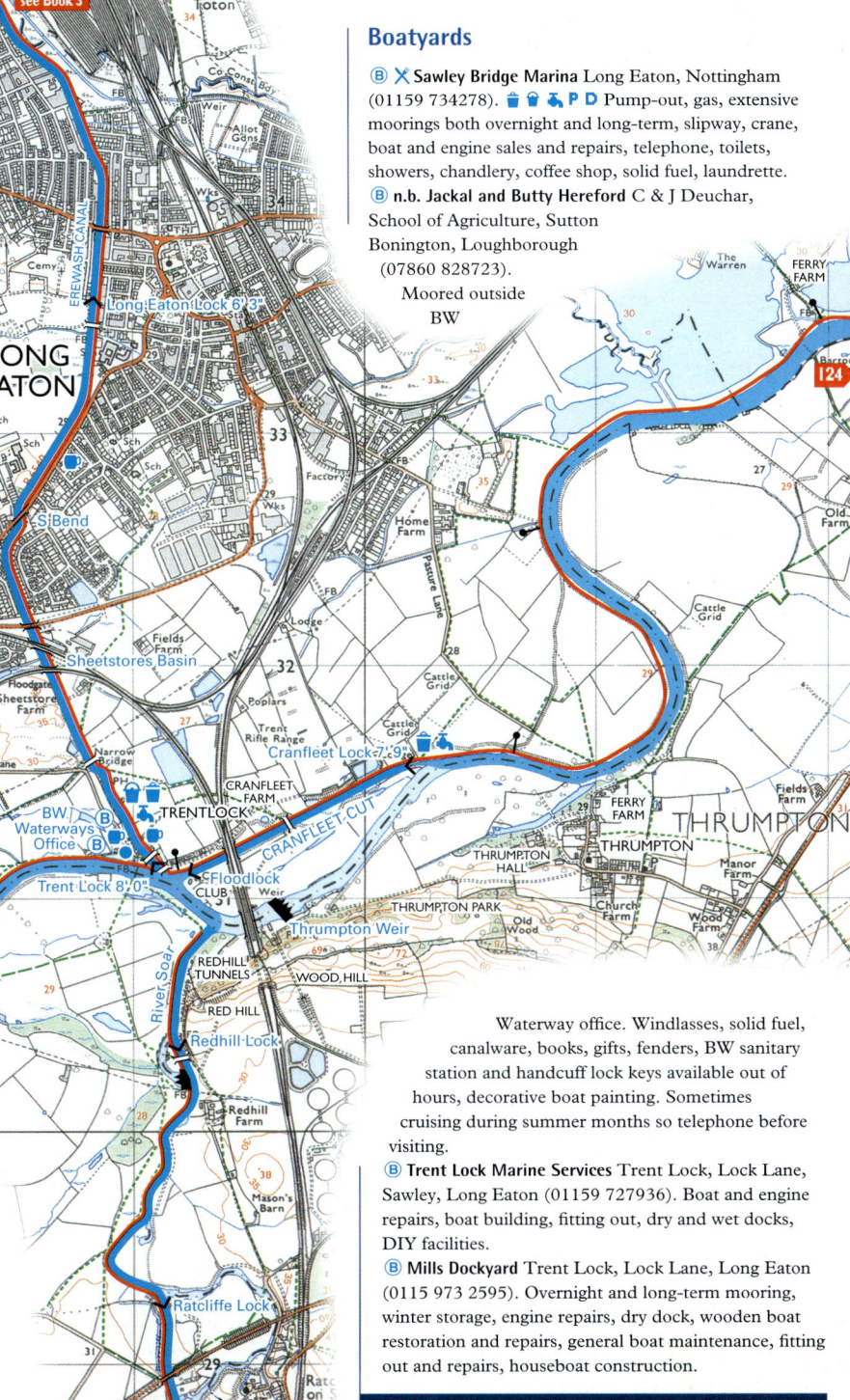

Boatyards

Ⓑ ✕ **Sawley Bridge Marina** Long Eaton, Nottingham (01159 734278). 🚽 🛢 ⚓ P D Pump-out, gas, extensive moorings both overnight and long-term, slipway, crane, boat and engine sales and repairs, telephone, toilets, showers, chandlery, coffee shop, solid fuel, laundrette.

Ⓑ **n.b. Jackal and Butty Hereford** C & J Deuchar, School of Agriculture, Sutton Bonington, Loughborough (07860 828723).

Moored outside BW

Waterway office. Windlasses, solid fuel, canalware, books, gifts, fenders, BW sanitary station and handcuff lock keys available out of hours, decorative boat painting. Sometimes cruising during summer months so telephone before visiting.

Ⓑ **Trent Lock Marine Services** Trent Lock, Lock Lane, Sawley, Long Eaton (01159 727936). Boat and engine repairs, boat building, fitting out, dry and wet docks, DIY facilities.

Ⓑ **Mills Dockyard** Trent Lock, Lock Lane, Long Eaton (0115 973 2595). Overnight and long-term mooring, winter storage, engine repairs, dry dock, wooden boat restoration and repairs, general boat maintenance, fitting out and repairs, houseboat construction.

Nottingham

The river winds on towards Nottingham passing the picturesque Barton Island (keep to the west of it), the old gravel pits of the Attenborough Nature Reserve and many sailing boats; this is clearly a popular stretch of the river. To the south runs a ridge of hills on which stands Clifton Hall. At the marina you should keep to the north side of the river to avoid the weir and enter Beeston Lock (where there are showers). This introduces the Beeston Canal or Beeston Cut which bypasses an unnavigable section of the River Trent. The canal passes first a housing estate and then Boots Estate, followed by Players' Horizon Factory designed by Arup Associates. East of the A52 bridge, the canal passes Lenton Chain. This marks the end of the short Beeston Canal for at this point the Nottingham Canal used to flow in from the north. The junction was called Lenton

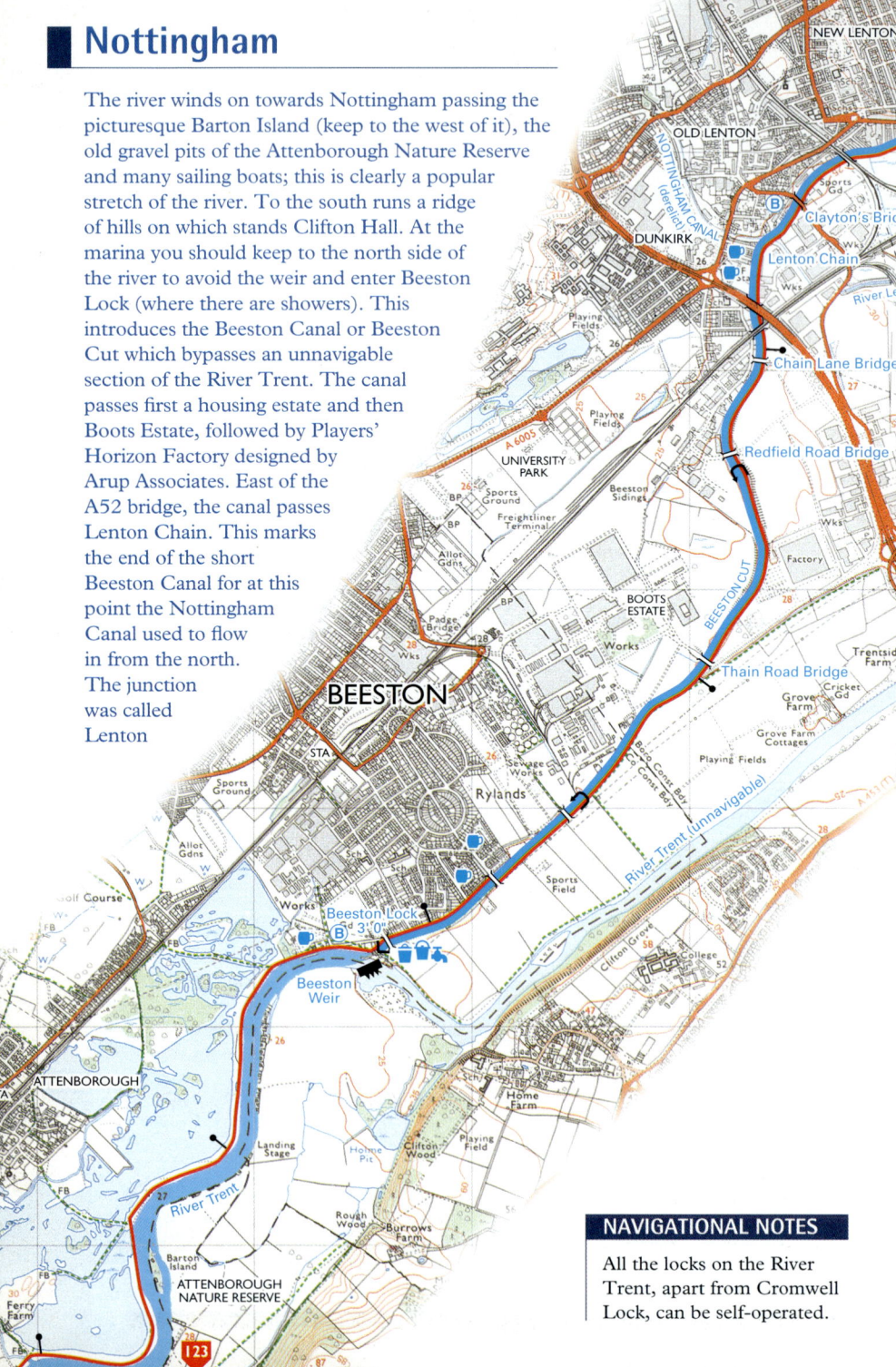

NAVIGATIONAL NOTES

All the locks on the River Trent, apart from Cromwell Lock, can be self-operated.

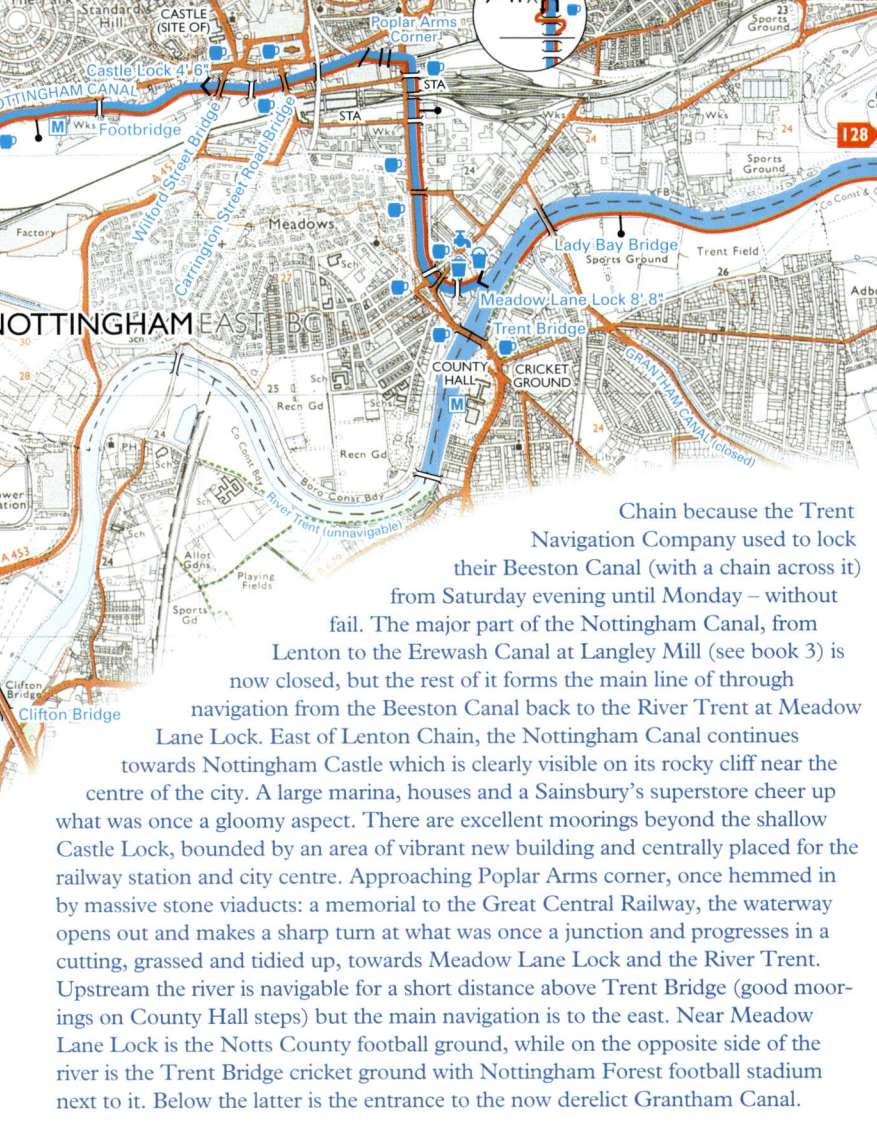

Chain because the Trent Navigation Company used to lock their Beeston Canal (with a chain across it) from Saturday evening until Monday – without fail. The major part of the Nottingham Canal, from Lenton to the Erewash Canal at Langley Mill (see book 3) is now closed, but the rest of it forms the main line of through navigation from the Beeston Canal back to the River Trent at Meadow Lane Lock. East of Lenton Chain, the Nottingham Canal continues towards Nottingham Castle which is clearly visible on its rocky cliff near the centre of the city. A large marina, houses and a Sainsbury's superstore cheer up what was once a gloomy aspect. There are excellent moorings beyond the shallow Castle Lock, bounded by an area of vibrant new building and centrally placed for the railway station and city centre. Approaching Poplar Arms corner, once hemmed in by massive stone viaducts: a memorial to the Great Central Railway, the waterway opens out and makes a sharp turn at what was once a junction and progresses in a cutting, grassed and tidied up, towards Meadow Lane Lock and the River Trent. Upstream the river is navigable for a short distance above Trent Bridge (good moorings on County Hall steps) but the main navigation is to the east. Near Meadow Lane Lock is the Notts County football ground, while on the opposite side of the river is the Trent Bridge cricket ground with Nottingham Forest football stadium next to it. Below the latter is the entrance to the now derelict Grantham Canal.

Boatyards

Ⓑ **Beeston Marina** Riverside, Beeston (0115 922 3168). 🚿 🚽 ♿ P D E Pump-out, gas, overnight mooring, long-term mooring, winter storage, slipway, 7 tonne crane, dry dock, chandlery, boat building, boat sales, engine sales and repairs, books, maps and gifts, groceries, toilets, showers, coffee shop, telephone. Also the Riverside Bar offering weekend entertainment.

Ⓑ **Trevethicks Boatyard** Lenton Chain, Nottingham (0115 978 3467). Boat building, boat and engine repairs, welding, dry dock, boat restoration, painting and sign writing.

Ⓑ **Nottingham Castle Marina** Nottingham (0115 941 2672). 🚿 🚽 ♿ D E Pump-out, gas, overnight mooring, long-term mooring, winter storage, slipway, chandlery, books, maps and gifts, boat sales, engine sales and repairs, solid fuel. telephone, toilets, laundrette and drying room. *24 hour* emergency call-out.

● **Attenborough Nature Reserve** Long Lane, Attenborough, Beeston (0115 922 1221). Worked out gravel pits, once derelict and unsightly, are now providing an interesting habitat for plant and animal life. There are comprehensive nature trails and a wooden observation hide. Now an SSSI. *Open during daylight hours.* Free.

● **Beeston Lock**
Nottingham (0115 925 4946). A splendidly kept lock where facilities are available for boats. The pretty cottages and the little backwater off the canal are a hint of its past importance; until some years ago there used to be a lock down into the river here, at right angles to the present lock. The river channel used to be navigable – by shallow-draft vessels – from here down to Trent Bridge, the Beeston Canal being cut to connect with the Nottingham Canal and to afford access into the middle of the town. But now the river is unnavigable as a through route and the canal is the only way.

● **Nottingham**
Notts. All services. The city's prosperity derives largely from the coal field to the north, and the long-established lace industry. John Player & Son make all their cigarettes here and Raleigh Industries turn out bicycles for the world. The city centre is busy and not unattractive – there is an imposing town hall in Slab Square – but little of the architecture is of note. Modern developments are encouraging, however, notably the superb Playhouse Theatre and the appearance of a variety of theme festivals spread throughout the year.
Angel Row Gallery Central Library Building, 3 Angel Row, Nottingham (0115 915 2869). The region's leading contemporary art and craft gallery. *Open Mon–Fri 10.00–18.00 (Wed 19.00). Closed B.Hols.* Free. Full disabled access.
Brewhouse Yard Museum Castle Boulevard, Nottingham (0115 915 3600). Re-created shops, period rooms and a shopping street from between the wars. *Open 10.00-16.00, otherwise admission details as per Nottingham Castle and the Museum and Art Gallery.* Limited disabled access.
Explorer Pass – one ticket, valid for a year, is available offering reduced admission charges to some of the attractions listed below. Available from the Tourist Information Centre or from one of the participating attractions.
Caves of Nottingham Drury Walk, Broadmarsh Shopping Centre (0115 924 1424). A unique honeycomb of caves explored on a self-conducted audio tour. *Open Mon–Sat 10.00–16.15, Sun 11.00-16.00. Closed 24-26 Dec & 1 Jan.* Charge.
Condemned! . . . At The Galleries of Justice Shire Hall, High Pavement, Lace Market, Nottingham (0115 952 0555). A major new crime and punishment experience. Visitors assume the identity of real 19th-C criminals, take part in a trial, visit the cells and finally the gallows New civil law and

children's activity centres. *Open Tue-Sun and B.Hols 10.00-17.00. Closed 24-26 Dec & 1 Jan. Last admission 1 hour before closing.* Charge. Disabled access.
Malt Cross Music Hall St James's Street, Nottingham (0115 941 1048). Next to the Old Market Square. Delightful little traditional music hall built in 1877 and one of the few surviving examples. Beautifully restored, including a wonderful glazed roof, it is open during the day and evening offering the opportunity to soak up the atmosphere of a bygone era. Evening entertainment to suit all tastes together with good food and real ales to suit all palates. *Open Mon–Sat from 10.00.* Free, but sometimes a modest charge for evening entertainments.
Museum of Costume and Textiles 51 Castle Gate, Nottingham (0115 915 3500). Nicely presented displays of 19th- and 20th-C costume in authentic, period settings. The unique Eyre Map tapestries of Nottinghamshire, textiles and fashion accessories. *Open Wed-Sun and B.Hols 10.00-16.00.* Free. Limited disabled access.
Museum of Nottingham Lace 3-5 HighPavement, The Lace Market, Nottingham (0115 989 7365). A fascinating new museum telling the story of lace from cottage craft through to the high-tech industry of today. A glimpse of life 100 years ago, live demonstrations, videos and an audio-guided tour. Also a lace shop and a coffee shop with, of course, lace tablecloths. *Open daily (inc B.Hols) 10.00-17.00. Closed Xmas & Box.* Charge for museum. Lace Market Visitor Centre free.
Nottingham Castle Nottingham (0115 915 3700). William the Conqueror's castle, which was notorious as the base of Robin Hood's unfortunate enemies while King Richard I was away crusading, has been destroyed and rebuilt many times during its tumultuous history. (It was a Yorkist stronghold in the Wars of the Roses and it was here that Charles I raised his standard in 1642, starting the Civil War.) Though the original secret caves beneath the castle still exist and can be visited on a guided tour, the present building dates only from 1674. It now houses the city's **Museum and Art Gallery** which includes fine displays of English pottery, silver and glass together with a collection of 17th-, 18th- and 19th-C paintings by artists including Rosetti, Le Brun and Nottingham artists Bonington and Sandby. Also the exciting interactive Circle of Life gallery. Café. *Open daily 10.00–17.00. Closed Xmas Day & B. Day, & Fri Nov-Feb.* Free, except weekends & B. Hols. Charge for caves tour. Disabled access except caves.
Nottingham Goose Fair The Goose Fair is now a conventional funfair but on a gigantic scale. It features traditional entertainments like boxing bouts (challengers invited to fight the house champ) as well as the usual mechanical fairground delights. The fair's original site was in the

town centre but now it is out on the Forest Recreation Ground, a mile to the north east (served by buses). The fair takes place in the *first week of Oct* and it is advisable to get there before the Saturday, when the prices are doubled.

Tales of Robin Hood Maid Marian Way, Nottingham (0115 948 3284). A 700-year adventure trip back into the sights, sounds and smells of history. Shoot the sheriff and search for Robin's true identity. Shop. *Open daily 10.00–18.00. Closed Xmas day & Box.* Charge. Disabled access.

Tourist Information Centre 1-4 Smithy Row, Nottingham (0115 915 5330).

● **Grantham Canal**
A long-disused but delightful canal from Trent Bridge, Nottingham, to Grantham. The canal was built purely to serve the agricultural communities of eastern Nottinghamshire, so it pursues a remarkably circuitous course through pleasant farmland, including the Vale of Belvoir (pronounced beever). Belvoir Castle, seat of the Duke of Rutland, is only about a mile from the canal at one point. A tramway was constructed to connect them in order to carry coal up to the castle using wagons drawn by horses. Traces can still be seen of this, one of Nottinghamshire's earliest railways. The Grantham Canal still feeds water down from secluded reservoirs at Knipton and Denton to the Trent. There are well-advanced plans for its complete restoration and re-connection to the River Trent. Details from 76 St Michael's Avenue, Gedling, Nottingham NG4 3PE (0115 953 1153). Also contact BW Trent Lock (0115 946 1017) for restoration information.

Pubs and Restaurants

🍺 **Jolly Anglers** Meadow Road, Beeston (0115 925 6497). North of Beeston Lock. Large pub with two comfortable lounges. Home and Theakston real ales and *lunchtime* food. Snacks only available *Sat & Sun.* Children's meals and play area.

🍺 **Boat & Horses** Trent Road, Beeston (0115 925 8589). North of Beeston Lock. Once a change-over station for barge horses. Fine traditional pub serving Home, Theakston and guest real ales. Traditional and inexpensive pub food always available. Quiz *Thur,* disco *Fri* and live entertainment *Sat.* Pub games.

🍺 **Johnsons Arms** Abbey Street, Nottingham (0115 978 6355). West of Lenton Chain. Friendly Shipstone's and Tetley's real ale establishment run by a landlord of the same name. No frills, student pub with log fires. Filled rolls available *lunchtimes and evenings.* Quiz *Wed.*

🍺 **Boat Inn** Priory Road, Nottingham (0115 978 6482). West of Lenton Chain. Theakston, Hook Norton and Home real ales in a single-bar pub. *Lunchtime* bar snacks. Quiz *Thur & Sun.*

🍺 ✗ **Boat House** Nottingham (0115 947 3419). Beefeater establishment with a surprising selection of real ales including Boddingtons, Flowers, Castle Eden, Whitbread (Fuggles), Marston's and guests. Not unattractive nautical decoration and Beefeater Fayre available *lunchtimes and evenings and all day Sat & Sun.* Quiz *Wed.*

🍺 **Navigation** 6 Wilford Street, Nottingham (0115 941 7139). Canalside by Castle Lock. Banks's, Camerons and Marston's real ales in a tastefully refurbished pub displaying a variety of canal memorabilia. *Lunchtime* bar food (*not Sun),* canalside seating and mooring below the lock. Children over 14 only.

🍺 **Trip to Jerusalem** 1 Brewhouse Yard, Castle Road, Nottingham (0115 947 3171). Set into the cliff face below the Castle, this is allegedly the oldest pub in England and is not without atmosphere. Hardys & Hansons and Marston's real ales together with *lunchtime* food served from an extensive menu *11.00–18.00.* Outside seating and storytelling *second Tue in month.* Pub games and B & B.

🍺 **F.M.C.** Canal Street, Nottingham (0115 950 6795). Next door to the Waterways Museum in the old Fellows, Morton & Clayton warehouse, this pub has its own real ale brewed around the back, plus Castle Eden, Boddingtons and Timothy Taylor real ales together with five guests. Restaurant for *lunchtime* meals adjoining. Outside seating and quiz *Sun.*

🍺 **Aviary** Trent Bridge, Nottingham (0115 986 1830). Young people's pub serving Boddingtons, Flowers, Morland and Marston's real ales. Bar food available *lunchtimes and evenings, 7 days a week.* Children and vegetarians catered for. Garden. Disco *every evening.*

🍺 **Sportsman** Trent Bridge, Nottingham (0115 927 5020). Hardys & Hansons real ale in a pub popular with football supporters. Family room and children's play area. Disabled access.

🍺 **T.B.I.** Trent Bridge, Nottingham (0115 982 2786). Large pub near the cricket ground. Ind Coope (Burton), Tetley's and Marston's real ales together with *lunchtime* bar meals (*not Sat).* Outside seating, no children. Disco *Fri* and live bands *Sun.*

Stoke Bardolph

Downstream from the railway bridge, the wide river soon leaves Nottingham behind and enters pleasant countryside. On the north bank are many boating centres and the Colwick racecourse. On the south side an exploration of the landscaped area will reveal the magnificent rowing course at Holme Pierrepont. Downstream are Holme Lock and sluices; the lock is on the south side (0115 981 1197). This section serves to establish the Trent's attractive rural character as it continues to sweep along through Nottinghamshire. Passing under a railway bridge (the Nottingham-Grantham line), one sees a very steep escarpment of tree-covered hills, effectively cliffs, rising out of the water. Radcliffe on Trent is concealed in the woods by the bend, but access is difficult. It is better to move on, down to the delightfully secluded Stoke Bardolph Lock (0115 987 8563), where there is a water point. The lock island is covered with trees. Below the lock, the river bends northwards and crosses over to the other side of the valley, leaving behind the woods and cliffs. At Burton Joyce the river rebounds from the side of the valley and turns east again. The water meadows that accompany the river serve to keep at bay any inroads by modern housing.

Pubs and Restaurants

🍺 **Manvers Arms** Radcliffe (0115 933 2404). Tetley's and Shipstone's real ales together with traditional pub food available *lunchtimes and evenings (not Sun evenings)*. Children's play area and beer garden. Pub games and quiz *Sun*.

🍺 **Royal Oak** Radcliffe (0115 933 3798). Cosy, village local dispensing Marston's, Morland, Timothy Taylor, Boddingtons, Castle Eden and guest real ales. Good bar food available *lunchtimes (daily) and evenings (Wed-Sun)*. Vegetarians and children catered for. Outside seating and real fires.

🍺 **Ferry Boat Inn** Stoke Bardolph (0115 987 1232). Riverside.

Good temporary mooring (ask permission). Shipstone's, Tetley's, Greenalls and guest real ales. Bar food available *all day, 7 days a week*. Large heated courtyard popular with families; indoor and outdoor children's play areas. *Tue* quiz.

🍺 **Earl of Chesterfield** Shelford (0115 933 2227). Bass real ale. Bar snacks available *lunchtimes (not Sun)*. Children welcome, outside seating.

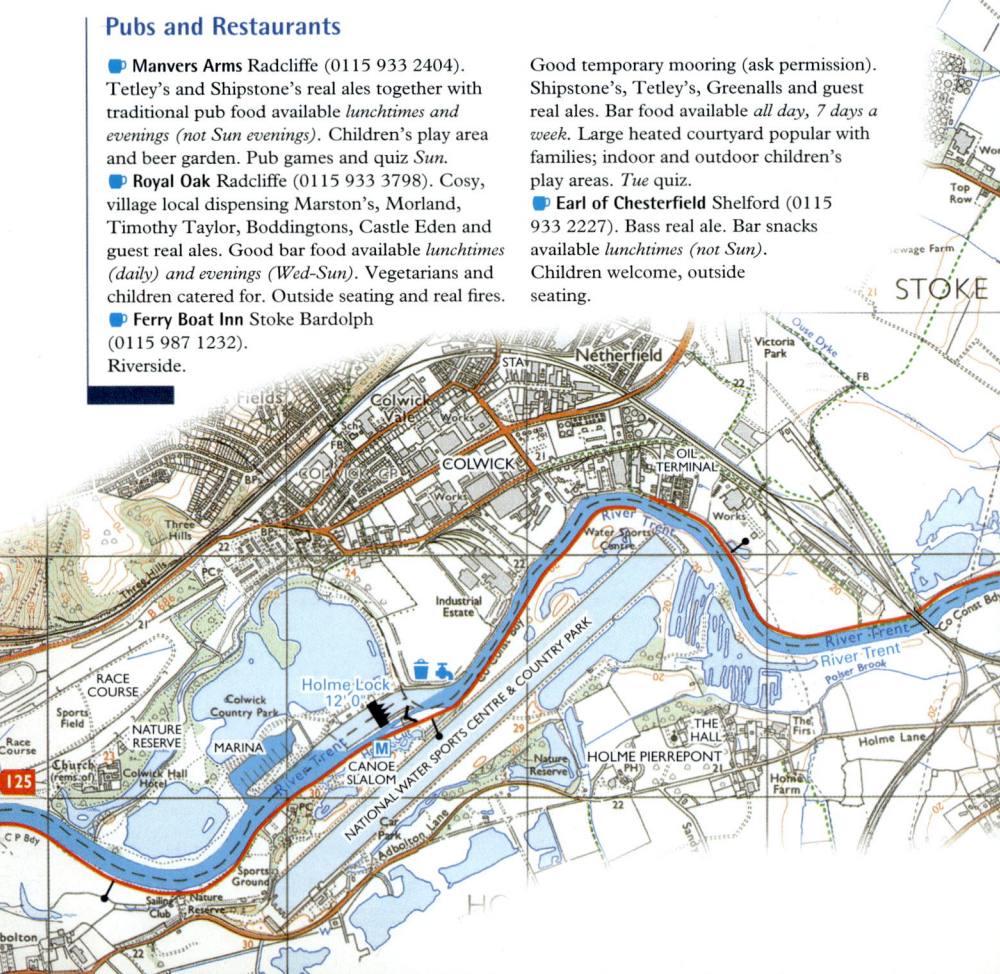

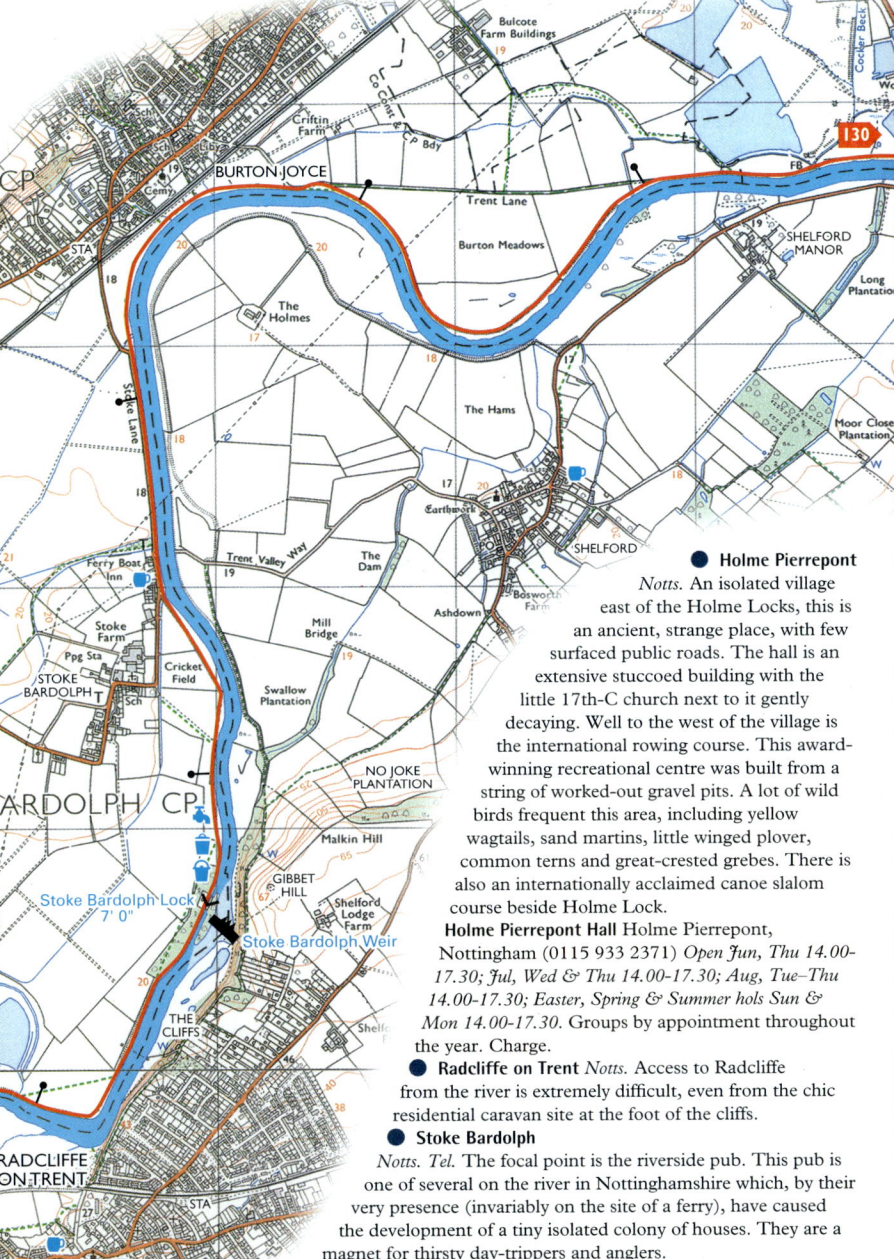

● **Holme Pierrepont**
Notts. An isolated village east of the Holme Locks, this is an ancient, strange place, with few surfaced public roads. The hall is an extensive stuccoed building with the little 17th-C church next to it gently decaying. Well to the west of the village is the international rowing course. This award-winning recreational centre was built from a string of worked-out gravel pits. A lot of wild birds frequent this area, including yellow wagtails, sand martins, little winged plover, common terns and great-crested grebes. There is also an internationally acclaimed canoe slalom course beside Holme Lock.

Holme Pierrepont Hall Holme Pierrepont, Nottingham (0115 933 2371) *Open Jun, Thu 14.00-17.30; Jul, Wed & Thu 14.00-17.30; Aug, Tue–Thu 14.00-17.30; Easter, Spring & Summer hols Sun & Mon 14.00-17.30.* Groups by appointment throughout the year. Charge.

● **Radcliffe on Trent** *Notts.* Access to Radcliffe from the river is extremely difficult, even from the chic residential caravan site at the foot of the cliffs.

● **Stoke Bardolph**
Notts. Tel. The focal point is the riverside pub. This pub is one of several on the river in Nottinghamshire which, by their very presence (invariably on the site of a ferry), have caused the development of a tiny isolated colony of houses. They are a magnet for thirsty day-trippers and anglers.

● **Burton Joyce**
Notts. All services. A long village extending along the A612. There is a railway station by the river (Nottingham-Lincoln line).

● **Shelford**
Notts. Tel. A flood bank protects this quiet and isolated village from the Trent. The old church has a wide Perpendicular tower which commands the Trent valley. There is a pub, but there is no obvious mooring place for boats to be left on the river.

Hoveringham

This is a stretch in which the presence of big old riverside pubs has far more effect on the river scene than do the villages that they represent. Passing Shelford Manor, one arrives at the sleek arches of Gunthorpe Bridge – the only road bridge over the river in the 24 miles between Nottingham and Newark. To the east of the bridge are the grand houses up on the hills of East Bridgford. Boats heading downstream should keep left to enter the mechanised Gunthorpe Lock (0115 966 3821) and avoid the foaming weir. On the west bank, just below the bridge, there is a BW mooring pontoon together with a full range of facilities including showers. The next 5 or 6 miles below Gunthorpe are probably the most beautiful and certainly the most dramatic on the whole river. On the east side, the wooded cliffs rise almost sheer from the flat valley floor to a height of 200ft, allowing here or there the presence of a strip of fertile land on which cattle graze. Only at two places does a track manage to creep down the perilous slope to the river; otherwise, access is impossible. On the west side, by contrast, the ground is flat for miles, across to the other side of the valley. The river continues along its superb isolated course, with the forested cliffs of the Trent Hills striding along the river's east bank, while on the other side the flat plain of the valley rolls away through green

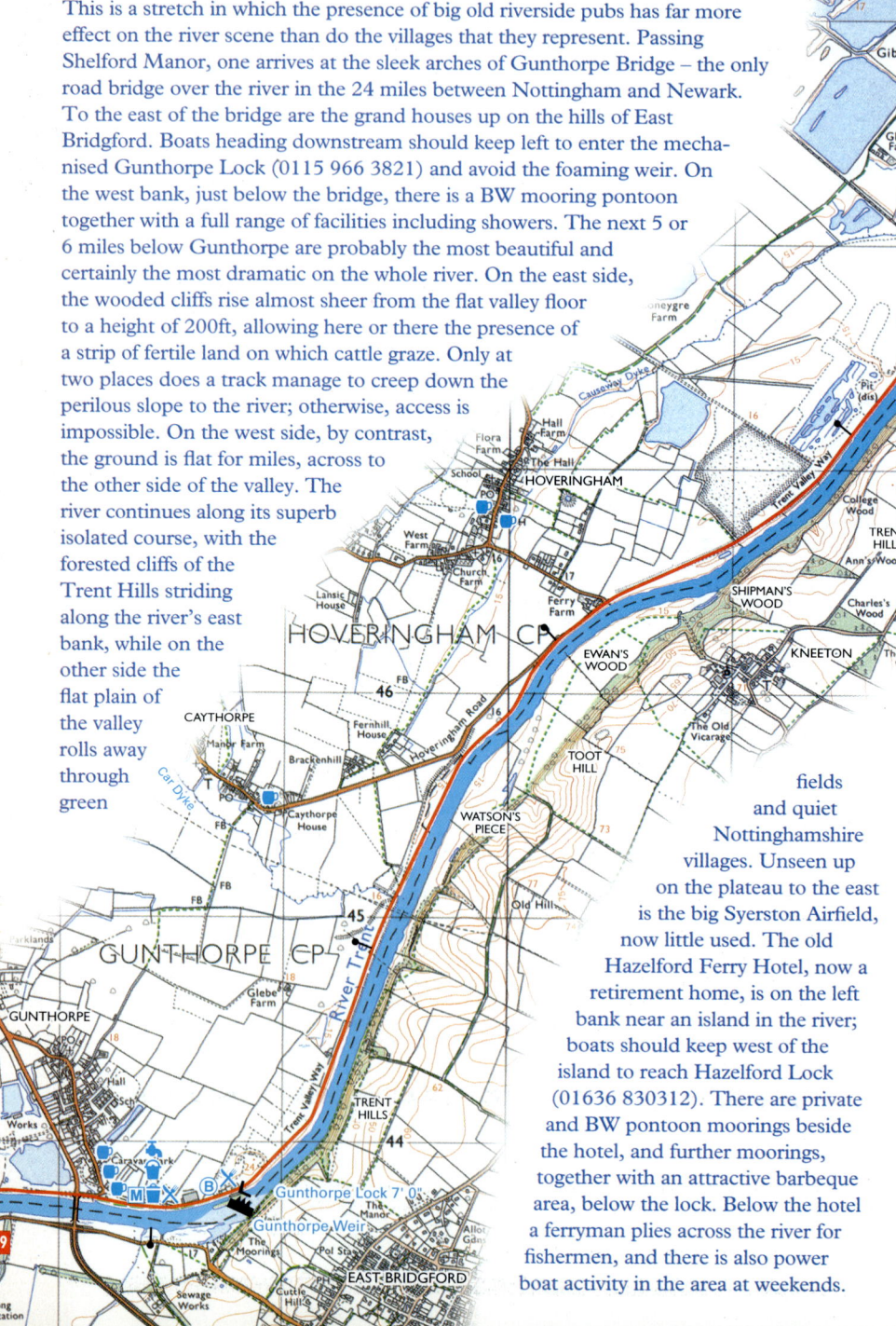

fields and quiet Nottinghamshire villages. Unseen up on the plateau to the east is the big Syerston Airfield, now little used. The old Hazelford Ferry Hotel, now a retirement home, is on the left bank near an island in the river; boats should keep west of the island to reach Hazelford Lock (01636 830312). There are private and BW pontoon moorings beside the hotel, and further moorings, together with an attractive barbeque area, below the lock. Below the hotel a ferryman plies across the river for fishermen, and there is also power boat activity in the area at weekends.

● **Shelford Manor** Near the river just west of Gunthorpe Bridge. The old manor was burnt down in 1645 after 2000 Roundheads attacked this Royalist stronghold. They massacred 140 of the 200 men inside. The manor was rebuilt in 1676. *Not open to the public.*

● **Gunthorpe**
Notts. PO, tel, garage. Gunthorpe has been an important river crossing point for over 2000 years. The bridge built in 1875 was replaced by the present one in 1927. Prior to this a ferry operated here. The riverside near the bridge and the pubs is often crowded with motorists and trippers. Speed boats buzz about on certain days when British Waterways relax the speed limit bylaw for particular clubs.

● **East Bridgford**
Notts. PO, tel, stores, garage. Accessible via a pleasant shady lane up the hill from the river. The church is pleasantly light. Rector Oglethorpe, one time incumbent of this parish, crowned Queen Elizabeth I.

Margidunum 1½ miles south east of East Bridgford is the site of Margidunum, a Roman town on the Fosse Way (the straightest road in England). Margidunum was probably located here to guard the ford at East Bridgford.

● **Hoveringham**
Notts. PO, tel, stores, garage. A village intimately linked with the gravel extraction industry.

● **Bleasby**
Notts. PO, tel, stores, station. Gas available at the caravan site between the village and the old Hazelford Ferry Hotel.

Pubs and Restaurants

● **Anchor Inn** Gunthorpe (0115 966 3291). Mansfield, Theakston, Home, Gale's, and Matthew Brown real ales served in this lively riverside pub which is *open all day.* A wide range of bar food available *12.00–21.00, 7 days a week.* Children and vegetarians catered for. Outside seating. Pub games. Quiz *Sun.*

● **Toll House** Gunthorpe (0115 966 3409). Attractive restaurant, serving *Sunday lunch and evening meals, 7 days a week. (Closed Sun & Mon evenings in winter.)* Children and vegetarians catered for. Non-smoking *until 21.30.*

● **Tom Brown's** Gunthorpe (0115 966 3642). A restaurant and bar, serving Home, Theakston and two guest real ales. An imaginative range of excellent food available *lunchtimes and evenings. (Restaurant closed Sun evenings.)* Children and vegetarians catered for. Outside seating.

● **Unicorn Hotel** Gunthorpe (0115 966 3612). Mansfield and guest real ales. A la carte meals *L & D and all day Sun.* Bar food available *at similar times.* Children and vegetarians catered for. Outside seating and quiz *Mon.* B & B. Bar *open all day.*

✕ **Gunthorpe Lock Tearoom** Gunthorpe Lock (0115 966 4283). Set in the old waterways workshops, the tea room is *open daily throughout the summer* serving breakfasts, tea, coffee, locally baked rolls, scones and cakes. *Limited opening during the winter.*

● ✕ **The Reindeer** Hoveringham (0115 966 3629). Marston's and guest real ales. Extensive menu, *served L & D except Mon D.* Pasta nights *Sun & Mon.* Vegetarians and children catered for; outside seating. Worth finding a mooring for.

● **Marquis of Granby** Hoveringham (0115 966 3080). Marston's and interesting guest real ales. *Lunchtime and evening* bar food. A mention of this guide may cause the landlord to reminisce.

● **Wagon & Horses** Bleasby (01636 830283). ½ mile north of Hazelford Ferry. Home, Theakston, Marston's and guest real ales. Inexpensive bar food available *lunchtimes Wed–Sat.* Vegetarians and children catered for. Outside seating and quiz *Sun.* Pub games. Moorings on BW pontoon.

Boatyards

Ⓑ **Trentside Marina** Trentside, Gunthorpe (0115 966 4283). ⚓ **D** Pump-out, gas, narrow boat hire, long-term mooring, winter storage, crane (½ tonne), boat and engine sales, boat and engine repairs (including outboards), boat fitting-out, chandlery, groceries, café, maps, gifts and *24 hour* emergency call-out.

Newark-on-Trent

Beyond Hazleford Lock the steep Trent Hills dwindle away and the river leaves the woods (near the battlefield of East Stoke) for Fiskerton. Downstream of Fiskerton, the river sweeps round past the parkland at Stoke Hall. The site of a 4-acre Roman fort is on the nearby Fosse Way. At Farndon, a pleasant riverside village with sailing clubs on either side and a small ferry, there is a BW mooring pontoon. The boat population is further increased by the use of some old gravel pits just north of Farndon as a mooring site for pleasure boats. Navigators must be especially careful to avoid the large Averham Weir which takes the main channel of the Trent to Kelham and round the north side of Newark. Boats heading downstream should keep right, steering by the 240 foot spire of Newark church. The waterway immediately becomes narrower east of this weir. This is the Newark Branch which takes boats straight into the middle of the town. On the way into Newark, the navigation passes an old windmill, a boatyard at the mouth of the River Devon (pronounced Deevon), some extensive old maltings, and a restored warehouse (now a museum and brasserie) with the words Trent Navigation Company in faded lettering on the side. Opposite is the British Waterways repair yard, followed by Newark Town Lock (01636 702226) and then below is the Waterways Office. Alongside the town lock are the remains of the old lock, half of which is now used as a mooring for pleasure boats while the rest is a covered dry dock. The townscape at this point is dominated by the north west wall of the ruined Newark Castle.

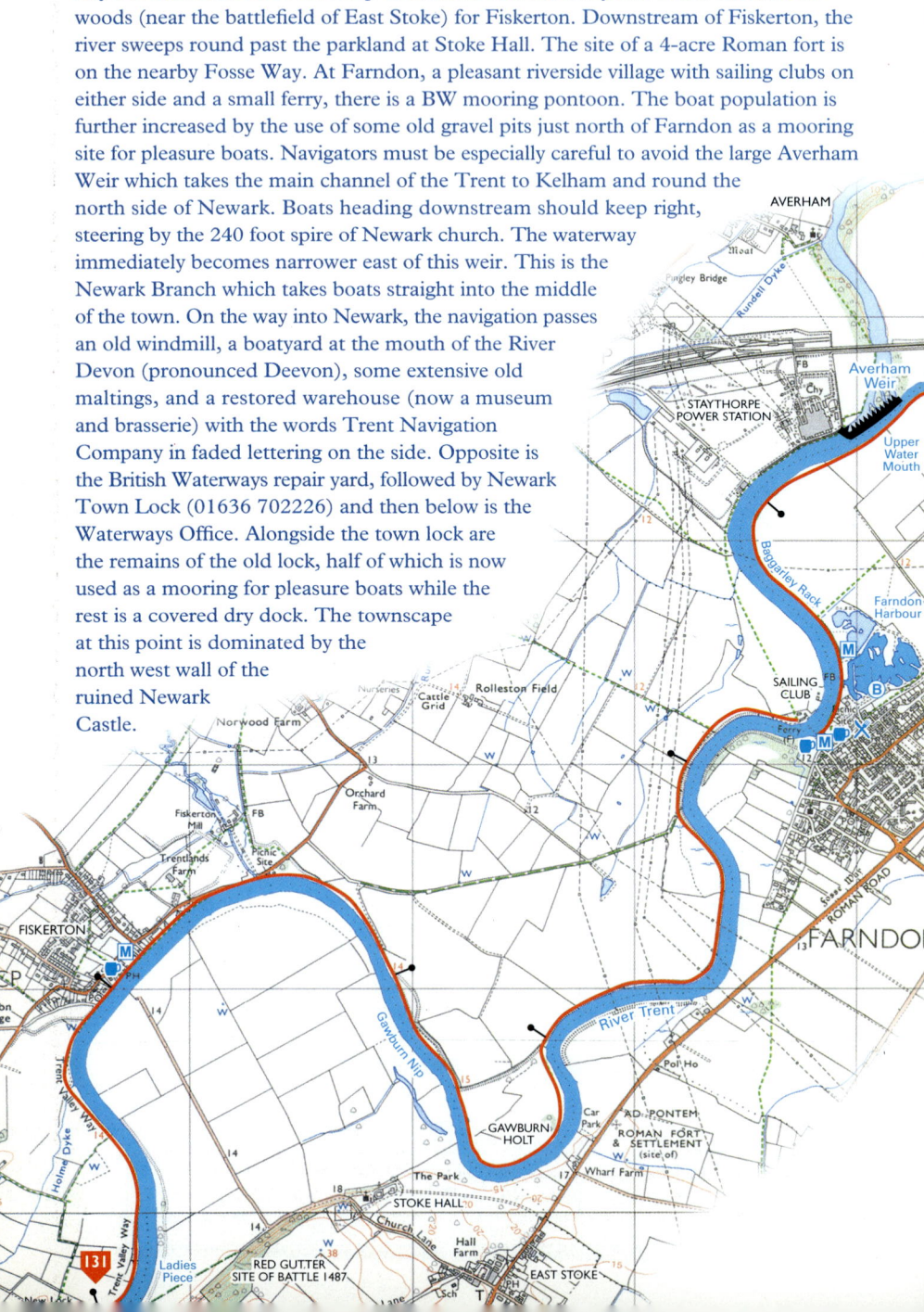

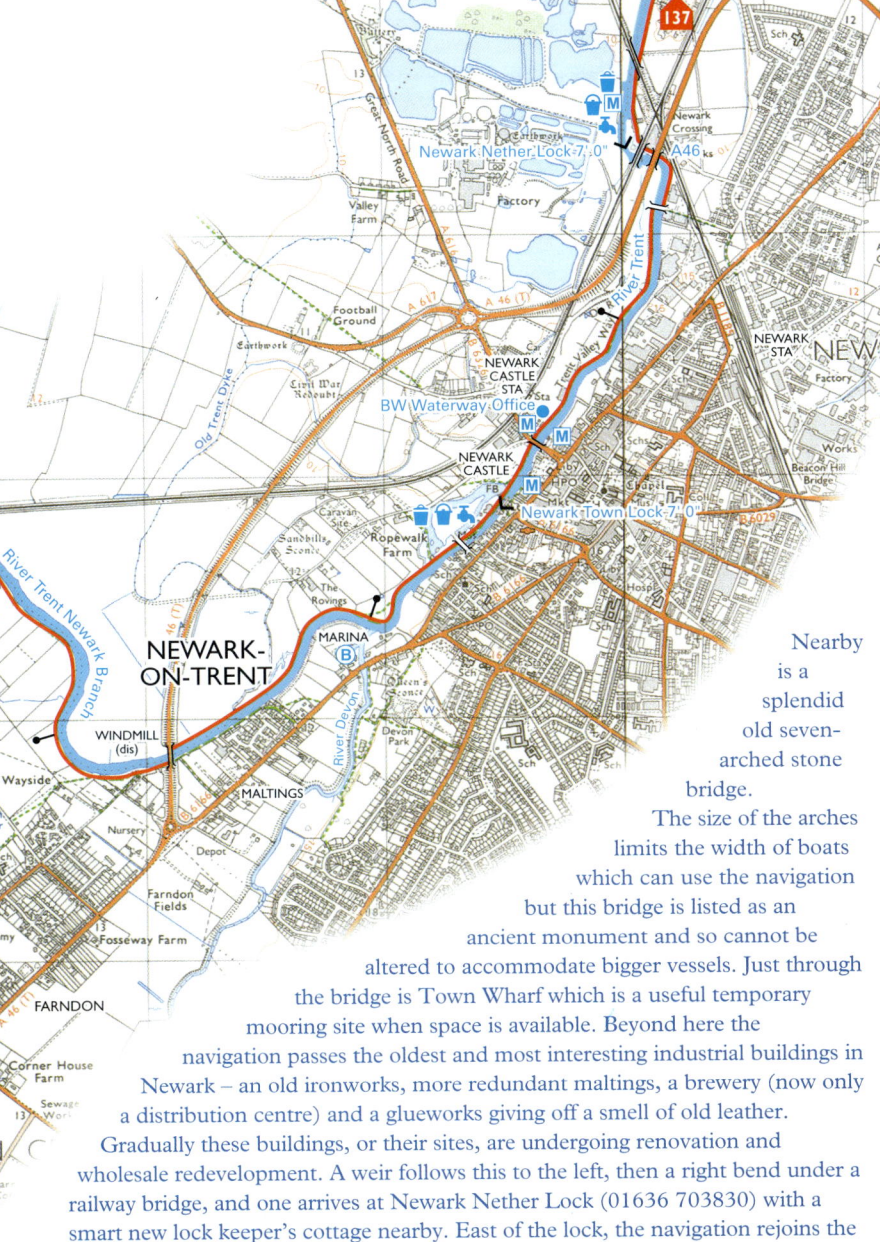

Nearby is a splendid old seven-arched stone bridge. The size of the arches limits the width of boats which can use the navigation but this bridge is listed as an ancient monument and so cannot be altered to accommodate bigger vessels. Just through the bridge is Town Wharf which is a useful temporary mooring site when space is available. Beyond here the navigation passes the oldest and most interesting industrial buildings in Newark – an old ironworks, more redundant maltings, a brewery (now only a distribution centre) and a glueworks giving off a smell of old leather. Gradually these buildings, or their sites, are undergoing renovation and wholesale redevelopment. A weir follows this to the left, then a right bend under a railway bridge, and one arrives at Newark Nether Lock (01636 703830) with a smart new lock keeper's cottage nearby. East of the lock, the navigation rejoins the main channel of the River Trent and proceeds north eastward under the graceful modern road bridge carrying the Newark bypass.

BOAT TRIPS
Newark Line departs from just below Newark Town Lock (01636 706479 or 525246 out of season). Pleasure and charter trips *each weekend Easter–Oct* plus *weekdays during peak periods* on *Sonning* and *River Prince*. Drinks and snacks available. Also jazz cruises, discos and summer barbecues.

● **Fiskerton**

Notts. PO, tel, stores, station. A charming riverside village with excellent access for boats. Although the normal river level is well below the wharf, all the buildings along the splendid front are carefully protected from possible flood by stone walling or a bank of earth.

● **Southwell**

Notts. Three miles north west of Fiskerton, this very attractive country town is well worth visiting in order to see its minster. The minster was founded at the beginning of the 12thC by the Archbishop of York, and is held by many to be one of the most beautiful Norman ecclesiastical buildings in England. Its scale is vast for Southwell, but it is set well back from the houses and is in a slight dip so it does not overawe the town centre, in spite of the two western towers and the massive central tower. Chief among the treasures inside the building are the naturalistic stone carvings in the late 13th-C chapter house, and the wooden carvings of the choir stalls.

● **East Stoke**

Notts. Tel. The village is nearly a mile from the river, and mooring is difficult. The dark and gloomy lane by the church and hall seems to brood on Stoke's violent past: in 1487 the concluding battle in the Wars of the Roses was fought here. Two years after the Battle of Bosworth Field (fought on a site near the Ashby Canal), where Henry Tudor defeated King Richard III and was proclaimed King Henry VII, the Earl of Lincoln set up Lambert Simnel – a ten-year-old lad – as the Earl of Warwick and proclaimed him King Edward VI. (The real Earl of Warwick was in fact locked up in the Tower of London.) With a 9000-strong army, comprising mainly German and Irish mercenaries, the rebels engaged the Crown's army at Stoke Field as the Earl of Oxford led Henry's 12,000 men away from Nottingham. The battle was short but sharp. After three hours most of the rebel leaders were dead and their army in total disarray. This effectively terminated the Wars of the Roses, although the last Yorkist claim to the throne was not extinguished until the real Earl of Warwick was executed in 1499. The appropriately named Red Gutter in Stoke is a reminder of the battle, although there is no physical trace.

● **Farndon**

Notts. PO, tel, stores. A local ferry still transports the fishermen to the far side of the river in this attractive village. The pub makes it a popular spot in summer as do the sailing boats. The extensive renovation of the 14th-C church in 1891 revealed a stone coffin containing a Saxon bronze sword.

● **Newark**

Notts. MD Wed, Fri, Sat. Two stations. Newark is magnificent, easily the most interesting and attractive town on the Trent, and it is very appealing from the navigation. Situated at the junction of two old highways, the Great North Road and the Fosse Way, the town is of great historical significance. During the Civil War it was a Royalist stronghold which was besieged three times by the Roundheads between March 1645 and May 1646. The defensive earthworks or sconces constructed by the Royalists are still visible. Today Newark, like everywhere else, is large, busy and surrounded by industry and modern housing. But the town centre is intact and still full of charm. Elsewhere antique stalls, markets and warehouses attract a steady flow of bargain hunters and collectors to the town. However, it is only the decaying, riverside maltings that give a hint of its past significance within the brewing industry.

British Horological Institute Upton Hall, Upton, Newark (01636 813795). Library, training and educational centre for all those interested in matters horological together with a fascinating museum open to the public. Housed in Upton Hall, built in 1828, the museum displays the original 'Six Pip' generator and the actual watch worn by Captain Scott on his final, disastrous expedition, amongst many other gems. *Open Easter–Aug, Sun–Fri 13.30–17.00.* Charge. Partial disabled access. Regular bus service from Newark.

Church of St Mary Magdalene The enormous spire is all that one can see of this elegant church from the market place, for the buildings on one side of the square hide the body of the structure. Inside, the church is made light and spacious by soaring columns and a magnificent 15th-C east window in the chancel. The building was begun in 1160 and completed about 1500. It is rich in carving, both within and without, but one of the church's most interesting features is a brass made in Flanders to commemorate Alan Fleming, a merchant who died in 1375. The monument is made up of 16 pieces of metal and measures 9 feet 4 inches by 5 feet 7 inches – one of the biggest of its type in England.

Market Place It is worth making a point of visiting Newark on market day to view the scene in the colourful old market. In opposite corners of the square once stood two ancient pubs: one of them, the White Hart, now resited elsewhere in the town, was built in the 15thC and is the oldest example of domestic architecture in the town; the other is the Clinton Arms where W.E. Gladstone made his first speech in 1832. He later became Prime Minister.

Millgate Museum 48 Millgate, Newark (01636 679403). Depicts the bygone social life of Newark, its trade and industry. Reconstruction of its streets, shops and house interiors set in an old waterside warehouse. *Open Mon–Fri 10.00–17.00, weekends & B. Hols 13.00–17.00.* Free.

Newark Castle Castle Gate, Newark (01636 611908). Only a shell remains, the one intact wall overlooking the river. The first known castle on this site was constructed around 1129, probably for Alexander, Bishop of Lincoln. The present building was started in 1173, with various additions and alterations in the 14th, 15th and 16thC – notably the fine oriel windows. King John died here in October 1216, soon after his traumatic experience in the Wash. The castle was naturally a great bastion during the Civil War sieges and battles that focused on Newark. When the Roundheads eventually took the town in 1646, they dismantled the castle. The ruins and the grounds are *open daily*. Free. The Castle Ranger offers conducted tours and can be contacted on 07971 248368.

Newark Gilstrap Centre Castle Gate, Newark (01636 678962). Castle exhibition and information centre. *Open all year except Xmas Day, Box. Day and New Year. Summer hours 09.00–18.00; winter hours 09.00–17.00.* Free.

Newark Museum Appleton Gate, Newark (01636 702358). A historical collection of local items, which includes several Civil War relics, a lead Roman coffin (and its original contents) and W.E. Gladstone's advertisement board ('Gladstone and the Conservative Cause') which he used at elections. During the early part of his career, Gladstone spent 14 years as MP for Newark. Half of the museum is in a schoolroom which is much as it was when built by Archbishop Magnus in 1529. There is also a display of long case clocks: the town was famed for their production in the past. *Open daily except Thu (all year) & Sun Oct–Mar.* Free.

Weston Mill Pottery Millgate, Newark (01636 676835). Terracotta ware in a working pottery. *Open daily.*

Tourist Information Centre Gilstrap Centre, Castlegate, Newark (01636 678962).

Boatyards

Ⓑ **Farndon Harbour** Farndon, nr Newark (01636 705483). 🚽 🚿 ⚓ D E Pump-out, gas, overnight mooring, long-term mooring, winter storage, slipway, crane (20 tonnes), chandlery, books and maps, boat building and repairs, boat fitting-out, DIY facilities, electrical repairs, boat sales, engine sales and repairs (including outboards), toilets, showers, gifts, telephone, café, laundrette. Boat transport by road. *24 hr* emergency call-out.

Ⓑ **Newark Marina** Farndon Road, Newark (01636 704022). 🚿 ⚓ D Gas, overnight mooring, long-term mooring, winter storage, slipway, crane (40 tonne), chandlery, books and maps, gifts, boat building and fitting-out, DIY facilities, boat sales and repairs, inboard and outboard engine sales and repairs, toilets and showers, emergency call-out.

Pubs and Restaurants

🍺 **Bromley Arms** Fiskerton Wharf (01636 830789). An attractive riverside pub, set beside the old wharf, serving Hardys & Hansons real ale. Inexpensive bar meals available *lunchtimes, 7 days a week and evenings Fri & Sat*. Vegetarians and children catered for. Riverside seating and quiz *Mon*. Pub games. Phone in advance to use moorings outside.

🍺 ✗ **Britannia** Northend, Farndon (01636 702416). Popular riverside pub, known for a long time as the Lazy Otter, serving Tetley's and guest real ales. Food available *lunchtimes and evenings*. Children welcome if dining. Moorings and patio. Pool, darts and skittles.

✗ **New Ferry Restaurant** Northend, Farndon (01636 76578). A Mediterranean-style restaurant with an exciting (although pricey) fish menu. L *12.00–14.00*. D *19.00–22.00*. More reasonably priced bar snacks available *Tue–Sat lunchtimes only. Closed Sun & Mon* except for private parties.

🍺 **Rose and Crown** Main Street, Farndon (01636 704334). Local pub dispensing John Smith's and guest real ales. Home-made bar meals available *lunchtimes and evenings Tue–Sun but not Sun evenings*. Children welcome if dining. Patio and pub games. Quiz *last Sun of the month*.

🍺 ✗ **Navigation Waterfront Brasserie** Millgate, Newark (01636 704763). Set in the old Trent Navigation Warehouse with a strong waterways theme, bare brickwork and beams, dispensing Everards and guest real ales. Also a strong emphasis on New World wines and Continental bottled lagers. Home-cooked food available *lunchtimes and an extensive self-service salad bar*. Vegetarian selection. Children welcome, patio seating. Live music *Sun*.

🍺 **Castle Barge** Newark Town Wharf (01636 77320). Floating pub in a 94 foot former Spiller's grain barge. The lower deck provides an atmospheric bar with lots of polished wood and an interesting display of pictures. However, many prefer to sit outside in the summer and enjoy the river. Mansfield real ale. Extended opening hours. Reasonably priced bar snacks available *lunchtimes and evenings except Sun evenings*. Top deck facilities for children.

🍺 **Old Malt Shovel** 25 Northgate, Newark (01636 702036). A cosmopolitan establishment, host to a wide ranging clientele, serving Timothy Taylor, Theakston and guest real ales from a bar set up in a one-time bakery. Food from a varied menu is served *lunchtimes every day and evenings Wed-Sun*. Children welcome. Pub games and outside seating. Disabled access.

Cromwell Lock

From Newark, the Trent follows a generally northerly course towards the Humber, which is still over 50 miles away owing to the very sweeping and tortuous line of the river. The villages of North Muskham and Holme face each other across the water and used to be connected by ferry. A mile or more below Holme is Cromwell Lock and Weir. On 28 September 1975 ten volunteers of the 131 independent parachute squadron of the Royal Engineers lost their lives here whilst taking part in Expedition Trent Chase. Cromwell has always been a significant place on the river; in the 8thC a bridge was built at this point. The lock here marks the beginning of the tidal section of the Trent, so navigation north of it requires a very different approach.

NAVIGATIONAL NOTES

1 Cromwell Weir is the largest on the Trent. It is buoyed and has a safety boom. All boats should keep to the west side of the river. The lock too is truly enormous; it is mechanised, and there is a lock keeper on duty every day *07.00-21.00* (01636 821213). Boaters can also book free passage through the lock outside these hours, to coincide with suitable tide envelopes, by giving 48 hours notice.

2 Boaters intending to break their passage to Torksey Lock, by staying on the pontoon mooring at Dunham, are requested to inform the lock keeper at Cromwell to avoid alarm at their non-arrival at Torksey. Similarly should you change your plans and subsequently stop at Dunham please contact a lock keeper to avoid unnecessary concern for your safety.

3 Commercial river traffic operate on channel 6 upstream of Keadby Bridge and it is useful for VHF users to monitor this channel to establish the whereabouts of large craft on the tideway.

Navigating the tidal Trent

A suitable boat is essential: proper navigation lights (compulsory on all the navigable Trent) and safety equipment (including an anchor and cable) is also compulsory. Navigation notes are available from British Waterways, Mill Lane, Mill Gate, Newark (01636 704481). The Trent Boating Association publish *Sissons Charts*, an excellent guide covering the tidal Trent and available from 16 Baker Avenue, Arnold, Nottingham, NG5 8FU (0115 926 2055). Deep-draughted boats should beware of shoals at low water and should avoid the inside of bends. The river banks are unsuitable for mooring and there are few wharves. Navigators who are more used to canals and non-tidal rivers will be more likely to treat the tidal Trent as a link route with the Fossdyke & Witham Navigation, the Chesterfield Canal, the South Yorkshire Navigations or the Humber Estuary. They should plan their trip with an eye to the tide table. The best approach is either to use a Hull tide table (available from local boatyards, fishing shops and newsagents) bearing in mind that the Trent floods for only about $2^{1}/4$ hours and ebbs for the remainder of the 12-hour period or, if in doubt, to ask the British Waterways lock keepers at the various junctions along the river. The relevant telephone numbers are listed below:

Cromwell Lock: (01636) 821213   West Stockwith Lock: (01427) 890204
Torksey Lock: (01427) 718202   Keadby Lock: (01724) 782205

In most cases it is advisable to plan your journey so that the tide is running with you, but bear in mind the lock operating times.

Pubs and Restaurants

Lord Nelson Winthorpe (01636 703578). Ruddles, Marston's, Courage and John Smith's. Bar and restaurant meals (both catering for vegetarians) *lunchtimes and evenings. Closed Mon.* Garden and children's play area. Barbecues during the *summer months.* Pool and pub games.

Muskham Ferry North Muskham (01636 704943). A riverside pub with mooring for patrons, fronted by a garden and children's play area. Morland and guest real ales together with inexpensive home-cooked food available *lunchtimes, evenings and all day Fri–Sun.* Games room.

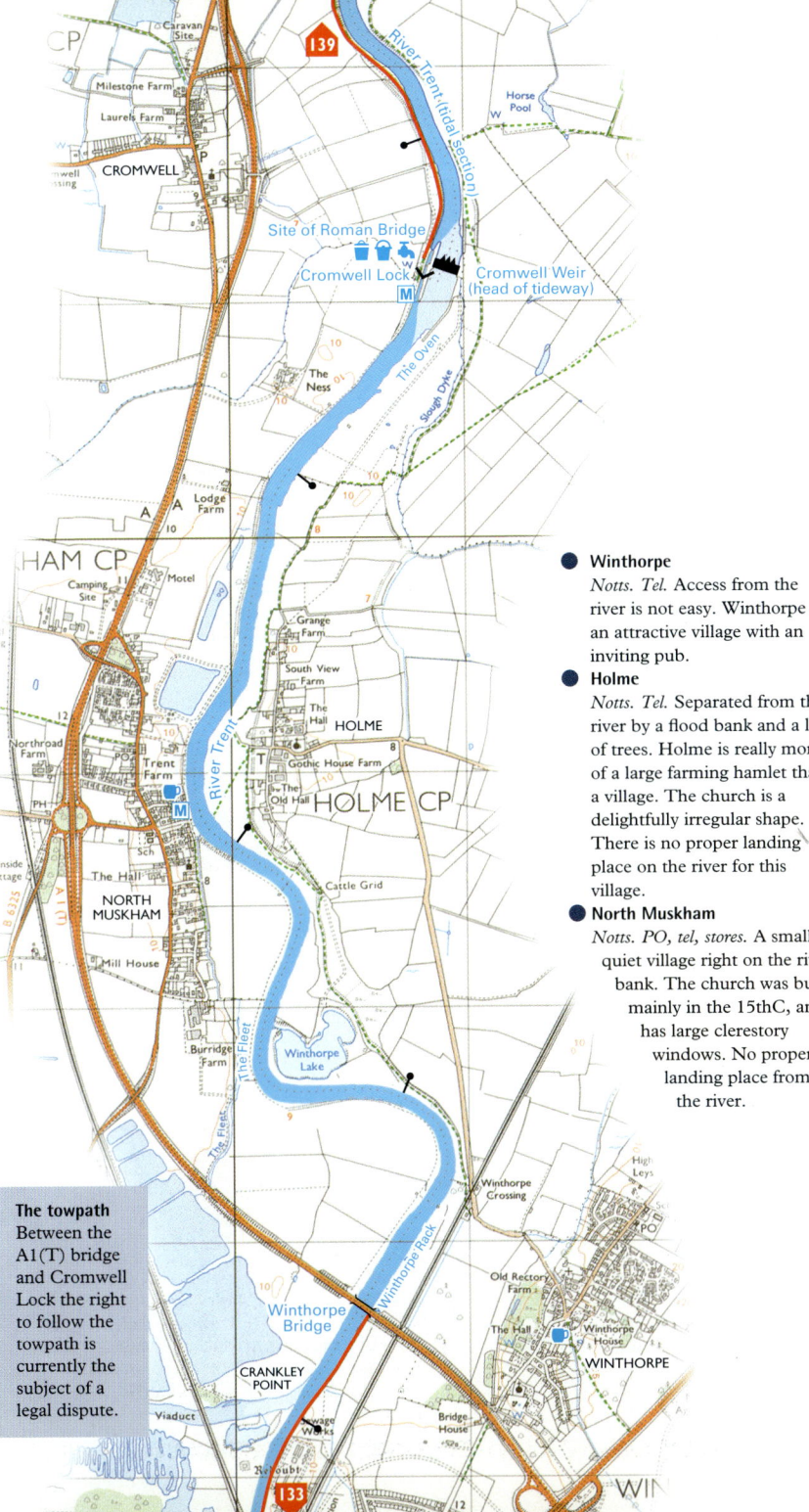

- **Winthorpe**
  Notts. Tel. Access from the river is not easy. Winthorpe is an attractive village with an inviting pub.
- **Holme**
  Notts. Tel. Separated from the river by a flood bank and a line of trees. Holme is really more of a large farming hamlet than a village. The church is a delightfully irregular shape. There is no proper landing place on the river for this village.
- **North Muskham**
  Notts. PO, tel, stores. A small, quiet village right on the river bank. The church was built mainly in the 15thC, and has large clerestory windows. No proper landing place from the river.

The towpath
Between the A1(T) bridge and Cromwell Lock the right to follow the towpath is currently the subject of a legal dispute.

Sutton on Trent

This is a typical stretch of the upper section of the tidal Trent. The river meanders along its northward course, flanked by flood banks and with no bridges. The land is largely grazed as permanent pasture nurtured by the high summer water table maintained by the winter flood (now of course contained). Evidence of an ancient landscape is glimpsed, often on the inside of a sweeping bend, in the form of isolated stretches of hedgerow. These are rich in an abundance of species including ash, willow, wild roses and hawthorn – a picture of white blossom in springtime. Apart from these tantalising views there is little to see save for the occasional sand barge. Elsewhere the land yields a vast quantity of glacial gravel quarried for building and road construction. A relatively interesting place is Girton Wharf, where there are still working barges to be seen, but the moorings here are not for pleasure boats. The village of Sutton on Trent is near this wharf; so is a large converted windmill. On the east bank is Besthorpe Wharf, which is used for feeding gravel from the adjacent pits into the river barges. The Trent valley can rightly be called the powerhouse of England: electricity generating stations operating within sight of the river currently produce more than a quarter of all electricity consumed in England and Wales. This area makes an ideal site for power stations with its plentiful supply of water for steam production, as well as for cooling the spent steam once it has passed through the generating turbines. A large reserve of coal to fire the boilers is also available from the nearby East Midlands coalfield, although several of the power stations are now converting to gas. Most of them have been built since 1950, and their huge cooling towers stand out as prominent features on an otherwise largely agricultural landscape. Approximately half of all the electricity generated in the Trent valley is transmitted, via the Supergrid of overhead power lines, to London, which as a large consumer is nevertheless poorly situated for large scale power production. Whilst waste cooling water is returned to the river, the vast output of fly ash has been used to fill nearby spent gravel pits. In an imaginative scheme it has also, in conjunction with soil from sugar beet washings, been used to reclaim worked-out clay pits at a Peterborough brick works. These have then been returned to agricultural use. In most cases mooring along the tidal Trent is not recommended.

The towpath

Under the 1792 Trent River Navigation Act hauling rights were granted in return for an annual rent. Since the 1930s craft using the river have been self-propelled and these rights have not been exercised. Custom and practice has led to paths following the flood banks rather than the water margins. BW's legal rights are for maintenance access only, whilst they also have an obligation to maintain and erect the numerous clapper gates as necessary. On the tidal stretch of the Trent it is often possible to follow a path on either flood bank; therefore the towpath indicated on the map represents only the most straightforward, continuous route to follow.

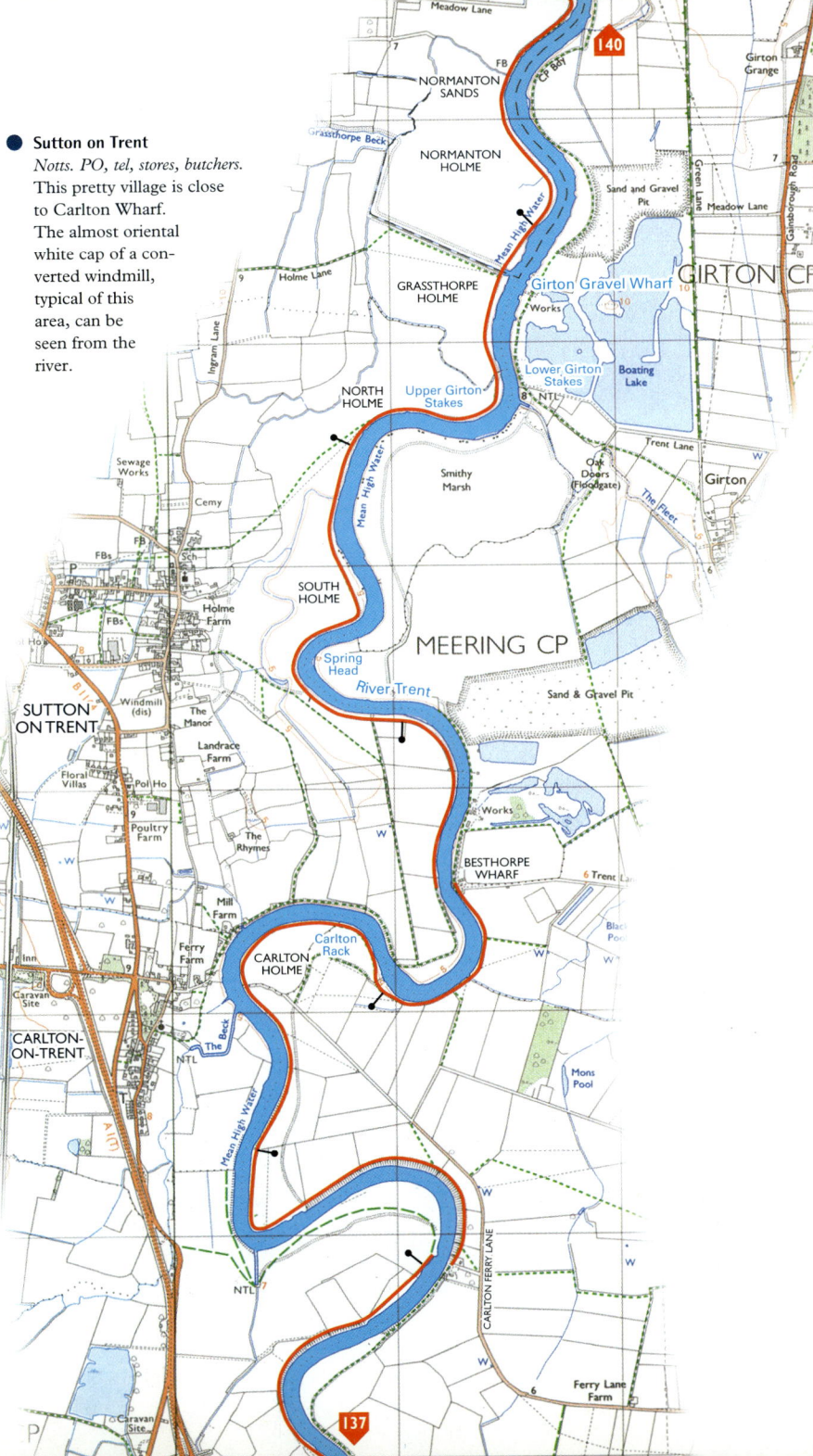

● **Sutton on Trent**
Notts. PO, tel, stores, butchers.
This pretty village is close
to Carlton Wharf.
The almost oriental
white cap of a con-
verted windmill,
typical of this
area, can be
seen from the
river.

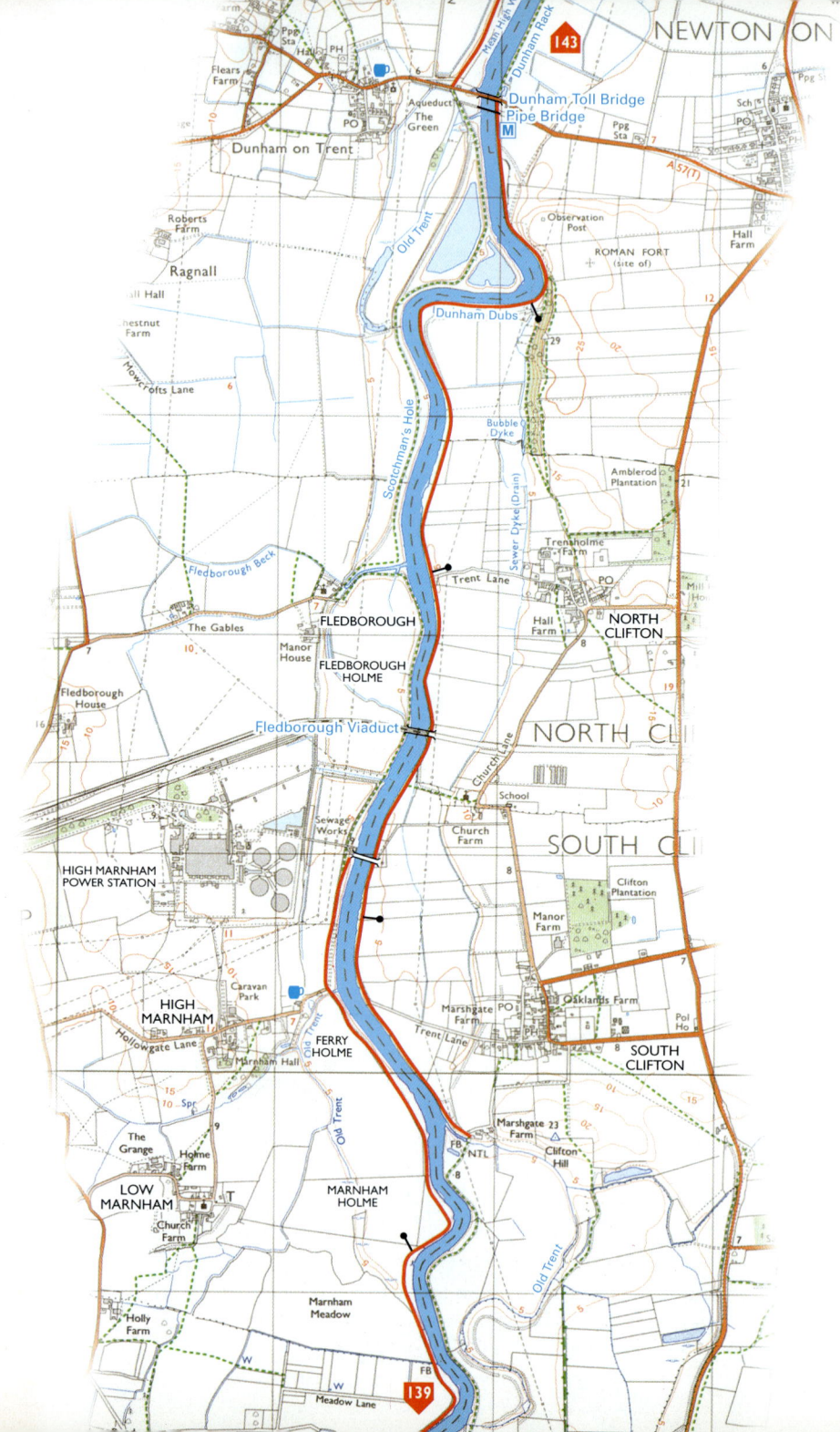

Dunham Bridge

Passing the nearby villages of High Marnham, Low Marnham and South Clifton, the river reaches the large cooling towers of High Marnham Power Station. There is a footbridge carrying a pipe across the river here; just north of it is the iron railway viaduct that carries the line supplying the power station. High Marnham was at one time two hamlets: Ferry Marnham and Church Marnham. The old hall which stood between them was demolished in 1800. It was the property of the Cartwright family who held many claims to fame. Dr Edmund Cartwright invented the power loom which revolutionised the weaving industry. One of his brothers was the engineer responsible for the construction of the Ramper Road leading into Newark over raised arches. Another was an admiral in Lord Nelson's navy. Near the railway viaduct is the isolated church of St George, situated equidistant between North and South Clifton in order to serve both parishes. North Clifton once had the use of a ferry which was free to its inhabitants. 1 1/2 miles further, the river describes a sharp S-bend as it passes a welcome little ridge of hills, pleasantly wooded. But the ridge fades away as one reaches Dunham Toll Bridge (the present structure replacing one built in 1832) and the iron aqueduct that precedes it. Once a market town, Dunham was notorious for its flooding. The Trent frequently caused buildings to be awash with up to ten feet of water. As a consequence most of the inhabitants were boat owners in order to maintain communications during the floods. Recent flood protection measures have, hopefully, made such events a thing of the past. The countryside resumes its flat and rather featureless aspect, while the river now forms the border between Nottinghamshire and Lincolnshire (as far downstream as West Stockwith). From Stapleford to Dunham the river is a birdwatcher's paradise of water meadows, pools and marshes. Mooring is available on a BW pontoon at Dunham, just upstream of the bridge on the east bank.

Pubs and Restaurants

Bridge Inn Dunham (01777 228385). West of toll bridge. Springhead and three guest real ales are served together with food *lunchtimes and evenings, 7 days a week*. Vegetarians and children catered for. Outside seating. B & B. Open all day Sun. Disabled access.

Brownlow Arms High Marnham (01636 822505). Recently refurbished, this family pub, with a large garden and children's play area, serves real ales and food *all day during the summer*. The landlord hopes to be able to establish moorings for patrons. Telephone for further details.

QUAY STRATEGY

Navigating the tidal Trent, the boater is constantly aware of the potential – both past and present – to effortlessly move large bulk loads. Evidence of the river's past glory as a waterways highway can be found at every tortuous twist and turn in the form of decaying wharves and jetties. The waterfront at Gainsborough, once heaving with barge traffic – often as many as three-deep – jostling for position to load or unload, is now moribund, locked in by concrete flood defences. This apparent shame at a past prosperity, one that was largely water-generated, is a telling indictment on the importance now attached to what was arguably the original form of green transport. Logic, it would appear, is completely lacking in a system that eschews the economies and scale of water transport in favour of diesel guzzling lorries. But, on reflection, is it? The more diesel consumed, the more revenue for the government. The greater the number of lorries cluttering up the roads, the greater the income from the road fund licence. Could it be that promoting the benefits of water transport would be to shoot the chancellor in the foot or, possibly, somewhere economically far more painful.

Torksey

At Laneham the traveller will enjoy a little relief from the Trent's isolation. Here there is a church and a few houses on a slight rise near the river. A farmhouse on the river bank was built on the site of the old manor. The cellars in the building are reputed to date back even further than this to the time when the land belonged to the palace of the Archbishops of York. To the north of the village, yet another power station – Cottam – appears as the river turns back on itself to the south before swinging northwards again at the junction of the Fossdyke Navigation (marked by a pumping station). Beside the power station is the loading wharf for Rampton Gravel Pit: unable to transport any of its output via the tortuous, local country lanes all the material produced is transhipped by barge to wharfs at Hull, Goole and Whitwood, near Leeds. *Watch out for large barges turning and manoeuvring on the sharp bend.* The lock up into the Fossdyke is just through the road bridge, mooring is below the bridge, and a pub, petrol station and shop are all near the lock. Torksey offers a haven for the boater navigating the tidal Trent with 72-hour pontoon moorings, water, toilets and showers, together with barbecue area and telephone. There is also a good restaurant in the village – for further information on Torksey see page 52. Nearing the railway viaduct at Torksey, one sees the gaunt ruin of Torksey castle standing beside the river. As at Newark, the façade that faces the Trent is the most complete part of the building, for the rest has vanished. (The castle has been abandoned since the 16thC.) For the first 15 feet or so from the ground, the castle is built of stone – above this it is dark red brick. In most cases mooring on the tidal Trent is not recommended.

NAVIGATIONAL NOTES

Boaters intending to break their passage to Cromwell Lock, by staying on the pontoon mooring at Dunham, are requested to inform the lock keeper at Torsey to avoid alarm at their non-arrival at Cromwell. Similarly should you change your plans and subsequently stop at Dunham, please contact a lock keeper to avoid unnecessary concern for your safety. The relevant telephone numbers are:

Cromwell Lock: (01636) 821213   Torksey Lock: (01427) 718202

Pubs and Restaurants

White Swan Torksey (01427 718202). Near the lock. Stones ale. Children's play area and garden. Also caravan and camping site.

Wheelhouse Restaurant Torksey Lock (01427 718301). Serving food *Tue–Sun lunchtimes and evenings*, (vegetarian food made to order). Children welcome.

Hume Arms Main Street, Torksey (01427 718613). A large, attractive old pub with two bars and carvery restaurant, situated 300yds from the junction of the Fossdyke and Trent navigations. A la carte menu with lots of fish specialities and a vegetarian menu served *lunchtime every day*. Garden. Children's room. B & B.

Ferry Boat Inn Church Laneham (01777 228350). Temporary moorings below the caravan park give access to this friendly pub which is just a short walk up from the river. Mansfield, Boddingtons and a variety of guest real ales are served at the bar along with bar meals and take-away food *lunchtimes and evenings, 7 days a week*. Traditional *Sunday* lunch. There is a family room and outside seating. *Mid-week* live music.

Butcher's Laneham (01777 228255). A short walk into the village from the Ferry Boat Inn. Village local serving Boddingtons and Stones real ales. Food is served in both the bar and the restaurant *lunchtimes and evenings, 7 days a week*, (vegetarians catered for). For those feeling in need of some exercise, or of spoiling themselves, there is an adjoining health studio with sauna, sun bed and gymnasium. Live music *Tue*.

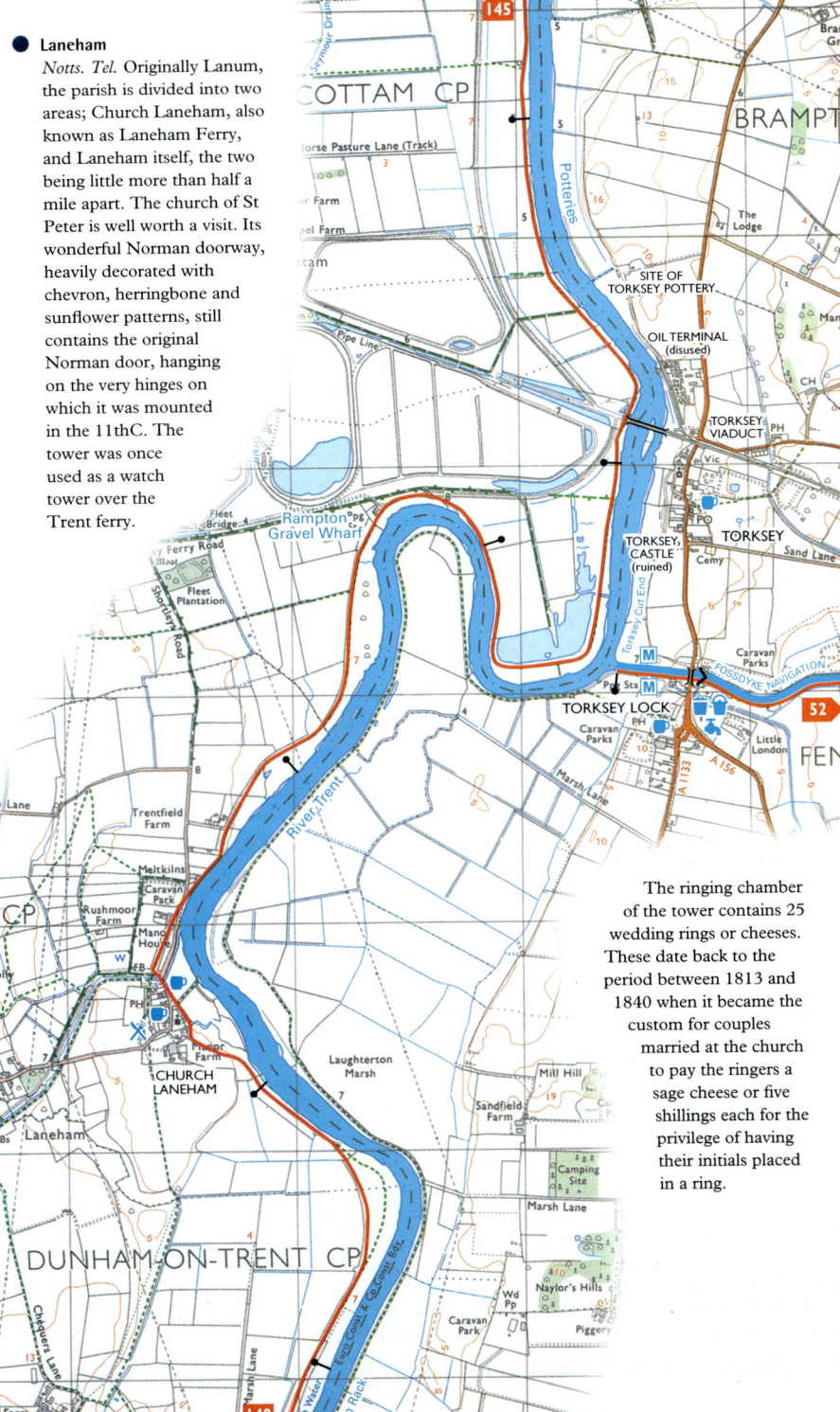

● **Laneham**

Notts. Tel. Originally Lanum, the parish is divided into two areas; Church Laneham, also known as Laneham Ferry, and Laneham itself, the two being little more than half a mile apart. The church of St Peter is well worth a visit. Its wonderful Norman doorway, heavily decorated with chevron, herringbone and sunflower patterns, still contains the original Norman door, hanging on the very hinges on which it was mounted in the 11thC. The tower was once used as a watch tower over the Trent ferry.

The ringing chamber of the tower contains 25 wedding rings or cheeses. These date back to the period between 1813 and 1840 when it became the custom for couples married at the church to pay the ringers a sage cheese or five shillings each for the privilege of having their initials placed in a ring.

Littleborough

From Cottam, the river continues to wind northwards towards Gainsborough. This is not as dull a stretch as those further south. A windmill marks the exaggeratedly named Trent Port, which is in fact the wharf for the small village of Marton. Speedboats operate from here, but owners of any larger boats will once again find it difficult to land. Marton was important in Saxon times because of its position near the ford where a Roman road (now the A1500) crossed the Trent. This ford marked the western boundary of the ancient kingdom of Lindsey. Many historians believe that Saint Paulinus baptised some of the first Saxon Christians here in 627. The church of St Margaret has evolved around an early Saxon church, side aisles being added to the original structure. The tapering Anglo-Saxon tower still reveals some fine herringbone masonry. In 1904 it was discovered that the entire structure was unsafe as it had been built on foundations only two feet deep made of sand and pebbles. The next place of interest is Littleborough, a tiny riverside settlement. Fortunately boats may moor temporarily at the floating jetty. Below Littleborough is a beautiful reach with steep wooded hills rising from the water's edge on the Lincolnshire side. The attractive brick and stone building set in the parkland is called Burton Château. A little further downstream, another clump of trees on the east bank at Knaith conceals a former nunnery and chapel, but mooring is only just possible here. On towards Gainsborough, the cooling towers of West Burton Power Station stand out prominently in the flat landscape on the west side of the river.

● **Knaith**
Lincs. Temporary mooring just possible. Among the trees is the hall and an interesting old church with a Jacobean pulpit. Both were part of a nunnery dissolved in 1539. The hall was the birthplace of Thomas Sutton, who founded Charterhouse School and Hospital.

● **Littleborough**
Notts. An attractive hamlet with reasonably good access from the river. The little church stands on a slight rise; it is a delightfully simple Norman structure and incorporates much herringbone masonry. It is assumed from various finds, including the perfectly preserved body of a woman dug up in the graveyard, that this was the site of the Roman camp Segelocum. The paved ford dating from the time of Emperor Hadrian became visible during a drought in 1933. King Harold's army crossed this ford on its way to Hastings in 1066.

BREAKFAST AT POTTERIES

Viewed from the wheelbox of a sand-carrying barge, the Romans and their ilk were untidy fellows. Clearly they thought nothing of tossing their rubbish into the river – to make a ford or empty a failed kiln – and might be considered the forerunners of the contemporary litter lout. A heavily-laden barge lumbers down this river with difficulty, banging the bottom on even the most generous ebb, unsure where she'll finally come to rest to await the next flood tide. History's cast-offs do nothing to help the situation and invariably result in an unscheduled halt, mid-river. Piling stones on the river bed, to form a ford, might have seemed a good idea to the Romans at the time. It is not, however, an opinion widely shared amongst barge skippers of today. Littleborough doubtless offers plenty to excite the archaeologist with its wealth of antiquity, whilst a short distance upstream, connoisseurs of porcelain can wax lyrical about the decorative output from the 19th-C Torksey Pottery. The common thread lies in the debris ejected into the tideway (commemorated in the name of this reach), making it a sure fire resting place for loaded barges and a regular bed and breakfast stop for their crew.

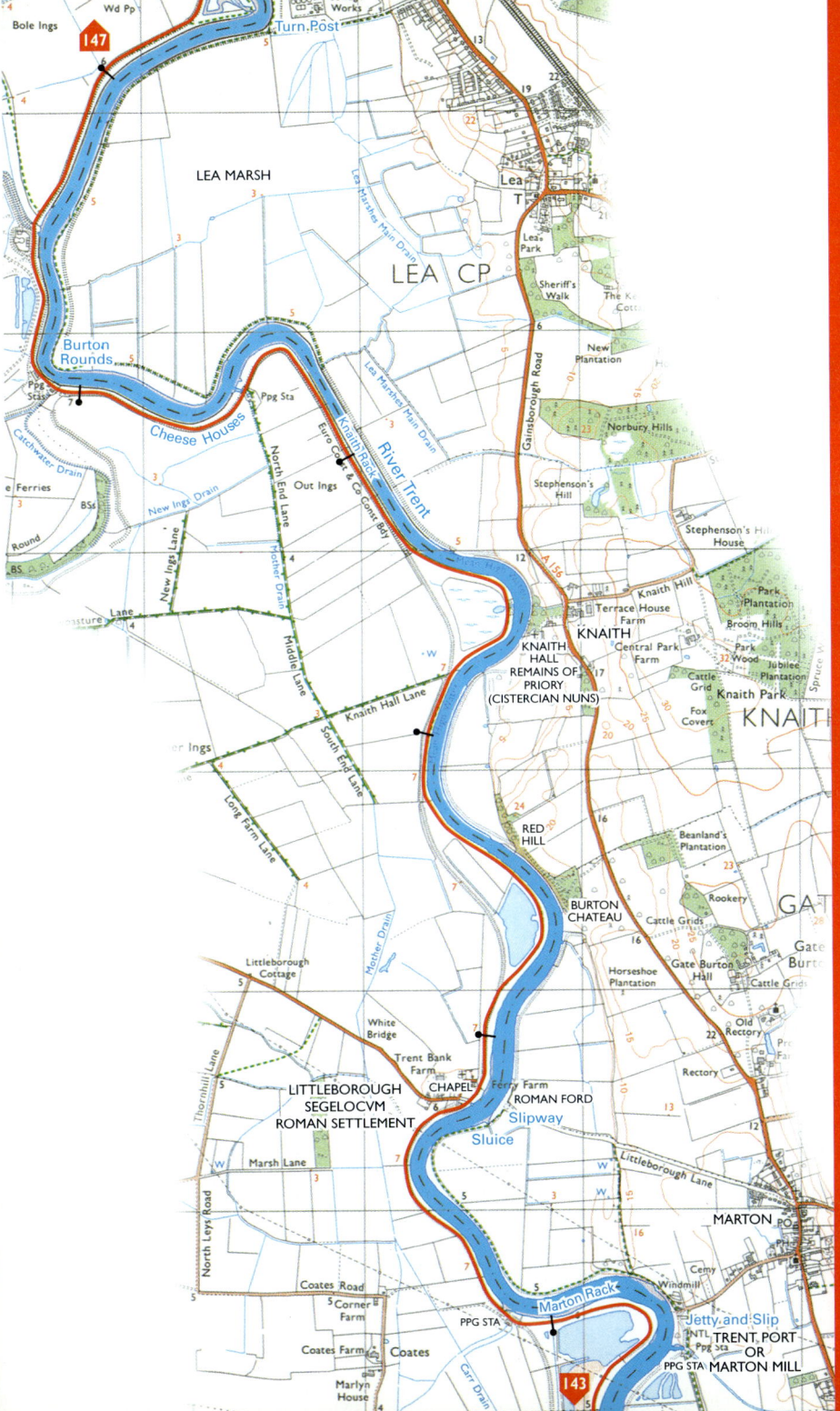

Bole Ings

Wd Pp

147

Turn Post

Sewage Works

LEA MARSH

Lea Marshes Main Drain

Lea Tre...

Lea Park

LEA CP

Sheriff's Walk

The Ke...
Cott...

New Plantation

Burton Rounds

PPG Sta

Ppg Sta

Gainsborough Road

Cheese Houses

Euro Cont & Co Const Bdy

Knaith Rack

River Trent

North End Lane

New Ings Drain

Lea Marshes Main Drain

Out Ings

Stephenson's Hill

Norbury Hills

Stephenson's Hi
House

New Ings Lane

Mother Drain

Middle Lane

Knaith Hill

Terrace House

Park Plantation

Broom Hills

KNAITH

Central Park Farm

Park Wood

Jubilee Plantation

Knaith Park

KNAITH

Pasture Lane

KNAITH HALL
REMAINS OF PRIORY
(CISTERCIAN NUNS)

Cattle Grid

Fox Covert

Spruce V...

Knaith Hall Lane

South End Lane

RED HILL

Beanland's Plantation

Rookery

GA...

Long Farm Lane

er Ings

Mother Drain

BURTON CHATEAU

Cattle Grids

Gate Burton Hall

Gate Burt...

Cattle Grids

Littleborough Cottage

Horseshoe Plantation

Thornhill Lane

White Bridge

Trent Bank Farm

CHAPEL

Ferry Farm

ROMAN FORD

Old Rectory

LITTLEBOROUGH
SEGELOCVM
ROMAN SETTLEMENT

Slipway

Sluice

Littleborough Lane

Rectory

Marsh Lane

MARTON

North Leys Road

Cemy

Windmill

Coates Road

Corner Farm

Marton Rack

MARTON

PPG STA

Jetty and Slip

NTL

Ppg Sta

Coates Farm

Coates

TRENT PORT
OR
MARTON MILL

PPG STA

Marlyn House

Carr Drain

143

Gainsborough

The river moves away from the wooded slopes, passes the power station (the northern-most on the river) and heads for Gainsborough, which is clearly indicated by a group of tall flour mills. Below the railway bridge, the river bends sharply before reaching the flour mills, the bridge at Gainsborough and the desolate wharfs. Mooring is difficult though just possible beside the supermarket. It will become even more difficult once the new flood defence scheme is put in place. The town is set entirely on one side of the river, and is worth visiting.

NAVIGATIONAL NOTES

1 Below Gainsborough Arches the River Trent ceases to be under the jurisdiction of BW and is controlled by the Humber Navigation bylaws. These are administered by Associated British Ports from whom a copy may be obtained by ringing (01482) 327171.

2 VHF marine band radio has become an important aid when navigating tidal commercial waterways. It allows the boater to know the whereabouts of other traffic and to maintain contact with lock keepers who listen out on channels 16 and 74, and work on channel 74. See note on page 136 for telephone contact.

3 BW request that boaters give lock keepers along the tidal river 24 hours notice of passage. Always seek advice from lock keepers and respect their skill and experience.

4 Charts are available for both the tidal and non-tidal sections of the Trent (and the River Ouse) and can be obtained from the Trent Boating Association on 0115 926 2055.

5 The Aegir, or tidal bore, a tidal wave of between one foot and five feet in height, and breaking at the sides, may be encountered between Keadby and Torksey. It is normally only seen on spring tides of over 25 feet (Hull), and arrives at the same time as the flood, although there can be a variation of half an hour each way. If you are on the river, keep a watch for it, and meet it head on, facing straight downstream and in the middle of the river. If you are anchored, use twice the normal length of warp. If you are moored, try to tie up to a barge or other large craft, which will itself rise and fall with the wave.

● **Gainsborough**
Lincs. MD Tue, Sat. All services, two stations.
Gainsborough is best seen from the river, where the old wharves and warehouses serve as a reminder of the town's significance as a port in the 18th and 19thC. Once qualifying as Britain's furthest inland port, there is now no evidence of the boats (of up to 850 tonnes deadweight) that used to carry animal feedstuffs, grain, fertilisers and scrap metals. Elsewhere industrial sprawl and Victorian red-brick housing tends to obscure the qualities of this old market town. There are several Victorian churches, but All Saints retains its Perpendicular tower. Gainsborough was a frequent battleground during the Civil War and George Eliot described it as St Ogg's in *The Mill on the Floss*.

The Old Hall Parnell Street, Gainsborough (01427 612669). An attractive manor house of the 15th and 16thC in the centre of the town: it contains a medieval kitchen and Great Hall. Here Henry VIII met Catherine Parr, later his sixth wife, who was the daughter-in-law of the house. The Pilgrim Fathers also met here. Now a folk museum. *Open Easter–Oct, Mon–Sat 10.00–17.00, Sun 14.00–17.30. Closed Nov–Easter on Sun.* Charge.

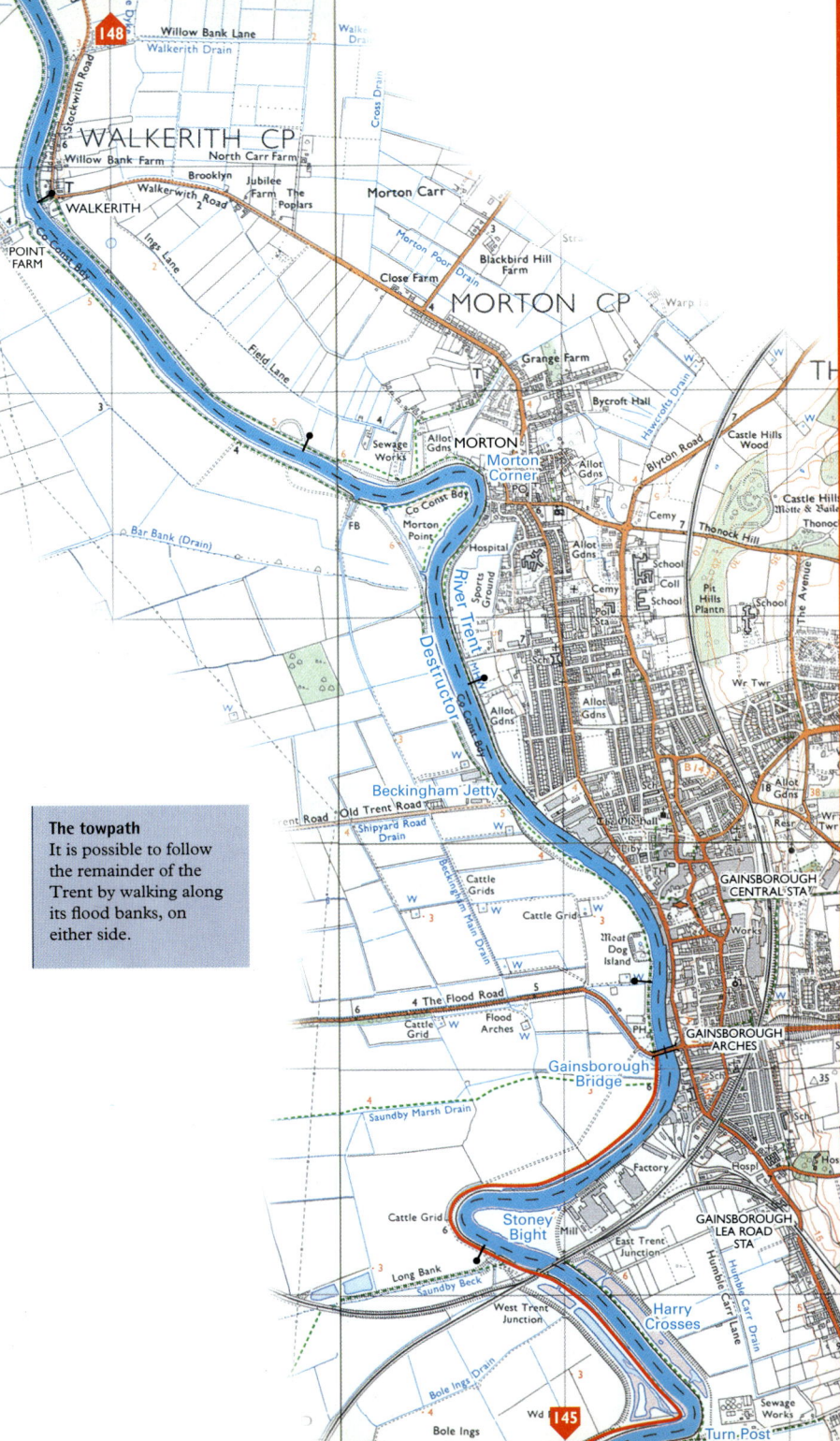

The towpath
It is possible to follow the remainder of the Trent by walking along its flood banks, on either side.

West Stockwith

On leaving Gainsborough the river passes the jetty of the Trent Wharfage and Storage Group on the left. This is the destination of the large coasters which occasionally ply the Trent above Gunness, where they discharge cargoes of ferro-metals, timber, fertilisers, bulk chemicals and animal feeds. They are able to carry loads of up to 1250 tonnes at a time, shipped from as far away as Sweden. Then the navigation bends sharply to the left, passing Morton Wharf with its Flemish gables, and winds its way past the hamlet of Walkerith towards West Stockwith. Immediately after the sharp right-hand bend in the river (below Farmers Jetty) the entrance lock into the Chesterfield Canal is visible on the left, giving access into the basin with its boatyard, moorings and friendly Yacht Club.

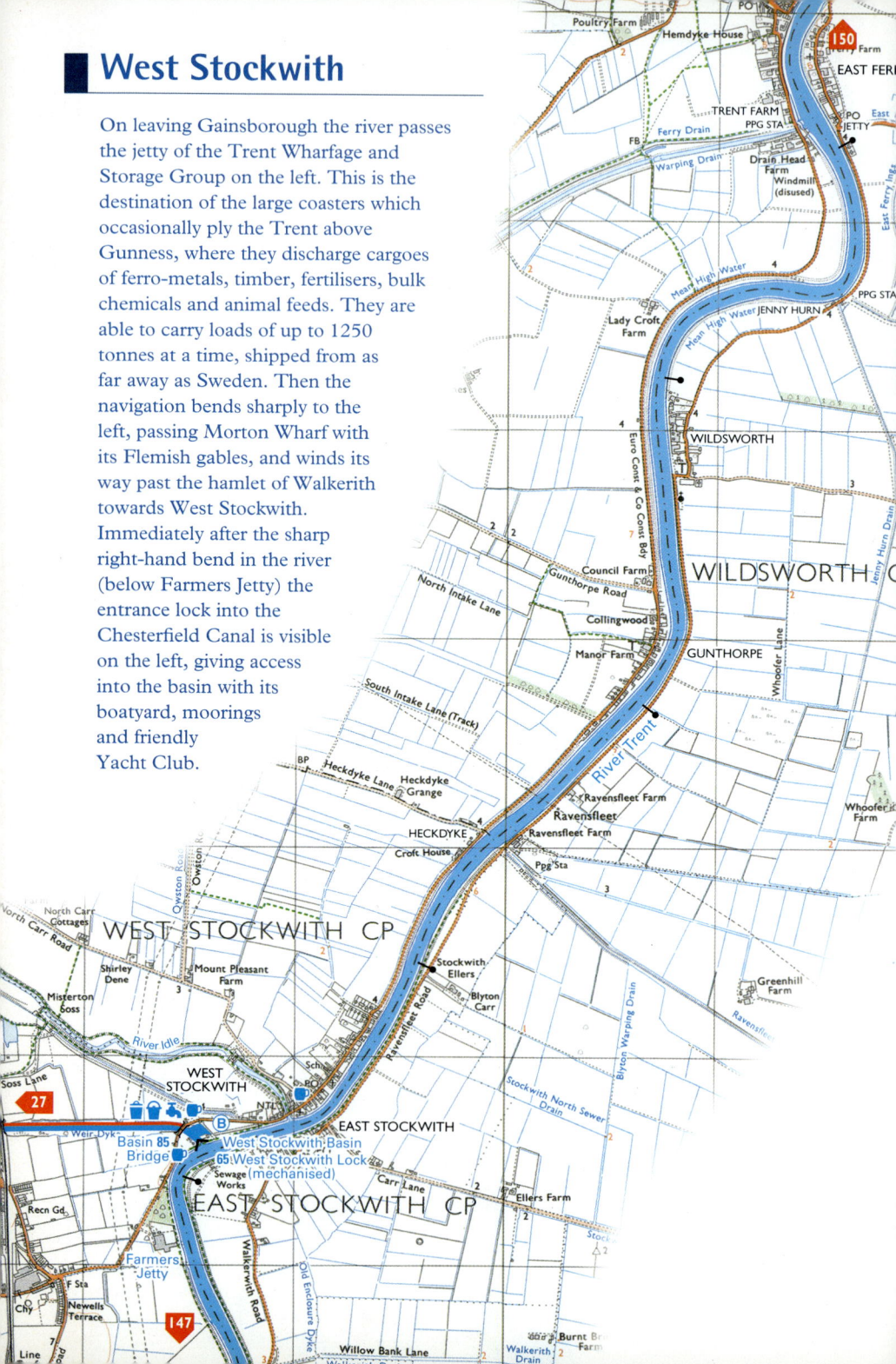

Just downstream from the basin the River Idle, barricaded in by steel flood doors, joins the Trent beside West Stockwith's unusual 18th-C Georgian church. This was once the main highway from the industrial areas of South Yorkshire, terminating at a large wharf in Bawtry. Goods travelled to and from the town by horse and cart and, before the development of the River Don as a reliable navigation, were dependent upon the river for onward transport. In draining the Isle of Axholme in the 17thC, Cornelius Vermuyden modified the course of the Idle and drastically reduced its effectiveness as a navigable waterway. From the river West Stockwith, now a conservation area, presents a closed-in, almost intimate, aspect with its many tall three-storey buildings. It is possible to catch the occasional tantalising glimpse into the village up tiny passages, or gunnels, running between the houses. Once a thriving boat building community – there were five boatyards only a hundred years ago – West Stockwith had a population of 5000 in the 1880s; it is now reduced to 240. The brick-built church, looking more like a chapel capped with a squat bell tower, is one of only three of its kind and was completed in 1722. Inside the plasterwork is classic Adam. See page 26 for further details on the village. Leaving West Stockwith the Trent follows a comparatively straight course passing the isolated hamlets of Gunthorpe and Wildsworth, barely visible to the boater hidden as they are below the river's flood banks. All this area bordering the river was, in AD 886, part of the Danelaw, and place names with *by* and *thorpe* endings are of Viking derivation. A sense of isolation and independence persists into the 20thC from a time when the Wash, the Trent and the Humber effectively cut this area off from the remainder of the country. In those times the inhabitants identified more with Denmark, Holland and the sea than with the rest of England.

NAVIGATIONAL NOTES

1 The lock at West Stockwith is keeper-operated. The operation of the lock is dependent on the height of the tide, but a passage can usually be made from $2^1/2$ hours before to $4^1/2$ hours after high water which is on average 2 hours after the time published for Hull.
2 Keepers at all the Trent locks can be contacted on marine band VHF radio: calling channel 16, working channel 74; or by telephone using the numbers listed below:
Cromwell Lock: (01636) 821213
Torksey Lock: (01427) 718202
West Stockwith Lock: (01427) 890204
Keadby Lock: (01724) 782205
3 Deep draught commercial traffic, especially coasters, require the deepest channel on the navigation at all times. Be prepared to give way to allow for this and do not necessarily expect to pass port to port when meeting craft head on.
4 Boaters intending to break their passage to Cromwell Lock, by staying on the pontoon mooring at Dunham, are requested to inform the lock keeper at West Stockwith to avoid alarm at their non-arrival at Cromwell. Similarly, should you change your plans and subsequently stop at Dunham, please contact a lock keeper to avoid unnecessary concern for your safety.

Owston Ferry

The conical tower of an old windmill on the left bank has been restored as part of a spacious new dwelling on a fairly grand scale – even to the point of having a helipad sited on an adjacent field. This feature, very much of the 20thC, contrasts strongly with the mellow buildings of Owston Ferry directly ahead. As the channel swings to the right the pleasing scale of the riverside houses becomes apparent. Skilfully constructed using local brick and tile, they are both solid and graceful in appearance. There is something reminiscent of a Dutch painting in the views over the river seen from the lower part of the village. The church, standing a little way from the waterway, is largely medieval, but with early 19th-C Gothic additions, and inside there is an attractive rood screen dating from 1897. Although modern executive dwellings have crept into the village, generally by way of infill, it is the largely three-storey, Dutch-influenced buildings that still predominate. At Robin Hood's Well to the north west, Roman coins have been found, indicating that this is a settlement of some antiquity. Flowing northwards the river regains its isolation amidst the flat, fertile countryside behind the flood banks. Throughout history this area has been known as the Isle of Axholme – once a wetland prone to seasonal flooding and in ancient times a forest, heath and then marsh. It is a tract of low flat land less than 100 feet above sea level, some 5 miles wide and running for approximately 18 miles along the Trent's western bank. In 1625 a Dutchman, Cornelius Vermuyden, was brought over to oversee the draining of the area at a cost of £56,000. The land's natural fertility was soon realised under the Dutch and French Protestant settlers that followed him, much to the disgust of the ousted native inhabitants. After lengthy litigation the land was finally divided in 1691, the locals receiving 10,532 acres and the settlers 2868 acres. The chief town in the area is Epworth, some 4 miles west of Kelfield and famous as the birthplace, in 1703, of John Wesley, founder of Methodism. His father was rector of the parish for 59 years. Over the years the pattern of agriculture in the area has varied, reflecting a changing society. At the time when the Wesley family lived at Epworth, flax and hemp, used in the manufacture of sacking and canvas, were amongst the principal crops. Walnut trees were plentiful along the east bank of the river, the nuts gathered as a further source of income. Today intensive vegetable growing, cereals and root crops predominate.

NAVIGATIONAL NOTES

The substantial mooring dolphins located on various reaches of the navigation – ie north and south of the M180 bridge – are for the safety of commercial craft and not to be used by pleasure vessels. They do not provide a way ashore.

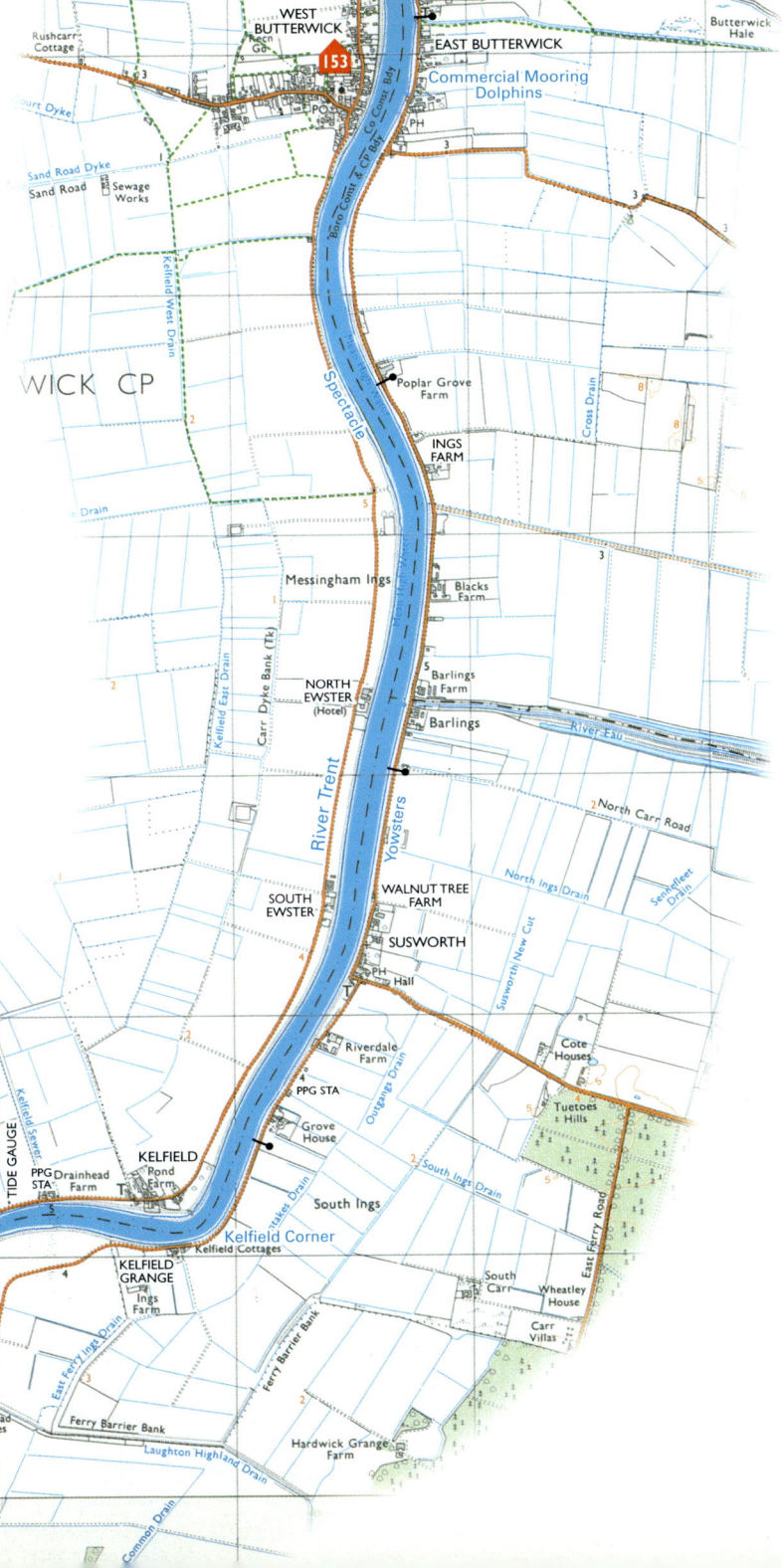

WEST BUTTERWICK
Beech Go
153
PO
EAST BUTTERWICK
Butterwick Hale

Rushcarr Cottage

Commercial Mooring Dolphins

Court Dyke

Sand Road Dyke
Sand Road
Sewage Works

Kelfield West Drain

WICK CP

Spectacle

Cross Drain

Poplar Grove Farm

INGS FARM

Drain

Messingham Ings

Blacks Farm

Carr Dyke Bank (Tk)

Kelfield East Drain

NORTH EWSTER (Hotel)

Barlings Farm

Barlings

River Eau

River Trent

Yowsters

North Carr Road

SOUTH EWSTER

WALNUT TREE FARM

North Ings Drain

Sandtoft Drain

SUSWORTH
PH Hall

Susworth New Cut

Riverdale Farm

Cote Houses

PPG STA

Outgangs Drain

Grove House

Tuetoes Hills

TIDE GAUGE

KELFIELD

Pond Farm

South Ings Drain

PPG STA
Drainhead Farm

Kelfield Sewer

Stakes Drain

South Ings

Kelfield Corner
Kelfield Cottages

KELFIELD GRANGE
Ings Farm

East Ferry Road

South Carr

Wheatley House

Carr Villas

East Ferry Ings Drain

Ferry Barrier Bank

Ferry Barrier Bank

Hardwick Grange Farm

Laughton Highland Drain

Common Drain

Keadby

The twin villages of East and West Butterwick now come into view, facing each other across the river. As seems so often to be the case on the lower part of the Trent, the village to the west is larger than its eastern counterpart. West Butterwick is another village with a strong Dutch influence evident in the local buildings. It has an attractive church built in 1841 from creamy white brick, deceptively stone-like from a distance. It follows the Gothic style, has a small octagonal spire together with period interior fittings. In contrast, East Butterwick is a plain place with a small church built in 1884 at a cost of £500. It was once described as being 'surrounded by root crops and often by fog'. Now the river begins to broaden out passing under the M180 viaduct, built in 1978, and rising out of the flat countryside to clear the navigation. The scale of the river is such that the boater can now begin to appreciate just how major a watercourse the Trent really is – 150 miles long, with a catchment area of over 4000 square miles. The river once flowed due east from Nottingham, discharging into the Wash. At some point in prehistory this channel became blocked and the river turned north, picking a course through the soft keuper marls, still evident in the many shoals along the navigation, to its present junction with the Ouse. Three thousand cubic feet of water a second discharge into the Humber, a volume greater than that from the Thames into the estuary. Throughout history the Trent has been exploited both as a trunk navigation and for its inherent fertility. For centuries farmers working the land beside the river have encouraged it to flood the fields during winter months, by directing its water along warping drains cut at right angles to the waterway. As the river water spread across the land the fertile sediment settled out, enriching the soil and raising the water-table to sustain rich summer grazing. North of the M180 two further villages sit opposite one another – behind flood embankments – before Keadby is reached. These are Burringham to the east, with its early Victorian brick and slate church squatting beside the river, and Althorpe to the west, where the church, with its late Perpendicular tower, nestles in with the houses. Dedicated to St Oswald, it owes its origins to Sir John Nevill whose 1483 tower and chancel are incorporated into a larger structure. Both his coat of arms, and that of the Mowbray family, appear in stone, carved on the ogee arch of the west door. Less than a mile downstream of these villages is the combined road and rail bridge, built in 1916, which was the only bridge into the Isle of Axholme before the construction of the motorway viaduct. When operational, it worked

NAVIGATIONAL NOTES

1 Three red lights are normally displayed at all times when Keadby Lock is not available. A green light will be shown when there is sufficient depth of water over the cill to work the lock. This is theoretically up to 7 hours after high water, but despite constant dredging a sand bar builds up in front of the lock and 5 hours is often the maximum realistic time after high water that passage can be effected.

2 Shelter passes are available from the lock keeper for non-registered craft using BW navigations and/or moorings for a limited period.

3 All locks and bridges on BW waterways west of Keadby Lock are now boater-operated using the sanitary station key.

4 Due to the number of craft requiring the lock and the varying tide envelope, please give the lock keeper 48 hours notice of your intention to use the lock.

5 Boaters intending to break their passage to Cromwell Lock, by staying on the pontoon mooring at Dunham, are requested to inform the lock keeper at Keadby to avoid alarm at their non-arrival at Cromwell. Similarly, should you change your plans and subsequently stop at Dunham, please contact a lock keeper to avoid unnecessary concern for your safety. VHF radio frequencies: calling channel 16, working channel 74; or telephone as below:

Keadby Lock: (01724) 782205   Torksey Lock: (01427) 718202
West Stockwith: (01427) 890204   Cromwell Lock: (01636) 821213

on the principle of water being pumped into the large counter balance tank on the upper structure of the eastern end of the bridge. Once filled with a mass of water greater than the weight of the bridge, the whole edifice proceeded to tip over into the open position. Boaters should follow the channel between the right-hand pier and the bank under the lifting section of the bridge, and beware of large vessels at Gunness Wharf immediately below. A further half mile below this bridge, on the left, is Keadby Lock (for further details of Keadby see page 118) leading into the Stainforth & Keadby section of the South Yorkshire Navigations. The entrance is often totally obscured by coasters unloading at the wharf between the sluice at the Three Rivers outfall and the lock itself.

Burton Stather

This final section of the river is host to serious continental shipping and is punctuated by a series of bustling wharves. Coasters come and go with the tides carrying steel, coal and fertilisers and the constant activity of cranes, on the busy jetties, warms the heart of the true waterways enthusiast. It is perhaps not insignificant that the wharves are all in private ownership and, although relatively modest, they are nonetheless efficient for this and are clearly most cost-effective enterprises. It is perhaps unique for the boater, used to the prosaic names of inland pleasure craft, to be passing hulls bearing the cyrillic inscriptions of vessels registered in Eastern European ports – and beyond. Water depth for these craft is critical, even so close to the mouth of the river, and all movements require very close correlation with the tide as well as expert pilotage. Always bear this in mind and pay close attention to the requirements of any large vessel on the move. It is in these situations that VHF radio is an invaluable aid; or at least a sound knowledge of the international sound signals. The wharves do not permit casual mooring (except in an emergency) so once past Keadby on a falling tide the boater, intending to head up the Ouse back into the inland waterways system, is, on reaching Trent Falls, committed to one of four courses of action:

1   Anchor under the lee of the training wall in the west channel, to the south of Trent Falls light.
2   Beach on Tackhammer flats.
3   Moor on Blacktoft Lay-by Jetty. *Charge.*
4   Punch the ebbing tide in the Ouse up to Goole (or beyond).

These options are examined in greater detail on the next page. Boaters passing Flixborough Stather, now predominantly engaged in steel traffic, may recall the disastrous explosion that occurred here when it was the site of a vast chemical works which was virtually flattened by the blast. To the north, beside the outfall from Meredyke, is a silt bank which, unusually, has built up on a straight section of the river, at the approach to the bite of a bend – BEWARE. Burton Stather was built and operated by Victor Waddington whose barges, moored on the Aire & Calder Navigation, cluster the outskirts of Goole docks awaiting incoming shipments of steel. Similarly his boats are to be found tied up several deep at Waddington Lock, on the South Yorkshire Navigations and are a testimony to his great commitment to waterways transport. His enthusiasm, often in the face of a less than co-operative bureaucracy, was only matched by the immense carrying capacity of his total barge fleet. He is alleged to have observed, about the perilous state of his home navigation, that 'The top's too near the bottom, the bottom's too near the top and there's nowt in between'. The unwary boater, failing to use the marked channel at Trent Falls, may well have occasion to reflect at some length on this observation.

Trent Falls

Now the steep wooded hills that have followed close to the east bank of the river start to peel away as the mouth of the Trent and its junction with the Ouse (to form the Humber) is approached. Large areas of low-lying ground – part mud flat, part rough grazing – accompany the waterway to its conclusion only to be dwarfed by the vast acreage of water that is the confluence of these two great rivers. There is a lonely eeriness about so much water with only the village of Alkborough in the distance to suggest human habitation. Strangely enough the River Don, now confined to its sterile, straight, tidal channel at Goole, used to have one of its two mouths here, just to the south of Anchor Drain. When Vermuyden set out to drain the Isle of Axholme he attempted to divert the river's entire output along its second branch, into the River Aire near Snaith. This was less than successful and his subsequent attempt produced the Dutch River as seen today. However the Don's channel to the Trent remained redundant except as the line still faithfully followed by the county boundary. Nowhere else in Britain will the inland navigator be exposed to so much water and so little bank. Many boaters, regaled with tales of the fearsome nature of these waters, will do anything to avoid passage, but in reality, in a properly equipped boat, in the right weather conditions and with informed planning, Trent Falls can be navigated with comparative ease. Before passing Keadby, with its safe haven in the Stainforth and Keadby canal, you should be clear about the channel (see reference to *Sissons Charts*, below), the tide and weather conditions and your strategy once the Humber is reached (technically the point where Trent and Ouse meet and all points east). You should also be clear that Trent Falls is also called Trent Mouth and Apex (Apex being the name given to the lighthouse at the end of the western training wall). All three names can be heard in regular use on local shipping radio traffic. Most boaters will choose to approach Trent Falls on an ebbing tide, low powered craft will have no option. Deep-draughted vessels will obviously plan to arrive well before low water. Only powerful boats will consider turning into the Ouse to push against the ebb to Goole. For the remainder the choices are set out below.

NAVIGATIONAL NOTES

1 Anchor in the western channel between South Trent Beacon and Anchor Drain, about 20 feet out from the training wall. There is a firm bottom here and you are clear of empty sand barges risking a short cut.
2 Flat bottomed boats can beach on Tackhammer Flats and await the flood. To perform this manoeuvre follow the eastern channel to a point roughly mid-way between South Trent Beacon and Apex Light, turn south east at right angles to your track and head square onto the flats. The ebb will draw your stern northwards, helping to lodge the vessel securely, whilst the flood will push it southwards and help to pull you off. **Note** (a) This is not a good strategy in rough weather. The western channel anchorage provides a modicum of shelter from westerly winds. (b) If attempted at night, remember that other vessels, especially large sand barges, may also have beached so look out for riding lights.
3 On the Ouse, west of Trent Falls (almost opposite West Ouse Beacon – the second flashing red light west of Apex Light) is Associated British Ports' (ABP) Blacktoft Lay-by Jetty which, for a fee, can be used between tides. Be prepared to share it with large commercial vessels and be sure that your vessel is powerful enough to reach it.
4 At all times read the above narrative and navigational notes in conjunction with a reputable chart such as *Sissons Charts* available from the Trent Boating Association (0115 926 2055). Be willing to take advice from BW lock keepers and ABP staff in Goole Docks. ABOVE ALL ELSE THE INLAND BOATER SHOULD NOT PASS KEADBY UNLESS HE FULLY UNDERSTANDS WHAT HE IS DOING.

● **Trent Falls**

The mouth of the Trent curves gently to the east as it meets the Ouse: a layout that is largely of man's doing as much as by nature's design. Between the wars an elaborate stone training wall was constructed on the western bank, easily visible at low water and marked by lights and wooden staffs at high water.

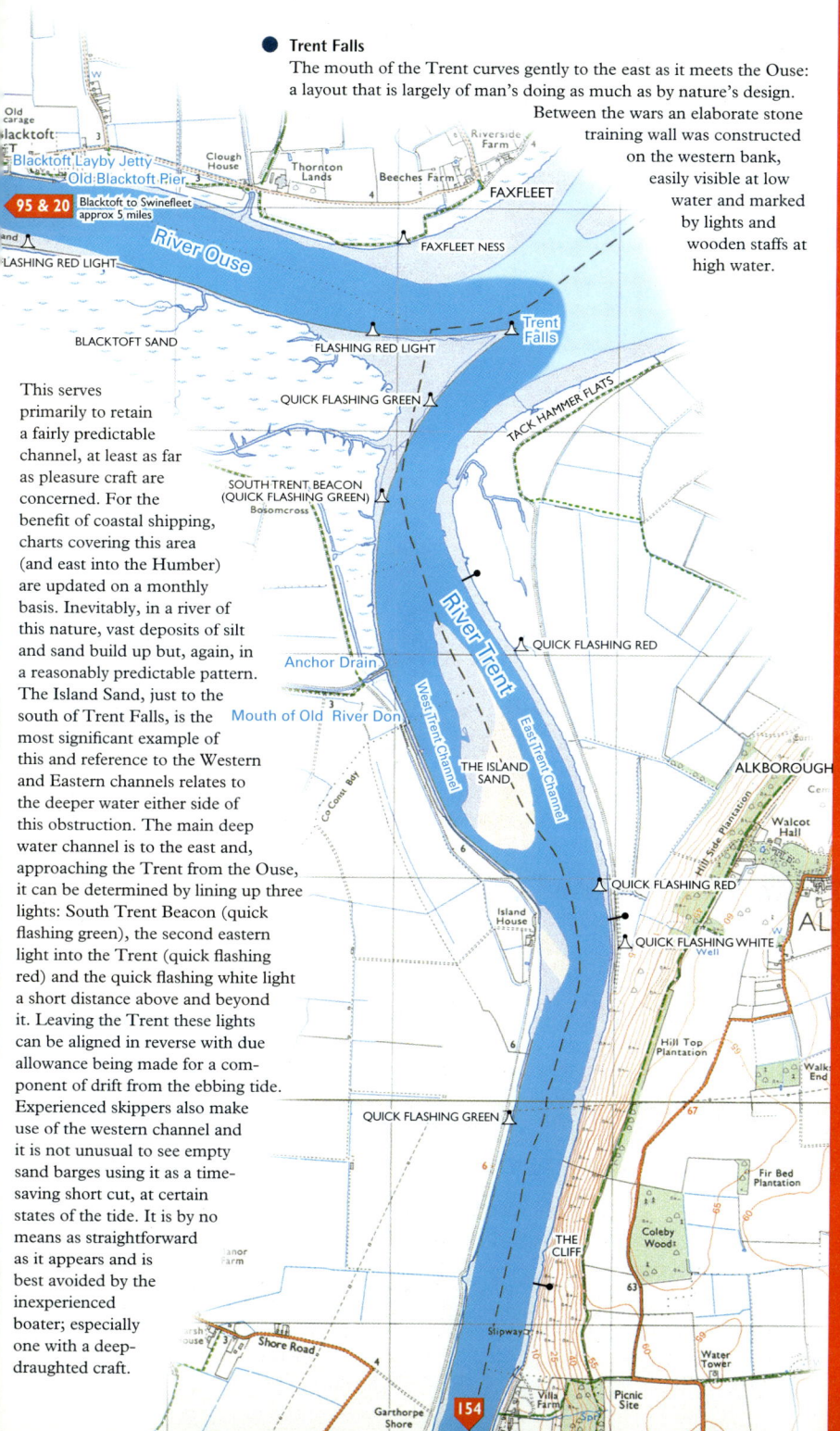

This serves primarily to retain a fairly predictable channel, at least as far as pleasure craft are concerned. For the benefit of coastal shipping, charts covering this area (and east into the Humber) are updated on a monthly basis. Inevitably, in a river of this nature, vast deposits of silt and sand build up but, again, in a reasonably predictable pattern. The Island Sand, just to the south of Trent Falls, is the most significant example of this and reference to the Western and Eastern channels relates to the deeper water either side of this obstruction. The main deep water channel is to the east and, approaching the Trent from the Ouse, it can be determined by lining up three lights: South Trent Beacon (quick flashing green), the second eastern light into the Trent (quick flashing red) and the quick flashing white light a short distance above and beyond it. Leaving the Trent these lights can be aligned in reverse with due allowance being made for a component of drift from the ebbing tide. Experienced skippers also make use of the western channel and it is not unusual to see empty sand barges using it as a time-saving short cut, at certain states of the tide. It is by no means as straightforward as it appears and is best avoided by the inexperienced boater; especially one with a deep-draughted craft.

INDEX